The Doctrine of Justification

Essays in Theology

Edited by JORDAN COOPER

and MATTHEW FENN

First published by The Weidner Institute: A Division of Just and Sinner 2021

Copyright 2021 Just and Sinner

All rights reserved. No part of this publication may be reproduced, stored or transmitted in any form or by any means, electronic, mechanical, photocopying, recording, scanning, or otherwise without written permission from the publisher. It is illegal to copy this book, post it to a website, or distribute it by any other means without permission.

www.JSPublishing.org

First edition

ISBN: 978-1-952295-43-0

Table of Contents

Introduction i
1. Justification: A Constellation of Concepts 1
2. Justification: "Objective" and "Subjective" 19
3. *Obedientia Christi Activa*: The Imputation of Christ's Active Obedience in the Lutheran Tradition and Scripture 75
4. Oswald Bayer and the Theology of Promise 103
5. Philipp Melanchthon's Use of Augustine in the Apology's Presentation of the Doctrine of Justification 119
6. "Payment for the Works of Charity": Finding Lutheran Soteriology in the Early Church 161
7. *Sola Fide* and the Council of Trent: Justification by Faith in the 16th Century and What Can Be Learned for Today's Ecumenical Dialogues 181
8. Defending God's Honor: The Righteousness of God in Light of Honor and Shame 221

Introduction

About This Series

The Weidner Institute's *Essays in Theology* series brings together writings from scholars and pastors on pressing theological issues that face the church today. The goal of these volumes is the promotion of classical Lutheran teaching as developed within the Protestant scholastic tradition beginning in the seventeenth century. The work in these books is not merely of historical interest, but it consists in the application of orthodox Lutheran thought to ecclesiastical and theological debates and concerns of the twenty-first century. It is the conviction of the Weidner Institute that classical Lutheran orthodoxy has the theological grounding and tools to address some of the most important issues of our day and that a recovery of the doctrines and method of the Protestant scholastics is necessary for the ongoing ministry of the church as it faces challenges both internally and externally.

This Volume

As we considered which topic should be chosen to launch this series, it seemed most appropriate to begin with what is often considered the most Lutheran of all doctrines: justification by faith alone. This idea was the center of Luther's Reformation and has since retained its status as the chief article of the Christian faith among Lutherans. Agreement regarding its centrality, however, does not mean that there has been a shortage of debate among Lutherans themselves over exactly what constitutes this teaching. Especially in a time when the heritage of Lutheran orthodoxy has been challenged as authors contend for discontinuity between Martin Luther and the later tradition, we felt it necessary to offer a defense of core elements of the perspective of Lutheran orthodoxy.

The introductory essay in this volume is not a scholarly treatment of the doctrine of justification but a conference presentation from the current Presiding Pastor of the American Association of Lutheran Churches, Curtis E. Leins. This talk is an explanation of the various ways in which the doctrine of justification can be presented and of some of the essential surrounding redemptive themes to be discussed alongside of forensic justification. This essay is an introduction to many of the major themes that are to be presented throughout this volume, and it challenges the oft-repeated claim that the Lutheran doctrine of justification flattens human salvation into a bare and impersonal forensic verdict. This paper also introduces the doctrine of justification from a practical perspective as it applies to the life and conscience of the average Christian. Justification is never to be taught as merely some theoretical idea to be endlessly debated, but instead it is to be taught as the saving act of God enacted in real time for real people.

Following this introduction, the next three articles address some particular areas of debate surrounding justification among Lutherans. First, David Jay Webber discusses the subject of objective justification. This element of the doctrine of justification was first given separate treatment among nineteenth-century American Lutherans, mostly within the Synodical Conference. As such, it has been a standard teaching in both the Lutheran Church—Missouri Synod and the Wisconsin Evangelical Lutheran Synod. However, in recent years, it has come under a bit of criticism, such as in statements set forth by the Evangelical Lutheran Diocese of North America. Webber presents the doctrine clearly by demonstrating its historical pedigree in Lutheran theology and correcting misconceptions surrounding the idea. Throughout this article, he responds to several common criticisms.

The second article which addresses a debated point in contemporary theology covers the role of the active obedience of Christ in justification. Jordan Cooper cites the various places where such challenges have arisen in the church, both outside of and within the Lutheran tradition. In view here are the New Perspective on Paul and Radical Lutheranism. For Gerhard Forde, the idea that Christ must fulfill the divine law in order to achieve human salvation is adherence to a "legal scheme," which he rejects as incompatible with the newness of the gospel in its total break from law. Cooper discusses the exegetical grounding of the active obedience of Christ, pointing out that some Reformation-era arguments are less than convincing today but positing that the doctrine remains a necessary element of Christ's fulfillment of the role of Israel within redemptive history.

The third debated theological point addressed in this volume is Oswald Bayer's conception of justification as a divine speech act. In his essay, David Scaer explains the recent prominence of John Austin's speech-act theory in explanations of justification. Oswald Bayer uses these philosophical developments to define Luther's concept of God's promise as that which does what it says. Scaer discusses some of the problems with the popularity of such an approach and questions whether it is really a beneficial theological shift for the Lutheran Church.

The next set of essays addresses historical concerns with regard to justification. Eric Phillips considers the relationship between Augustine's soteriology and that which was developed by Luther and Melanchthon. In particular, he interacts with two mischaracterizations of the relationship between Augustine and the Reformation. First is the claim of Robert Koons (among others) that Melanchthon completely misrepresents the North African theologian by ripping a set of quotes out of context. Second are those Lutherans who present an exact identification between Augustine and the Reformation on the doctrine of justification. Phillips navigates the way between these extremes by demonstrating that the Lutheran Reformation depended upon Augustine's soteriology in significant ways but also diverged from him in some specifics.

Also addressing the question of justification by faith in the works of the church fathers, Peter Daniel Fawcett discusses the difficulty of harmonizing statements that affirm *sola fide* (whether explicitly or implicitly) in the works of the church fathers with their insistence that God rewards almsgiving, often seemingly giving the act a salvific effect. Through quotes from Melanchthon, Luther, and Chemnitz, Fawcett demonstrates that early Lutherans were not opposed to attaching promises of some kind to the act of almsgiving as the fathers were. He contends that one can even speak of a sacramental quality in good works, wherein they are signs that assure one of God's promises. While Fawcett's conclusion may be controversial here, he forces the reader to reckon with some statements about good work that appear in the Lutheran confessional documents.

The final historical essay included in this volume is an overview of the views of justification within Rome during the Council of Trent. Laurin Fenn demonstrates the existence of a variety of perspectives on the topic at the council, rather than a single unified opposition to the Reformation teaching. She then puts forward the conclusions of Trent and discusses the relationship between Lutherans and Roman Catholics in light of current ecumenical efforts, such as the *Joint Declaration on the Doctrine of Justification*. Fenn puts forth a vision for dialogue between Roman Catholics and Lutherans that does not minimize significant differences remaining between these two traditions.

At the end of this book is the only strictly exegetical essay, which covers the much-debated subject of "the righteousness of God" in the book of Romans and presents a way to harmonize some of the exegetical conclusions of the New Perspective on Paul with the classical Lutheran view. Matthew Fenn argues for a restoration of the concept of honor in its Anselmic formulation underlying Paul's construction of God's righteousness. Fenn places honor and shame in their classical context, addresses the theme in Lutheran theology, and gives an exegetical defense of the use of such an idea in Paul's Letter to the Romans.

This book does not address every concern related to justification in the modern context, but it does provide a way forward on a number of questions of debate. Through this book, one will gain an understanding of some of the most relevant issues facing Lutheran theology in our time and an appreciation of the practical and pastoral nature of this central doctrine.

As an aside, it is to be noted that not every author agrees with all conclusions of each of the other essays. This includes the two series editors: Jordan Cooper and Matthew Fenn. The goal of this volume is not to put forth one single unified conception of all particulars of justification but is instead to present constructive essays from those who are seeking to be faithful within the classical Lutheran tradition. The series editors themselves are not in agreement about the meaning of God's righteousness in Paul's thought (Fenn is more sympathetic to N.T. Wright's view and Cooper to Lee Irons's take), yet both acknowledge that the other remains confessionally Lutheran despite an exegetical disagreement.

May this work point you to the source of your salvation and righteousness which is *extra nos*: Jesus Christ crucified and risen for you.

The Series Editors

Justification: A Constellation of Concepts

By Curtis E. Leins[1]

INTRODUCTION

Romans 3:28: "For we maintain that a man is justified by faith apart from works of the law." The Greek word *dikaioo* is often translated to "justify." However, *dikaioo* is translated in other passages to "declare righteous." We believe that a person is justified or declared righteous before God by faith alone, apart from any works of the law. In the court of divine law, those who have faith in Jesus Christ are made completely right before God. They are fully justified in the face of God's judgment, solely on account of faith in Christ Jesus.

Three Clarifiers in this Discussion

Satisfactio vicaria,[2] *vicarious satisfaction*: This ecclesiastical term refers to Jesus having vicariously satisfied the righteous demands of God's law. God's law demands perfect obedience. Jesus offered perfect obedience and fulfilled the law of God. He did so in our place, vicariously. Furthermore, not only did he perfectly keep the law (active obedience), but Christ also took the full extent of God's punishment for our sins (passive obedience) because we did not keep God's law. For this reason, the complete wrath of God was poured out

---

[1] Special thanks: The format that I have chosen for this presentation is based in large measure on a publication by Jacob A. O. Preus titled *Just Words*.[1] This brief text, approximately 220 pages long and published in the year 2000, is as imaginative and inspiring as it is confessional and comprehensive.

[2] Francis Pieper, *Christian Dogmatics*, vol. 1 (Saint Louis, MO: Concordia Publishing House, 1951), 344.

upon him, and God was completely appeased on account of him. Therefore, there is nothing more that can or should be added to the completely sufficient sacrifice of Christ for our salvation. We dare not think that something is lacking in his act of vicarious satisfaction such that we might add our works or our obedience to his. This would be idolatry, putting ourselves in the place of Christ. Moreover, it would be futility itself because, in so doing, we would once again place ourselves under the demands of God's law, which we cannot keep. No! We will gladly trust and rely upon *satisfactio vicaria*. This is Christ's obedient sacrifice, which perfectly satisfied God's law and completely assuaged God's wrath on our behalf.

Divine monergism,[3] *divine work alone*: This term makes clear that our justification unto salvation is in no way a product of our own work. Our justification is solely God's work. However, one may argue that "Christ did the work of our justification, but can we not claim credit at least for the faith that we have in him? Even though Christ did the work of salvation, didn't we do the work of believing?" No! (1) The idea that the unbeliever can choose saving faith is called Pelagianism (an early fifth-century heresy). Scripture teaches that the unconverted person is spiritually dead (Eph. 2:5, Col. 2:13). In Luther's response to Erasmus, *On the Bondage of the Will*, Luther explained that prior to conversion, the will is bound. The unconverted cannot choose God or faith in Christ. (2) The idea that God and the unbeliever work together in such a way that the human begins the process and God completes the conversion is Semi-Pelagianism. This too is a false teaching. (3) The idea that God begins and a person

---

[3] Ibid., 471–492.

completes their own conversion is called Synergism. This is another false teaching in which Christ's saving work is deemed incomplete. (4) But, we believe, teach, and confess that the unconverted person is dead in their sin. They cannot choose God or saving faith in Christ. God comes in his word and creates faith *ex nihilo* ("out of nothing").[4] "Faith comes by hearing and hearing by the word of Christ" (Rom. 10:17). The human will is not active toward producing conversion; it remains purely passive.[5] This is a great comfort to believers. For if saving faith were our own work in any way, not only would Christ's work be insufficient, but our salvation would be dependent upon our own fatally flawed efforts to complete it. How could we ever be assured of salvation if it were dependent upon ourselves? We could not be! The doctrine of divine monergism teaches that our salvation is from start to finish the completed work of Christ alone.

Opinio legis,[6] *opinion of the law*: This is the default position of the human religious mind. It is the opinion that if a person does a good thing, they should rightly be rewarded with divine grace. Likewise, when they do an evil thing, they should receive retribution. If sin is what separates a person from God and if someone rejects sin and does good, they logically should merit or earn God's grace and favor. This faulty theology asserts that a person's moral actions and good works can satisfy God's law, thereby producing reconciliation with God and earning the person eternal salvation.

With this basic vocabulary in mind, let's explore the meaning of justification through the examination of six interrelated topics:

---

[4] Ibid., 455–456.
[5] Ibid., 457.
[6] Ibid., 483–484.

JUSTIFICATION: A CONSTELLATION OF CONCEPTS

redemption, identity, marriage, sacrifice, salvation, and birth. Together, they form a constellation of meaning that provides a more complete understanding of God's act of justification.

A CONSTELLATION OF CONCEPTS
Redemption (Person in Chains)

One of the primary concepts used to describe the justifying work of Christ is the idea of payment. As St. Peter writes in his first epistle, "Know[ing] that you were not redeemed with perishable things like silver or gold from your futile way of life inherited from your forefathers, but with precious blood, as of a lamb unblemished and spotless, the blood of Christ" (1 Pet. 1:18–19). A divine transaction has taken place in order to purchase and liberate a great number of slaves. The transaction is, as Jesus says in Matthew 20:28, a ransom. It is paid not with silver or gold but with the most precious commodity in heaven or on Earth—the blood of the Lamb of God.[7]

The *Exsultet* is a hymn of praise dated as early as the fifth century and not later than the seventh century. It was sung during the procession of the Paschal candle during the Great Vigil of Easter. This ancient hymn declares,

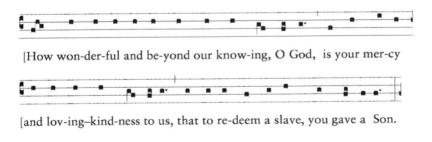

[How won-der-ful and be-yond our know-ing, O God, is your mer-cy

[and lov-ing–kind-ness to us, that to re-deem a slave, you gave a Son.

---

[7] Preus, *Just Words*, 80.

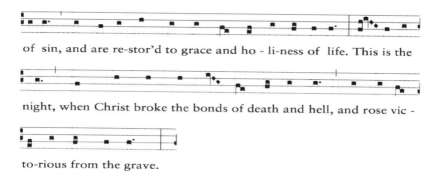

of sin, and are re-stor'd to grace and ho-li-ness of life. This is the night, when Christ broke the bonds of death and hell, and rose victo-rious from the grave.

"To redeem a slave, you gave a Son." From this holy transaction, we are to understand a number of truths. First, we should know with assurance that we are of inestimable value to God. We literally cannot comprehend our great value to our heavenly Father, but we begin to recognize some of our worth to him when we see the great cost he is willing to pay in order to set us free from our enslavement to sin, death, and the devil. Second, we should understand that his is an intimate love for us. This is not some "at arm's length" business transaction. It is a vicarious payment accomplished when Jesus, the Son of God, took our place. He has fully identified himself with us. "Surely, our griefs He Himself bore, and our sorrows He carried . . . He was pierced through for our transgressions, and He was crushed for our iniquities; The chastening for our well-being fell upon Him, and by His scourging we are healed" (Isa. 53:4–5).

Finally, we must know that because this ransom was paid by God himself in Jesus Christ, it is a completed transaction. There is nothing that can or should be added to it, *satisfactio vicaria*. To the idea that a ransom that is paid should be added the reality of a redemption, that is accomplished. The divine price that was paid has had a dramatic effect upon those who were purchased. Before, you may have felt as though you were free, but you were in reality enslaved. Now, you have been set free from slavery, though you are indeed servants of God. The effect of Christ's redemption is a happy exchange, a *communicatio idiomatum* ("communication of attributes").[8] Christ has taken upon himself the attributes of sinful humanity. These attributes have been applied to him and nailed to the cross. At the same time, the holy attributes of Christ have been imputed to those who believe. Now you are "a chosen race, a royal priesthood, a holy nation, a people for God's own possession" (1 Pet. 2:9). You have become children of God and inheritors of eternal life.

As God's own possessions, you are no longer slaves. You are truly free. You have been washed in the waters of regeneration, have been clothed in the robes of Christ's righteousness, and have been seated in the heavenly places.

This is included in the word *justification*.

Identity (Father's Embrace)

Though *justification* is often seen as a legal or forensic term, its application is intensely personal, and its significance affects one's identity, earthly consequence, and eternal inheritance.

> Blessed be the God and Father of our Lord Jesus Christ, who has blessed us with every spiritual blessing in the heavenly places in Christ, just as He chose us in Him before the

---

[8]Ibid., 90.

foundation of the world, that we would be holy and blameless before Him. In love He predestined us to adoption as sons through Jesus Christ to Himself, according to the kind intention of His will, to the praise of the glory of His grace, which He freely bestowed on us in the Beloved. (Eph. 1:3–6)

For you have not received a spirit of slavery leading to fear again, but you have received a spirit of adoption as sons by which we cry out, "Abba! Father!" The Spirit Himself testifies with our spirit that we are children of God, and if children, heirs also, heirs of God and fellow heirs with Christ, if indeed we suffer with Him so that we may also be glorified with Him. (Rom. 8:15–17)

The commission of sin leaves one stained with guilt and shame. Guilt is addressed through the justification that is ours through faith in Jesus. Literally, justification declares that we are "not guilty" before God. The work of Christ, applied to us by grace through faith, renders a guilty person right with God. Under the law of God, the believer is not guilty. Unfortunately, a not-guilty person may still be filled with shame. The issue at hand is not their action but their identity. Guilt is a condition in relation to the law; shame is a condition in relation to another. The glory of God's work in Christ is that the redeemed are not only declared not guilty in relation to the law, but they are also transformed into beloved children in relation to God. What is changed is not only the verdict for what they have done but the value of who they are.

St. Paul writes that Christ Jesus continually intercedes for us (Rom. 8:33–34). Christ is our defender, our mediator, and our intercessor. More than that, Jesus is the lover of our souls. He will allow nothing to separate us from the love of God. "Neither death nor life, nor angels nor principalities nor powers, nor things present, nor things to come, nor height, nor depth, nor any other creature will be able to separate us from the love of God which is in Christ Jesus our Lord" (Rom. 8:37–39). Nothing is able to defeat God's grace, remove Christ's mercy, or separate us from his love. This changes not only the verdict of our actions but the identity of our lives. Our new identity is adopted children of the Most High!

This is included in the word *justification*.

Marriage (Wedding Day!)

In both the Old and New Testaments, God uses the image of marriage to speak of his commitment to and love for human beings. Hosea the prophet becomes a living example of God's faithfulness in his covenant relationship with an adulterous wife. In Ephesians 5, the language of God's faithfulness is even more explicit; "For this reason a man shall leave his father and mother and shall be joined to his wife, and the two shall become one flesh. This mystery is great; but I am speaking with reference to Christ and the church" (5:31–32).

In Christ, God has left the celestial glory of heaven and his perichoretic intimacy (from *perichoresis*, "the interpenetration of the three Divine Persons") with the Father and the Spirit and has become incarnate, enfleshed. Now as the fully God-Man, he takes upon himself the sin of the world. He who knew no sin not only takes the punishment and endures the curse, but he literally becomes sin. What a conundrum: perfect and holy God became sin. In fact, Jesus became more sinful than all the sins of all humanity of all time. Much worse, he became sin itself. He took all sin unto himself. He bore all punishment upon himself. He suffered all wrath within himself. Though this was the very will of God and was the glory and righteousness of God, at the same time it yielded a forsakenness from God. These two ideas are incomprehensible together: God's wrath and God's love simultaneously displayed. What suffering and sorrow for all three of the Divine Persons. This is the extent to which God will go in order to be reconciled and reunited with a sinful and adulterous humanity that neither then nor now truly understands what he has done and what it has cost him.

What we understand is seen "as through a glass, darkly" (1 Cor. 13:12). That is to say, we know in part—as though our eyes cannot truly see, our ears cannot truly hear, and our hearts cannot truly receive—what has been given to us. Jesus uses words like *peace*: "Peace I leave with you; My peace I give to you; not as the world gives do I give to you. Do not let your heart be troubled, nor let it be fearful" (John 14:27). But we do not truly understand. Who among us today knows peace in their heart or life? Who can explain what it is to experience this gift of Christ, that we have the very peace that is in him, his peace, living in us?

Through this unity, this holy marriage of faith in Christ, we have been given another gift: forgiveness. This is no partial forgiveness or superficial cleansing. It is absolute and complete merciful absolution; it is divine, entire, and eternal cleansing. There is no spot or wrinkle, no blemish of sin, guilt, or shame that remains. This is a promise given and accomplished through the Savior's death to all those joined to the Bridegroom by faith. But who among us has danced with head held high and tear-filled eyes streaming with the glorious certainty of this cleanliness from sin? Who has understood, even for an instant, the heavenly declaration *"Te Absolvo*, I forgive you. You are clean. You are *mine!"*?

Regardless of whether we comprehend it or not, the fact—the historical fact—of the crucifixion of Jesus stands, and thereby the reconciliation of a sinner with a loving and merciful God also stands.[9] This marriage, this atonement, this new and abiding unity of Christ and his bride, of your Lord and you, has already taken place.

This, too, is included in the word *justification*.

Sacrifice (Judge)

The first three concepts that we have explored have been astounding and wonderful. God has *redeemed* us; we are slaves set free. God has *embraced* us; we are adopted as his own children. God has *reconciled* us; we are married to him as a bride to a husband.

However, we have a multifaceted God. He also is a jealous God, a holy God, and a God of judgment. In order for a person to be in relationship with him, God requires perfect cleanliness, perfect obedience, and perfect righteousness. If a person does not meet God's requirements, that person will meet a God of wrath.

> The kings of the earth and the great men and the commanders and the rich and the strong and every slave and free man hid themselves in the caves and among the rocks of the mountains; and they said to the mountains and to the rocks, "Fall on us and hide us from the presence of Him who sits on the throne, and from the wrath of the Lamb; for the great day

---

[9]Ibid., 138-142.

of their wrath has come, and who is able to stand?" (Rev. 6:15–17)

The ancient Requiem, the Mass for the dead used among Lutherans, Anglicans, and Roman Catholics, declares,

Dies illa, dies irae, calamitatis, et miseriae; ("That day, day of wrath, calamity, and misery;")

Dies illa, dies magna, et amara valde, ("That day, day of great and exceeding bitterness,")

Dum veneris iudicare sæculum per ignem. ("When thou shalt come to judge the world by fire.")

Jacob A. O. Preus writes,

> All this is only a window on a more profound and troubling uncleanness that affects us all. Before God, all people are unclean, tainted, polluted. God is holy, and our filthiness is a personal offense to Him. We never will have access to Him, He will never come near us, as long as we remain contaminated. Try as we might, we cannot purify ourselves. God declares, "Although you wash yourself with soda and an abundance of soap, the stain of your guilt is still before Me" (Jeremiah 2:22).[10]

What is to be done? God himself will provide a way for us to be clean. In the Hebrew scriptures, we read that God provided a sacrificial system that enabled his priests and people to come before

---

[10]Ibid., 184.

him and participate in a holy, covenant relationship. Countless sheep, lambs, goats, rams, bulls, oxen, doves, and pigeons were offered as blood sacrifices to appease a God of wrath who required a holy people. But God's people proved themselves to be sinfully unfaithful again and again. Finally, God provided a sacrifice that forever satisfied his righteous requirements and perfectly assuaged his holy anger: the crucifixion of his own son, the Lamb of God. Through this pure and holy sacrifice, humans have expiation of their sins. That is, the guilt of their sin is removed. This sacrifice provides complete propitiation. That is, the anger of God's wrath is fully satisfied.[11] These ideas are hard for human beings to face. In former ages, we read and revered certain scriptures more than we do today. Still, and even now, we must know that justification by grace through faith includes a sacrificial substitute for our sin, a God-Man whose blood sacrifice both expiates and propitiates. Only by the shed blood of this Lamb of God is the righteous anger of a holy God's judgment appeased and is a people of God cleansed and justified forever.

This is included in the word *justification*.

Salvation (Christus Rex of Washington Basilica)

We are Americans! We are the can-do people. With hard work and honest effort, we can do anything, fix anything, be anything. Right? We have a bootstrap mentality. If we fall or find ourselves in a bad situation, we pull ourselves up by our bootstraps. It is called making it on your own. We are free to do just that. We are responsible for our own lives and our own choices. Anyone can grow up to become

---

[11]Ibid., 170.

President of the United States. I can be anything that I truly want to be. It's up to me. Right? It is all a matter of choice. This is true in career, finances, education, and even religion. Take faith; it's a free choice. I get to choose. I either believe or I do not. It's up to me. And when it comes to heaven or hell, that's up to me too. I've lived a pretty good life. Compared to some other people, I'm not such a bad guy. So I'm going to heaven. Right? The point is that I am free.

What I have just expressed is *opinio legis*, the opinion of the law. It is the default position of the human spiritual condition. The human thinks that they are free and determine their own spiritual destiny. The problem is that this is a lie. The human is not free. They are a slave in bondage to sin and death. There is nothing that they can do to set themself free from sin. The truth is they are spiritually dead. They cannot choose fear of God, faith in God, or love of Christ. They cannot choose to live a holy life, have holy thoughts, or stand holy before God's righteous judgment. You see, to be guilty of one sin is to be guilty of all sins. Moreover, if a person wants God to judge them on account of their good works, they will also be judged on account of their bad ones. There is no escape. There is no liberation from this slavery to sin. And, as the Bible says, "The wages of sin is death," eternal, tormenting, isolating, terrifying death.

Opinio legis is a lie. You and I cannot save ourselves. The truth is, we need a Savior, a Liberator, a Victor! We need a mighty warrior who is able to set us free from our captivity to sin, death, and the power of the devil. "Through Christ Jesus the law of the Spirit of life set me free from the law of sin and death" (Rom. 8:2).

Let me tell you about this mighty warrior. When he is dressed for battle, he does not wear a helmet of salvation; he is salvation. He wears no belt of truth; he is truth. He wears no breastplate of righteousness; he is righteousness. He wears no shoes of peace; he is peace. He carries no sword of the Spirit; he is the word of God. And he needs no shield of faith, because all the faith that we will ever need is in him. He is the mighty warrior. Dressed in nothing but a crown of thorns and covered in his own blood, he reigns from the throne of his cross. He takes the full weight of sin and death; he bears the full assault of the devil's fury. This paschal Lamb is not Satan's spectacle. It is Christ the conqueror who is making a public spectacle of his enemies. It is Christ the Lord who has vanquished sin and death and set his people free.

Ruling from his heavenly throne, the Savior has set us free *from* a life of sin and death. He has set us free *for* a life of discipleship filled with the Holy Spirit.[12] As Preus writes, "Christians don't need their good works; they have the perfect good works of Jesus as their own through faith. We are free to give our good works away to others, who do need them, sometimes desperately."[13]

This is included in the word *justification*.

Birth (Holy Baptism)

For much of our discussion, we have been talking about a forensic decision that takes place in a divine court of law. How can sinful human beings be counted as righteous before God, the holy Judge? We have learned that through faith in the crucified Son of God, a divine exchange takes place—a *communicatio idiomatum* (a "communication of attributes"). The soul sickness, selfish idolatry, sin, and death that

---

[12] Ibid., 198.
[13] Ibid., 199.

belong to us are imputed to Christ. The righteousness, sonship, inheritance, and eternal life that belong to Christ are imputed to us. This is a great miracle. But I am going to tell you of a miracle that is even greater.

"Blessed be the God and Father of our Lord Jesus Christ, who according to His great mercy has caused us to be born again to a living hope through the resurrection of Jesus Christ from the dead . . . for you have been born again not of seed which is perishable but imperishable, that is, through the living and enduring word of God" (1 Pet. 1:3, 22). The greater miracle is that we who have faith in Christ are not only judged as if we were God's children, but we are reborn and truly transformed into being God's children. There is a change not only of the verdict placed upon us but of the very spirit living within us. As the word of Jesus declares, "Truly, truly, I say to you, unless one is born again [(ἄνωθεν, alternate translation, from above)] he cannot see the kingdom of God . . . Truly, truly, I say to you, unless one is born of water and the Spirit he cannot enter into the kingdom of God. That which is born of the flesh is flesh, and that which is born of the Spirit is spirit. (John 3:3, 5)

The Lord Jesus uses many different word pictures to convey this new reality: death to life, darkness to light, empty to full, parched to satisfied, born from above.[14] We struggle to find words when words are simply inadequate. The reality is literally beyond our ability to verbalize. It is too big for our language. Instead, we must use story or song or some kind of analogy—"rescued us from the domain of

---

[14]Ibid., 63–76.

darkness, and transferred us to the kingdom of His beloved Son" (Col. 1:13).

The reality is that we have been justified by grace through faith, and in that divine transaction, we have been changed. We have been altered. It is not only that we are looked upon differently but that we are different. This is not only a forensic or judicial change, but it is also an ontological one. At the level of our deepest being, the word of God has penetrated us, faith has laid hold of us, and the Spirit has transformed us. This is something that no human being can do to themself. This is monergistic, an act of God alone!

This, too, is what it means to be justified.

CONCLUSION

God promised this in Holy Scripture centuries before the birth of Jesus. We read in the Psalms,

> In You, O Lord, I have taken refuge; Let me never be ashamed;
> In Your righteousness deliver me. Incline Your ear to me, rescue me quickly;
> Be to me a rock of strength,
> A stronghold to save me. (Ps. 31:1–2)

> In You, O Lord, I have taken refuge; Let me never be ashamed;
> In Your righteousness deliver me and rescue me; Incline Your ear to me and save me.
> Be to me a rock of habitation to which I may continually come;
> You have given commandment to save me,
> For You are my rock and my fortress. (Ps. 71:1–3)

The gift of our justification and the declaration and transformation into new righteousness in Jesus Christ were foretold from the time of David. However, it was Paul who most fully explained it to us.

> But now apart from the Law the righteousness of God has been manifested, being witnessed by the Law and the Prophets, even the righteousness of God through faith in Jesus Christ for all those who believe; for there is no distinction; for all have sinned and fall short of the glory of God, being justified as a gift by His grace through the redemption which is in Christ Jesus; whom God displayed publicly as a propitiation in His blood through faith. This was to demonstrate His righteousness, because in the forbearance of God He passed over the sins previously committed; for the demonstration, I say, of His righteousness at the present time, so that He would be just and the justifier of the one who has faith in Jesus. (Rom. 3:21–26)

Paul expressed this glorious irony and unexpected incongruity: God demonstrated and displayed the enormity of his righteousness. He did this not by being a terrifying and distant judge who dispassionately adjudicates our eternal fate. No! May it never be! God demonstrated and displayed the enormity of his righteousness by spanning the distance, becoming one of us, bearing our sin and death, and making us righteous through the atonement of Christ in spite of ourselves. This is righteousness, God's righteousness. Remember, the word *righteous* and the word *justify* are the same Greek word. The word for righteousness and the word for justification are the same. God justifies himself; he displays and proves his righteousness. "In

JUSTIFICATION: A CONSTELLATION OF CONCEPTS

Your righteousness, deliver me," says the Psalmist. God has demonstrated that he alone is righteous. How? God has made a way to be just and holy and to be the Justifier and Savior of sinners at the same time. He has justified himself by justifying even the likes of you and me.

This is what it means to be justified.

Justification: "Objective" and "Subjective"
By David Jay Webber

The terms *objective justification* and *subjective justification* do not have a long and deep pedigree in Lutheran theological history. They are not Reformation-era terms. But the truths that these terms are intended to express certainly do have such a pedigree. In summarizing the meaning and application of St. Paul's statement in his Second Epistle to the Corinthians, that "in Christ God was reconciling the world to himself, not counting their trespasses against them, and entrusting to us the message of reconciliation" (2 Cor. 5:19 ESV[1]), the Lutheran theologian Johann Quistorp the Elder (1584–1648) offered these observations: "The word *justification* and *reconciliation* is used in a twofold manner: 1) in respect of the acquired merit, 2) in respect of the appropriated merit. Thus all are justified and some are justified. All, in respect of the acquired merit; some, in respect of the appropriated merit."[2]

These dual truths are summarized in a 1981 statement that served to settle a controversy regarding the teaching of objective justification within the Lutheran Church—Missouri Synod:

> When the Lord Jesus was "justified" (I Timothy 3:16) in His resurrection and exaltation, God acquitted Him not of sins of

---

[1]Scripture quotations marked "ESV" are from the English Standard Version.
[2]Johann Quistorp as quoted in Friedrich A. Schmidt, *Justification: Subjective and Objective*, trans. Kurt E. Marquart (Fort Wayne, IN: Concordia Theological Seminary Press, 1982), 21.

JUSTIFICATION: OBJECTIVE AND SUBJECTIVE

His own, but of all the sins of mankind, which as the Lamb of God He had been bearing (John 1:29), and by the imputation of which He had been "made ... to be sin for us" (II Corinthians 5:21), indeed, "made a curse for us" (Galatians 3:13). In this sense, the justification of Jesus was the justification of those whose sins He bore. The treasure of justification or forgiveness gained by Christ for all mankind is truly offered, given, and distributed in and through the Gospel and sacraments of Christ. Faith alone can receive this treasure offered in the Gospel, and this faith itself is entirely a gracious gift and creation of God through the means of grace. Faith adds nothing to God's forgiveness in Christ offered in the Gospel, but only receives it. Thus, "He that believeth on the Son hath everlasting life: and He that believeth not the Son, shall not see life; but the wrath of God abideth on Him" (John 3:30).[3]

By God's design and according to God's saving plan, Jesus was the representative and stand-in for mankind in his death and resurrection. Therefore, Jesus's justification was, in this sense, the vicarious "justification" of mankind. But Jesus's justification was not in *every* sense the justification of mankind, because each human being is not as a consequence now destined for heaven. mankind's justification in Christ's justification is not universalism. For the personal salvation of the individual, justification in the sense of a

---

[3] Walter A. Maier made this statement to the Board of Control of Concordia Theological Seminary in Fort Wayne, Indiana, on January 30, 1981. It was quoted in Robert D. Preus, "Objective Justification," *Concordia Theological Seminary Newsletter* 2 (1981).

personal *reception* of "the treasure of justification" by faith is necessary.

The use of the "objective" and "subjective" terminology became somewhat standardized within the Missouri and Norwegian Synods in North America in the second half of the nineteenth century in the context of a renewed study of, and appreciation for, the proper relationship between absolution and justification. But other terms were also used: *general* and *individual* justification; *universal* and *personal* justification; and objective and subjective *reconciliation*.

The use of such terminology, and the embracing of this way of explaining the two sides of justification, were not limited to Lutherans in the Missouri and Norwegian Synods. For example, Carroll Herman Little (1872–1958), a theological professor in the United Lutheran Church in America, taught that "Objective Justification may be defined as God's declaration of amnesty to the whole world of sinners on the basis of the vicarious obedience of Christ, by which He secured a perfect righteousness for all mankind, which God accepted as a reconciliation of the world to Himself," and that "Subjective, or Personal or Individual Justification, or the act of God by which, out of pure mercy and grace for Christ's sake, He pronounces the believer free from guilt and punishment and actually clothed with the imputed righteousness of Christ while he is in a state of faith, is the actual acceptance by faith of the Objective Justification."[4]

The specific word *forgiveness* and the specific word *justification* do not mean exactly the same thing. To forgive the sin of someone is to send off, or remove, the sin from that person. To justify

---

[4] C. H. Little, *Disputed Doctrines* (Burlington, IA: Lutheran Literary Board, 1933), 60–61.

JUSTIFICATION: OBJECTIVE AND SUBJECTIVE

someone is forensically to declare that person to be righteous. In forgiveness, something bad is taken away; in justification, something good is given or credited. But in biblical, Lutheran theology, "forgiveness" and "justification" are functionally synonymous. Forgiveness and justification are basically two ways of looking at, and describing, the same thing—albeit from slightly different angles.

The Apology of the Augsburg Confession accordingly states that "To obtain the forgiveness of sins is to be justified according to [Ps. 32:1]: 'Blessed are those whose transgression is forgiven'" (*Ap. AC* 4:76, in *BC*, 133)[5]. In the context of elaborating on the distinction between law and gospel, and the difference between faith and works, the Apology also reminds us that

> since justification takes place through a free promise, it follows that we cannot justify ourselves ... And since the promise cannot be grasped in any other way than by faith, the gospel (which is, strictly speaking, the promise of the forgiveness of sins and justification on account of Christ) proclaims the righteousness of faith in Christ, which the law does not teach.... For the law requires of us our own works and our own perfection. But the promise freely offers to us, who are oppressed by sin and death, reconciliation on account of Christ, which is received not by works, but by faith alone... . Therefore it follows that personal faith—by which an individual believes that his or her sins are remitted on account of Christ and that God is reconciled and gracious on account of

---

[5]This and all citations from the *Book of Concord* are from the Kolb and Wengert translation unless otherwise noted.

> Christ—receives the forgiveness of sins and justifies us. (*Ap. AC* 4:43–45, in *BC*, 127)

And in the Formula of Concord, the following declaration is made:

> Regarding the righteousness of faith before God, we unanimously believe, teach, and confess . . . that poor sinful people are justified before God, that is, absolved—pronounced free of all sins and of the judgment of the damnation that they deserved, and accepted as children and heirs of eternal life—without the least bit of our own "merit or worthiness," apart from all preceding, present, or subsequent works. We are justified on the basis of sheer grace, because of the sole merit, the entire obedience, and the bitter suffering, death, and the resurrection of our Lord Christ alone, whose obedience is reckoned to us as righteousness. The Holy Spirit conveys these benefits to us in the promise of the holy gospel. Faith is the only means through which we lay hold of them, accept them, apply them to ourselves, and appropriate them. Faith itself is a gift of God, through which we acknowledge Christ our redeemer in the Word of the gospel and trust in him. Only because of his obedience does God the Father forgive our sins by grace, regard us as upright and righteous, and give us eternal salvation.[6] (*FC SD* 3:9–11, in *BC*, 563–64)

---

[6]Punctuation slightly revised.

JUSTIFICATION: OBJECTIVE AND SUBJECTIVE

When the Lutheran Confessions speak of a Christian's new standing before God, they often jump back and forth unselfconsciously between the two terms "justified" and "forgiven." And therefore today, a Lutheran discussion of justification and a Lutheran discussion of forgiveness, or absolution, are really two aspects of the same discussion.

As noted, the original focus of the nineteenth-century deliberations in the Missouri and Norwegian Synods was not on justification *per se* but was on the nature and character of absolution *in relation to* justification. Is absolution merely an expression of God's wish for someone's forgiveness, which may or may not be fulfilled depending on whether the condition of faith is met? Or is absolution a powerful impartation of a forgiveness that already exists for the world in Christ, which is either received by faith or rejected by unbelief? Theodore Julius Brohm made a presentation to the 1860 convention of the Missouri Synod, "Concerning the Intimate Connection of the Doctrine of Absolution with that of Justification." Among the theses that he set forth in this presentation were these:

1. Absolution, or the forgiveness of sins, is, according to Luther's teachings, the Gospel, whether it is proclaimed to many or to few....
4. Absolution consists: (a) not in a judicial verdict of the confessor; (b) nor in any empty announcement of, or wish for, the forgiveness of sins; but (c) in a powerful impartation of [the forgiveness of sins].
5. The effect of Absolution (a) does not depend upon man's repentance, confession, and atonement, (b) but Absolution

demands faith, creates and strengthens faith; (c) without faith it profits a man nothing; (d) although it is not therefore a "failing key."

In the discussion that followed his presentation, Brohm emphasized that

> it is necessary to recognize, before all else, that this great treasure of the Gospel, the redemption which has come to pass for all men through Christ and the forgiveness of sins acquired thereby, is also presented to all men, according to Christ's command: "Preach the Gospel to every creature." To all who hear it, whether they believe or don't believe, forgiveness of sins is announced and presented. When a preacher announces the Gospel he always speaks an absolution, and truly also to those who do not believe, because absolution is a divine act and [is] not dependent on the belief or unbelief of men. The unbeliever, therefore, quite certainly rejects that which came to him also by the preaching of the Gospel, and precisely for this reason (his rejection), [he] forfeits it.

The preaching of the gospel and the pronouncing of absolution today are not merely reminders of a past pardon for all that was issued by God long ago in conjunction with the death and resurrection of Jesus. Rather, according to Brohm,

> Where the preaching of the Gospel is announced, there the dear Lord himself steps before the sinner and says, "I am

reconciled and herewith announce to you that all your sins are forgiven you." Just as this would be no mere announcement but a powerful impartation of forgiveness if God so spoke to the sinner without means, thus the preaching and Absolution of the pastor is also truly nothing else than an announcement of forgiveness, but such an announcement as actually brings and gives the forgiveness it announces.[7]

Brohm's theses, and his explanation of his theses, were shaped largely by Martin Luther's teaching on absolution and the power of the keys, especially as found in his treatise *On The Keys* from 1530 and in a letter that he and Philip Melanchthon wrote to the city council of Nürnberg in 1533. The "keys" terminology originates in Jesus's solemn declaration to Peter in Matthew 16:19 (ESV), "I will give you the keys of the kingdom of heaven, and whatever you bind on earth shall be bound in heaven, and whatever you loose on earth shall be loosed in heaven." Yet when Jesus fulfilled this pledge after his resurrection and gave to Peter the authority to bind and to loose, he did not give that authority *only* to Peter. We read in John 20:22–23 (ESV) that Jesus told *the disciples*, "Receive the Holy Spirit. If you forgive the sins of any, they are forgiven them; if you withhold forgiveness from any, it is withheld."

---

[7]Theodore Julius Brohm, "Concerning the Intimate Connection of the Doctrine of Absolution with that of Justification," in *Proceedings of the Convention of the Missouri Synod* (1860), pp. 41–42 as quoted in Rick Nicholas Curia, *The Significant History of the Doctrine of Objective or Universal Justification among the Churches of the Former Evangelical Lutheran Synodical Conference of North America* (1983), pp. 16–17.

In *The Keys*, Luther described the objective content of the keys and the source of their power to forgive when he stated that "hidden in the keys of Christ [lie] his blood, death, and resurrection, by which he has opened to us heaven, and thus imparts through the keys to poor sinners what he has wrought through his blood." The office of the keys is, therefore, "a high and divine office, aiding our souls to pass from sin and death to grace and life; it grants them righteousness without any merit of works, solely through forgiveness of sins."[8] Further on in the treatise, Luther addresses his readers personally with these words of encouragement and instruction:

> Rely on the words of Christ and be assured that God has no other way to forgive sins than through the spoken Word, as he has commanded us . . . Do you believe he is not bound who does not believe in the key which binds? Indeed, he shall learn, in due time, that his unbelief did not make the binding vain, nor did it fail in its purpose. Even he who does not believe that he is free and his sins forgiven shall also learn, in due time, how assuredly *his sins were forgiven, even though he did not believe it.* St. Paul says in Rom. 3[:3]: "Their faithlessness [does not] nullify the faithfulness of God." We are not talking here either about people's belief or disbelief regarding the efficacy of the keys. We realize that few believe. We are speaking of what the keys accomplish and give. *He who does not accept what the keys give receives, of course, nothing. But this is not the key's fault.* Many do not believe the gospel, but this does not

---

[8] Martin Luther, *The Keys*, in *Luther's Works*, vol. 40 (Philadelphia, PA: Fortress Press, 1958), p. 328.

mean that the gospel is not true or effective. A king gives you a castle. If you do not accept it, then it is not the king's fault, nor is he guilty of a lie. But you have deceived yourself and the fault is yours. The king certainly gave it.[9]

The loosing key flows out from the objective forgiveness of all for whom Jesus died, and it announces that forgiveness to everyone who hears the spoken word of absolution. The means of grace in general, and the loosing key in particular, do not create God's forgiveness. They carry, convey, and deliver God's forgiveness as it already exists in Christ. The forgiveness that Christ won is in the gospel, and in the absolution, so that it can be conferred upon those who believe this divine pardon. Of course, those who do not believe it do not receive it and so remain in their lost condition. But, even for unbelievers, their forgiveness was there for them in the gospel. Christ won it on the cross for them and for everyone and has placed it in his Word for them and for everyone. And that is why a person who persists in his rejection of Christ will someday learn—on Judgment Day, if not before—"how assuredly his sins were forgiven, even though he did not believe it."

The objective truth of God's forgiveness of *redeemed* humanity *in* Christ does not contradict the continuing reality of God's condemnation of *fallen* humanity *outside of* Christ. The gospel does not contradict the law but coexists with it in symbiotic tension within God's ongoing conversation with humanity. Therefore objective justification—which is an important component of the gospel—does

---

[9] Martin Luther, *The Keys*, in *LW* 40:366–67. Emphases added.

not contradict the law either. These words of John the Baptist continue to be true: "Whoever believes in the Son has eternal life; whoever does not obey the Son shall not see life, but the wrath of God remains on him" (John 3:36 ESV).

Yet in his explication of what believers do in fact believe, *these* words of John the Baptist *also* continue to be true: "Behold, the Lamb of God, who takes away the sin of the world!" (John 1:29 ESV). When John the Baptist said this, Jesus was still walking the earth, on a pathway that was taking him to Calvary and to the empty tomb. Now, during the Easter season each year—as the church looks back upon the finished work of Christ—it joyfully prays in the Easter Preface, ". . . chiefly are we bound to praise You for the glorious resurrection of Your Son Jesus Christ, our Lord; for He is the very Paschal Lamb, *which was offered for us and has taken away the sins of the world.*"[10]

In settling a dispute in the city of Nürnberg on the relative desirability or propriety of public absolution as compared to private absolution, Luther and Melanchthon wrote a letter to the Nürnbergers in which they point out that

> The preaching of the holy gospel itself is principally and actually an absolution in which forgiveness of sins is proclaimed in general and in public to many persons, or publicly or privately to one person alone. Therefore absolution may be used in public and in general, and in special cases also in private, just as the sermon may take place publicly or privately, and as one might comfort many people

---

[10]Proper Preface for Easter, in *Evangelical Lutheran Hymnary* (Fenton, MO: MorningStar Music Publishers, 1996), p. 73. Emphasis added.

JUSTIFICATION: OBJECTIVE AND SUBJECTIVE

> in public or someone individually in private. Even if not all believe [the word of absolution], that is no reason to reject [public] absolution, for each absolution, whether administered publicly or privately, has to be understood as demanding faith and as being an aid to those who believe in it, just as *the gospel itself also proclaims forgiveness to all men in the whole world and exempts no one from this universal context.* Nevertheless the gospel certainly demands our faith and *does not aid those who do not believe it;* and yet the universal context of the gospel has to remain [valid].[11]

This reference to the "universal context" of a gospel that proclaims forgiveness to "all men in the whole world" is just another way of acknowledging that there is a universal justification of all people in Christ, which is made known and applied in preaching and absolution. The gospel does not proclaim anything that is not true. And so, if the gospel "proclaims forgiveness to all men in the whole world and exempts no one from this universal context," then there must be a forgiveness in existence for all people in the whole world. And the fact that this gospel "demands our faith" proves that the gospel, and the forgiveness it proclaims, exists prior to faith, and that the gospel, and the forgiveness it proclaims, is "an aid" for salvation only to those who believe in it.

Luther emphasizes some of these same points in a sermon for Easter Tuesday, in which he says that

---

[11]Martin Luther and Philip Melanchthon, "Letter to the Council of the City of Nürnberg" (1533), in *LW* 50:76–77. Emphasis added.

we should preach also forgiveness of sins in his name. This signifies nothing else than that the Gospel should be preached, which declares unto all the world that *in Christ the sins of all the world are swallowed up*, and that he suffered death to put away sin from us, and arose to devour it, and blot it out. All this he did, that whoever believeth, should have the comfort and assurance that it is reckoned unto him, even as if he himself had done it; that his work is mine and thine and all men's; yea that he gives himself to us with all his gifts to be our own personal property. Hence, as he is without sin and never dies by virtue of his resurrection even so I also am if I believe in him . . . [12]

In all of this, we are reminded of what the Augsburg Confession teaches: that faith "is brought to life by the gospel or absolution" and that "faith believes that sins are forgiven on account of Christ..." (*Ap. AC* 7:5, in *BC*, 45). Absolution comes before faith and gives birth to faith. Kurt E. Marquart comments on this passage from the Augustana: "Absolution can exist without faith (although its benefits of course go to waste unless faith receives them), but faith cannot exist without absolution."[13]

---

[12]Martin Luther, "Sermon for Easter Tuesday," in *Complete Sermons of Martin Luther* (Grand Rapids, MI: Baker Books, 2000), Vol. 1, pt. 2, p. 316. Emphasis added.

[13]Kurt E. Marquart, "The Reformation Roots of Objective Justification," in *A Lively Legacy: Essays in Honor of Robert Preus*, ed. Kurt E. Marquart, John R. Stephenson, and Bjarne W. Teigen (Fort Wayne, IN: Concordia Theological Seminary, 1985), p. 118.

JUSTIFICATION: OBJECTIVE AND SUBJECTIVE

Within the Missouri and Norwegian Synods of the mid-nineteenth century, the teaching of the Lutheran theologian Johann Gerhard (1582–1637) that Christ was absolved of humanity's sin in his resurrection was also influential in how their way of explaining the objective and subjective aspects of forgiveness and justification took shape.[14] In commenting on the Epistle to the Romans, Gerhard writes that "the heavenly Father, by delivering Christ into death for the sake of our sins, condemned sin in His flesh." Gerhard goes on to explain that God the Father "punished our sins in Christ, which were imposed on Him and imputed to Him as to a bondsman," and that "by raising Him from the dead, by that very deed He absolved Him from our sins that were imputed to Him, and consequently has also absolved us in Him, so that, in this way, the resurrection of Christ may be both the cause and the pledge and the complement of our justification."[15]

Elsewhere, in one of his theological disputations, Gerhard explains the saving significance of the death and resurrection of Christ in a similar way. In this disputation, he speaks first of how the Lord's resurrection assures Christians that their sins truly are forgiven. He writes that "Because Christ arose, we are therefore no longer in sins, since most assuredly full and perfect satisfaction has been made for them, and because in the resurrection of Christ we are absolved of our sins, so that they no longer can condemn us before the judgment bar

---

[14]This can be seen especially in C. F. W. Walther's Easter sermon "Christ's Resurrection – The World's Absolution," in *The Word of His Grace: Occasional and Festival Sermons* (Lake Mills, IA: Graphic Publishing Company, Inc., 1978), 229ff.

[15]Johann Gerhard, *Adnotationes ad priora capita Epistolae D. Pauli ad Romanos* as quoted in Paul A. Rydecki, "The Forensic Appeal to the Throne of Grace in the Theology of the Lutheran Age of Orthodoxy: A Reflection on Atonement and Its Relationship to Justification" (2013), p. 36.

of God." As he continues to unfold the blessings of the resurrection of Christ for believers, Gerhard goes on to say that "This power of the resurrection of Christ includes not only the application of the righteousness that avails before God, but also the actual absolution from sins, and even the blessed resurrection to life, since by virtue of the resurrection of Christ we are freed from the corporal and spiritual death of sins." But then, as the text of this disputation continues, Gerhard cites "the apostolic teaching in 1 Timothy 3:16, *God was manifested in the flesh, justified in the Spirit* (namely through the resurrection by God the Father)" and explains that when the divine Son was in this way justified,

> *he was absolved of the sins of the whole world, which he as Sponsor took upon himself,* so that he might make perfect satisfaction for them to God the Father. Moreover in rising from the dead he showed by this very fact that satisfaction has been made by him for these sins, and all of the same have been expiated by the sacrifice of his death.[16]

The reason why each of us is able to know from the gospel that we are absolved of all our sins in the resurrection of Christ is because

---

[16] Johann Gerhard, *Disputationes Theologicae* 20:1450, trans. Kurt E. Marquart (1655) as quoted in Jon D. Buchholz, "Jesus Canceled Your Debt!" (2012), p. 10. Emphasis added. In a separate commentary on 1 Timothy 3:16, Gerhard similarly states that "He was justified" means, among other things, that "He was declared to be righteous, since in and by means of the resurrection Christ was absolved of the sins of men that He took upon Himself as Guarantor in order to make satisfaction for them to the Father." Johann Gerhard, *Adnotationes ad Priorem D. Pauli ad Timotheum Epistolam*, trans. Paul A. Rydecki. Translation slightly revised.

the whole world was so absolved in the resurrection. The sins of the whole world were placed upon Christ, and in his death he made satisfaction for them to God the Father. And now, in his resurrection, Christ is *absolved* of the sins of the whole world, which he had carried to the cross. In God's tribunal, they are all lifted and removed from him. Since Christ, both in his death and in his resurrection, was humanity's bondsman, sponsor, and representative before God, this lifting of humanity's sins *from him* was, before God, the lifting of humanity's sins *from humanity*. An individual human being is obviously a part of "the whole world" and of the human race. An individual human being can therefore be certain that he is included both in Christ's perfect satisfaction before the Father and in the Father's absolution of Christ.

Gerhard never expresses himself in this way—concerning Christ's absolution on our behalf and our collective absolution in Christ—without also always recognizing the necessity of a personal absolution, and faith in the same, for the justification of the believing individual.[17] This is because the whole point of talking about

---

[17] In commenting on Romans 5:19, Gerhard explains that "a distinction must fully be made between the acquisition and the application of the merit of Christ; or between the benefit itself and participation in the benefit. The acquisition of the merit, or the benefit itself obtained by the death of Christ, is general. For as Adam, by his disobedience, enveloped all of his posterity in the guilt of sin, so Christ, who suffered and died for the sins of all, also *merited and acquired righteousness for all*. But this benefit is only *applied* to those who are grafted into Christ by *faith*, and only they become participants in this benefit." Johann Gerhard, *Adnotationes ad priora capita Epistolae D. Pauli ad Romanos* as quoted in Paul A. Rydecki, "The Forensic Appeal to the Throne of Grace in the Theology of the Lutheran Age of Orthodoxy: A Reflection on Atonement and Its Relationship to Justification," p. 27. Emphases added.

humanity's absolution in Christ's resurrection is to lay the foundation for and give substance to the absolutions that are by necessity spoken to specific human beings here and now by their pastors. And faith is the only means by which these absolutions, and the justification in Christ that they convey, are received. There is, then, no contradiction whatever between Gerhard's teaching that in raising Jesus from the dead, God the Father "absolved Him from our sins that were imputed to Him, and consequently has also absolved us in Him," and his teaching in another place that

> the merits of Christ are *received* in no other way than through faith, not to mention that it is impossible to please God without faith, Hebrews 11:6, let alone to be received into eternal life. In general, St. Paul concludes concerning this matter in Romans 3:28, "Thus we hold then that *a man* becomes righteous without the works of the Law—only through faith."[18]

The discussions of objective forgiveness, objective absolution, and objective justification that began in the Missouri Synod spread also into the Norwegian Synod, where the clarity and comfort with which Brohm and others in Missouri had explained these things were greatly appreciated. But almost immediately, the Norwegians were criticized for their embracing of this form of teaching by many within the Augustana Synod and later by George Fritschel and others in the

---

[18]Johann Gerhard, *A Comprehensive Explanation of Holy Baptism and the Lord's Supper*, trans. Elmer Hohle (Decatur, IL: Johann Gerhard Institute, 1996), 165. Emphases added.

JUSTIFICATION: OBJECTIVE AND SUBJECTIVE

Iowa Synod. Friedrich A. Schmidt, in the essay on justification that he delivered at the first convention of the Evangelical Lutheran Synodical Conference in 1872, demonstrates the unsound foundation on which these criticisms were based by pointing out that

> when G. Fritschel claims: "In the Gospel God shows the sinner a way out, which *can* redeem him from death and damnation and *bring about the forgiveness of his sins*," he thereby denies that justification has already been accomplished by Christ and that thus the righteousness which avails before God already exists. But thus teach not only the Scriptures but also the Confessions of our church, as in the 6th article of the Augsburg Confession, where it says, following the Latin: "forgiveness of sins and justification *are apprehended by faith*" [AC 6:2], and, "grace, forgiveness of sins, and justification *are apprehended by faith*" [AC 20:22]. Thus also the Apology: "Faith *accepts the forgiveness of sins*" [Ap. AC 4:62]. Further: "Justification is something promised freely for Christ's sake alone, wherefore it is accepted always and only by faith before God" [Ap. AC 4:217].
>
> These quotations show clearly that a justification must first be in existence, which faith can accept, [and] that faith does not have to bring it about first, but that it embraces it as already existing. But if someone were to say: Yes, forgiveness of sins indeed already exists, but not justification, he would have to be ignorant of our Confessions, which expressly teach that justification and forgiveness of sins are the same. "We believe, teach, and confess that according to the usage of Holy

Scripture, the word justify in this article means absolve, that is, acquit of sins" [FC Ep. 3:7].[19]

Norwegian Synod Pastor Herman Amberg Preus explains and defends his synod's teaching in an 1874 article that included a section on "The justification of the world." As Preus summarizes the confession of his synod on "the justification of the world," or "as it is more often called, objective, universal justification," he states:

> By this we understand that by raising Christ from the dead God declares him righteous, and at the same time acknowledges and declares all people, the whole world— whose Representative and Substitute Jesus Christ was, in his resurrection and victory as well as in his suffering and tribulation ("He was delivered for our offenses and raised for our justification")—as free from guilt and punishment, and righteous in Christ Jesus. At the same time, we maintain and teach, in agreement with the Scriptures, that the individual sinner must accept and appropriate by faith this righteousness earned for everyone by the death of Christ, proclaimed by his resurrection, and announced and bestowed through the Gospel, to himself, for his comfort and salvation; and that for the sake of Christ whose righteousness the troubled sinner grasps and makes his own in faith, God justifies the believer and counts his faith to him for righteousness. We teach therefore that the expressions

---

[19]Friedrich A. Schmidt, "Justification: Objective and Subjective," 22. Emphases in original.

> "justification" and "to justify" are used in Scripture and in the Lutheran Church in a twofold way: 1) that justification has come to *everyone*, namely when we mean that justification *is earned* for everyone by Christ, and 2) that only the *believer* is justified, when a person is talking about the righteousness being *received*.

Preus goes on to demonstrate that "our doctrine of justification in the first sense, as a justification of everyone through the resurrection of Christ from the dead, is biblical" by pointing out that "it is expressly taught in Romans 5:18.19, where it says, 'Therefore, as by the offense of one judgment came upon all men to condemnation; even so by the righteousness of one the free gift came upon all men unto justification of life. For as by one man's disobedience many were made sinners, so by the obedience of one shall many be made righteous.'" Preus continues by showing how "the correctness of this teaching" about the justification of the world in Christ is confirmed "from the biblical teaching about redemption," and he observes that

> Scripture teaches that Christ "is the propitiation for our sins; and not for ours only, but also for the sins of the *whole world*" (1 Jo. 2:2); that he is "the Lamb of God who takes away the sin of *the world*" (Jo. 1:29); and that in Christ God reconciled *himself with the world, because he did not impute their trespasses unto them* (2 Co. 5:19). If Christ has borne the sin of the world and atoned for it, then in the sight of him who gave the ransom for it, the world is loosed and free from sin and its

punishment—although it remains in bondage and under the wrath of God if it remains in unbelief.[20]

In their teaching on "objective" or "universal" justification, the pastors and theologians of the Missouri and Norwegian Synods were consciously drawing on the writings of Luther, Gerhard, and other orthodox Lutheran theologians of the past. They were not influenced by, and were not trying to reproduce, the erroneous teaching of Samuel Huber (1547–1624), a convert from Calvinism to Lutheranism and for a time a professor at Wittenberg, who had used similar terminology. Schmidt states,

> When a king pardons a group of criminals, then they all are from the king's side acquitted of guilt and punishment, but whoever among them does not accept the pardon, must continue to suffer for his guilt; it is the same with sinners in the justification which has happened through Christ's death and resurrection. Yes, if God had not written and sealed the letter of pardon, then we pastors would be liars and seducers of the people if we said to them: Only believe, then you are righteous. But now that God has through the raising of His Son signed the letter of pardon for the sinners, and sealed it with His divine seal, we can confidently preach: the world is justified, the world is reconciled with God, which latter expression too would be impermissible if the former were not

---

[20] Herman Amberg Preus, "The Justification of the World," in *Evangelisk Luthersk Kirketidende*, trans. Herbert Larson, 1874. Emphasis in original. Punctuation slightly revised.

JUSTIFICATION: OBJECTIVE AND SUBJECTIVE

true. Our old dogmaticians too would themselves have used the expression more—since they believed and taught the substance—had not *Huber* shortly before Gerhard's time taught that God had not only justified all men already, but had also elected them to eternal life. In order to avoid the appearance of agreement with this erroneous doctrine, they used the expression only rarely . . . The Wittenberg theologians (Gesner, Leyser, Hunnius, and others) did not want to tolerate Huber's expression: . . . "Christ imparted the redemption to the entire human race *in the proper sense*," because the *actual imparting*, "as it is taken in the theological schools," refers to the *appropriation* (See Wittenberg *Consilia* I, 642 ff.). Nevertheless we find not a few unimpeachable theologians who speak of a universal justification or absolution.[21]

Christ's atonement for all human sin, which absolution reveals and applies, did not merely put God into a neutral state—no longer wrathful against humanity but not yet reconciled to humanity either until and unless specific human beings repent and believe. The righteousness that avails before God, which Jesus acquired for humanity in his death and resurrection, is not an inert righteousness. It is a justifying righteousness which exists in Christ *for* everyone and which is offered in the means of grace *to* everyone. As Robert D. Preus explains,

---

[21]Schmidt, "Justification: Subjective and Objective," 20–21. Emphasis in original.

The doctrine of objective justification is a lovely teaching drawn from Scripture which tells us that God, who has loved us so much that He gave His only to be our Savior, has for the sake of Christ's substitutionary atonement declared the entire world of sinners for whom Christ died to be righteous (Romans 5:17–19).

Objective justification, which is God's verdict of acquittal over the whole world, is not identical with the atonement; it is not another way of expressing the fact that Christ has redeemed the world. Rather, it is *based upon* the substitutionary work of Christ, or better, it is a part of the atonement itself. *It is God's response to all that Christ did to save us;* God's verdict that Christ's work is finished, that He has been indeed reconciled, propitiated. His anger has been stilled and He is at peace with the world, and therefore He has declared the entire world in Christ to be righteous.

According to all of Scripture Christ made a full atonement for the sins of all mankind. Atonement (at-one-ment) means reconciliation. If God was not reconciled by the saving work of Christ, if His wrath against sin was not appeased by Christ's sacrifice, if God did not respond to the perfect obedience and suffering and death of His Son for the sins of the world by forgiveness, by declaring the sinful world to be righteous in Christ—if all this were not so, if something remains to be done by us or through us or in us, then there is no finished atonement. But Christ said, "It is finished." And God raised Him from the dead and justified Him, pronounced Him, the sin bearer, righteous (I Timothy 3:16), and thus in

JUSTIFICATION: OBJECTIVE AND SUBJECTIVE

Him pronounced the entire world of sinners righteous (Romans 4:25).[22]

Being careful about how these things are understood, preached, and applied is not merely a matter of ivory-tower hairsplitting. The gospel must not be proclaimed as if it were a conditional message about a potential justification. Such a "gospel" would not calm the fears of a troubled conscience. Quite simply, a conditional message about a potential justification cannot forgive sins. In this regard, Ken R. Schurb makes an important pastoral observation:

> A crushed unbeliever must be told that God is no longer angry with him in Christ, that all his sins are forgiven, that God has declared him "not guilty" (i.e., justified him)—or he will not believe. Simply to tell him, "God loves you, and Christ died for you," is not sufficient. Even a 16th century Roman Catholic could say this much. Urging a penitent unbeliever to have faith on such a basis is fruitless. He must know that Christ's atonement directly affects God's attitude toward him in such a way that God no longer wants to punish him, but loves and forgives him. In other words, he must know objective justification.[23]

---

[22]Robert D. Preus, "Objective Justification," *Concordia Theological Seminary Newsletter*, no. 2 (1981). Emphases added. Punctuation slightly revised.
[23]Ken R. Schurb, *Does the Lutheran Confessions' Emphasis on Subjective Justification Mitigate Their Teaching of Objective Justification?* (1982), 32.

As interesting as it is to review the private writings of Luther and Gerhard that the American Lutherans of the nineteenth century found so helpful on this issue, as well as the private writings of respected twentieth-century theologians who explained and defended this teaching, these private writings are nevertheless not a part of the official confessional corpus of Lutheranism as found in the *Book of Concord*. Is this teaching on objective and subjective justification, forgiveness, and reconciliation also found in the Confessions? Yes, it is.

The Augsburg Confession is the most universal symbol of the Lutheran Reformation and of the Lutheran Church. It does not have a section explicitly expounding on the objective and subjective aspects of justification and forgiveness. But a recognition of these two aspects of justification and forgiveness is implicit in everything that it does say about Christ's saving work and about the Christian's saving faith. The Augsburg Confession declares:

> . . . it is taught that we cannot obtain forgiveness of sin and righteousness before God through our merit, work, or satisfactions, but that we receive forgiveness of sin and become righteous before God out of grace for Christ's sake through faith when we believe that *Christ has suffered for us* and that *for his sake our sin is forgiven and righteousness and eternal life are given to us.* For God will regard and reckon this

JUSTIFICATION: OBJECTIVE AND SUBJECTIVE

faith as righteousness in his sight, as St. Paul says in Romans 3[:21–26] and 4[:5]. [24] (*Ap. AC* 4:1–3, in *BC*, 39–41)

Note the construction. The saving truth of Christ that is to be believed is this: Christ has suffered for us, and for his sake our sin is forgiven and righteousness and eternal life are given to us. This saving truth is the essential content of the gospel. And this is what we believe when we believe the gospel, because it is true. It is already true for everyone for whom Christ died when it is preached, even before it is believed. It is not true *because* we believe it or only *as* we believe it. And according to the Augsburg Confession, when we do believe this gospel—that for Christ's sake our sin is forgiven—we then *receive* forgiveness of sin and *become* righteous before God out of grace for Christ's sake through faith. The forgiveness of sin in its objective dimension is the forgiveness that is "given"—in and through the means of grace. The forgiveness of sin in its individual and personal dimension is the forgiveness of sin that is "received"—by faith.

With reference to consciences that have already been terrified by the preaching of the law of God, the Apology states that

> in the midst of these terrors, *the gospel about Christ (which freely promises the forgiveness of sins through Christ)* ought to be set forth to consciences. They should therefore believe that *on account of Christ their sins are freely forgiven.* This faith uplifts, sustains, and gives life to the contrite, according to the passage [Rom. 5:1]: "Therefore, since we are justified by faith,

---

[24] Emphases added.

we have peace with God." This faith receives *the forgiveness of sins*. This faith justifies before God, as the same passage testifies, "since we are justified by faith." This faith shows the difference between the contrition of Judas and Saul on the one hand, and Peter and David on the other. The contrition of Judas or Saul was useless for the reason that it lacked the faith that grasps *the forgiveness of sins granted on account of Christ*. Accordingly, the contrition of David and Peter was beneficial because faith was added, which apprehends *the forgiveness of sins given on account of Christ*.[25] (*Ap. AC* 7:35–36, in *BC*, 192–93)

Faith is of crucial importance in the doctrine of justification. But faith is important and necessary not so much because of what it *is* but because of what it *receives* and *grasps*—namely, the forgiveness of sins. And the forgiveness of sins that is given by God so that it can be received and grasped is not given on account of faith, or because of faith, but is "given on account of Christ." What faith embraces is not just a divine proposal for a possible forgiveness and justification that do not yet actually exist but that may be brought into existence if certain conditions are met. Forgiveness and justification in Christ are already there, in the preached gospel. They are real and can be grasped. And by faith, they *are* grasped. If they are *not* grasped by someone for whom Christ died, they still were graspable. In the objective sense, they were still true and real. The gospel was *for* that person, even if the gospel was never *received by* that person.

---

[25]Emphases added.

JUSTIFICATION: OBJECTIVE AND SUBJECTIVE

Again, with reference to Luke 24:47, in which "Christ commands the preaching of repentance and the forgiveness of sins in his name," the Apology acknowledges that God's Word, in law and gospel,

> accuses all people of being under sin and subject to eternal wrath and death, and for Christ's sake offers the forgiveness of sins and justification, which are received by faith. The proclamation of repentance, which accuses us, terrifies consciences with genuine and serious terrors. In the midst of these, hearts must once again receive consolation. This happens when they believe the promise of Christ, namely, that on his account we have the forgiveness of sins. This faith, which arises and consoles in the midst of those fears, receives the forgiveness of sins, justifies us, and makes alive.[26] (*Ap. AC* 4:62, in *BC*, 130)

So, faith "justifies us," not because justification is *completed* by faith, but because justification is *"received* by faith."

The Formula of Concord—in the context of setting forth a sound explanation of the doctrine of the person and work of Christ—also explains the relationship between what is offered in the gospel, and the faith that relies upon what is offered in the gospel, when it confesses that

---

[26]Punctuation revised.

the entire obedience of the entire person of Christ, which he rendered to the Father on our behalf unto the most shameful death of the cross [Phil. 2:8], is reckoned to us as righteousness. For the human nature alone, apart from the divine nature, could not satisfy the eternal, almighty God neither through its obedience nor through its suffering for the sins of the whole world. On the other hand, the deity alone, without the humanity, could not mediate between God and us. However, because, as has been stated above, the obedience is that of the entire person, *it is a perfect satisfaction and reconciliation of the human race, which satisfied God's eternal, unchangeable righteousness, revealed in the law. Thus, it is our righteousness before God and is revealed in the gospel. On this righteousness faith relies before God*, and God reckons it to faith, as is written in Romans 5[:19]: "For just as by one man's disobedience the many were made sinners, so by one man's obedience will the many be made righteous," in 1 John 1[:7]: "The blood of Jesus his Son cleanses us from all sin," and in Habakkuk 2[:4]: "The righteous will live by faith." For this reason, neither the divine nor the human nature of Christ in itself is reckoned to us as righteousness, but only the obedience of the person, who is at the same time God and a human being. Therefore, faith looks to the person of Christ, as this person submitted to the law for us, bore our sin, and in going to his Father performed complete and perfect obedience for us poor sinners, from his holy birth to his death. Thereby he covered all our disobedience, which is embedded in our nature and in its thoughts, words, and deeds, so that this disobedience is not reckoned to us as condemnation but is pardoned and forgiven by sheer grace, because of Christ alone.[27] (*FC SC* 3:56-58, in *BC*, 572-73)

The Concordists are responding to Andreas Osiander's teaching regarding the Christian's righteousness before God, which attributed the Christian's righteousness to the indwelling of Christ's essentially righteous divinity. In the face of this error, they emphasize that sinners are justified by Christ's obedience to his Father and not by his mere existence as God's incarnate Son or by his mystical indwelling of the believer. And they emphasize that sinners receive Christ—and everything he earned, accomplished, and brought into existence for their salvation—by means of faith.

The focus of what the Concordists are teaching here is not on the act or receptiveness of faith, but it is on that which faith receives. Faith receives a righteousness that is tied to the objective saving work of Christ in real history. Faith is not the context or setting for God's creation of an individualized righteousness for each believing person. It is instead the passive reception of a righteousness before God that was objectively brought into existence for the human race by the obedience of our divine-human Savior; and that is revealed, made known, and delivered to us in the gospel. Our faith does not rely on a potential righteousness or even on a righteousness that may in some way exist but that is not yet "our righteousness" before God. Faith

---

[27]Emphasis added. For a fuller discussion of this section of the Formula of Concord and of the entire subject of objective and subjective justification, see David Jay Webber, "Our Righteousness before God . . . Is Revealed in the Gospel. On This Righteousness Faith Relies," *The Emmaus Conference* (2015).

relies on, and receives, Christ's "perfect satisfaction and reconciliation of the human race." This is "our righteousness" in Christ, even before we receive it, because our Savior has procured it for *us* and established it for *us*.

Our faith does not contribute, in whole or in part, toward bringing our righteousness into existence. Jesus brought our righteousness into existence by his obedience and by his vicarious death on the cross for the sins of humanity. This is what it means to say, as the Formula of Concord does say, that God reckons this righteousness—this already-existing perfect satisfaction and reconciliation of the human race—"to faith." Our Lutheran forefathers had emphasized, in response to scholastic Roman error, that we are justified by *faith* and *not* by *works*. In this context, our Lutheran forefathers now also emphasize that we are justified *by* faith and not just *in* faith or *because of* faith. In other words, "our righteousness," which is established and defined by the work of God in Christ, and not by the work of God in us, is received *by means of* faith.[28]

What Luther writes in the *Large Catechism* regarding the petition for forgiveness in the Lord's Prayer speaks more directly to the distinction between objective and subjective forgiveness, as this

---

[28]This would seem to be what Martin Luther is driving at in these theses: "1. [To say] that the Son of David is sitting at the right hand of God [Ps. 110:1; Matt. 22:42–45] means that the Son of God is risen from the dead. 2. His resurrection from the dead is our justification [Rom. 4:25], through faith alone. 3. [To say] that we are justified by faith alone means that all the righteousnesses of the Law and of human beings are condemned." Martin Luther, "Disputation on Justifying Faith and Miracle-Working Faith and That We Are Justified by Faith Alone," in *LW* 73:378 (Saint Louis, MO: Concordia Publishing House, 2020). See also Tom G. A. Hardt, "Justification and Easter: A Study in Subjective and Objective Justification in Lutheran Theology," in *A Lively Legacy*, 52ff.

JUSTIFICATION: OBJECTIVE AND SUBJECTIVE

distinction would be applied to the daily struggles and daily comfort of a Christian:

> Although we have God's Word and believe, although we obey and submit to his will and are nourished by God's gift and blessing, nevertheless we are not without sin. We still stumble daily and transgress because we live in the world among people who sorely vex us and give us occasion for impatience, anger, vengeance, etc. Besides, the devil is after us, besieging us on every side and, as we have heard, directing his attacks against all the previous petitions, so that it is not possible always to stand firm in this ceaseless conflict. Here again there is great need to call upon God and pray: "Dear Father, forgive us our debts." *Not that he does not forgive sins even apart from and before our praying; for before we prayed for it or even thought about it, he gave us the gospel, in which there is nothing but forgiveness.* But the point here is for us to recognize and accept this forgiveness.[29] (*LC* 3:86–88, in *BC*, 452)

The forgiveness that Christ won *for* humanity is offered *to* humanity in the gospel. The recognition and acceptance of this forgiveness by those who believe is a recognition and an acceptance of something that already exists. God's forgiveness is not triggered or brought into existence by our praying for that forgiveness or by our thinking about it and desiring it. The forgiveness of sins is already in the gospel for everyone, before anyone prays for it or thinks about it. This is true of

---

[29]Emphasis added.

the gospel whenever and wherever it is offered and given to someone, whether for the first time—for the kindling of faith—or as a part of the Christian's baptismal life of daily dying to self and daily rising in Christ.

Luther had spoken in his 1521 treatise *Against Latomus* in a way that was similar to how he speaks in the *Large Catechism*. In the treatise, he draws a comparison between what Christ did for everyone in his death and resurrection, and what the Holy Spirit does and will do for Christians in their life of faith and in their own future resurrection. He begins by quoting St. Paul's words from the Epistle to the Romans, "For the law of the Spirit of life in Christ Jesus has set me free from the law of sin and death" (8:2). With a desire to explain the difference between being objectively set free from the *law* of sin and death and being subjectively set free from sin and death *in actuality*, Luther then asks,

> Why does he not say that, "It has set me free from sin and death"? Has not Christ set us free from sin and death once and for all? Paul, however, is speaking of the proper operation of the law of the Spirit, which does what Christ has merited. Indeed, *Christ once and for all absolved and freed everyone from sin and death when He merited for us the law of the Spirit of Life.* But what did that Spirit of Life do? He has not yet freed us from death and sin, for we still must die, we still must labor under sin; but in the end He will free us. Yet He has already liberated us from the *law* of sin and death, that is, from the kingdom and tyranny of sin and death. Sin is indeed present, but having lost its tyrannic power, it can do nothing; death

JUSTIFICATION: OBJECTIVE AND SUBJECTIVE

indeed impends, but having lost its sting, it can neither harm nor terrify.[30]

In his propitiatory sacrifice and in his resurrection, Christ merited for a humanity enslaved to sin and mired in death "the law of the Spirit of Life"; that is, he merited *for* the world the way of salvation that is implemented and enacted by the Holy Spirit *in* the world. In terms of what Christ *merited* for "everyone"—with respect to humanity's needed liberation from sin and death—"everyone" has been objectively "absolved" from sin and "freed" from death, "once and for all." "Everyone" in this context does not mean everyone who believes, because not everyone for whom Jesus meritoriously died and rose again does eventually believe. The absolution of everyone is attached to the Son's *earning* of salvation and not only to the Holy Spirit's *application* of salvation. And yet, it is only *in the application* that believers are liberated from the *power* of sin and the *sting* of death in *this* life; and it is only in the faith which the Holy Spirit works in Christians that they are able to look forward in hope to their ultimate liberation from sin and death *itself* in the *next* life. Without the converting and regenerating work of the Spirit through the means of grace, the absolution of "everyone" does not actually *benefit* everyone. What Christ *merited for* all is, sadly, not *received by* all.

In Luther's Smalcald Articles, we see an even clearer presentation of this doctrine, both in terms of the justification and reconciliation that exist in Christ for all, and in terms of the personal faith that allows individuals to know and experience this justification

---

[30]Martin Luther, *Against Latomus*, in *LW* 32:207 (Philadelphia, PA: Fortress Press, 1958). Emphasis added.

and its saving benefits. He begins his summary of "the first and chief article" of the Christian religion by describing certain objective truths that "must be believed" and that are "obtained or grasped" by faith alone.

> Here is the first and chief article: That Jesus Christ, our God and Lord, "was handed over to death for our trespasses and was raised for our justification" (Rom. 4[:25]); and he alone is "the Lamb of God, who takes away the sin of the world" (John 1[:29]); and "the Lord has laid on him the iniquity of us all" (Isa. 53[:6]); furthermore, "All have sinned," and "they are now justified without merit by his grace, through the redemption that is in Christ Jesus ... by his blood" (Rom. 3[:23-25]). (SA 2, 1:1–5, in *BC*, 301)

Note in particular how Luther selectively quotes from Romans 3:23–25. In the biblical text, immediately after saying the things that Luther does quote, St. Paul also says that these truths and blessings are "to be received by faith." But Luther very deliberately does not quote that statement. Luther's purpose in citing some of this passage but not all of it, at this point in his presentation, is to show which portions of the passage speak of the objective aspect of justification. Apart from and before anyone believes in these things, Luther confesses that all have sinned and that all are now justified by God's grace through the redemption that is in Christ Jesus. The sinfulness of all and the justification and redemption of all can be considered and reflected upon in their own right as theologically significant facts, before the progression of thought goes on to a consideration of the means by

JUSTIFICATION: OBJECTIVE AND SUBJECTIVE

which this redemption and this justification are received by an individual. And that is exactly what Luther is doing here.

But then, right after his summary of what is to be believed, obtained, and grasped by a Christian, Luther does describe the believing, the grasping, and the obtaining that allow these objective truths to be received for justification by the individual:

> Now because *this must be believed* and may not be obtained or grasped otherwise with any work, law, or merit, it is clear and certain that this faith alone justifies us, as St. Paul says in Romans 3[:28,26]: "For we hold that a person is justified by faith apart from works prescribed by the law"; and also, "that God alone is righteous and justifies the one who has faith in Jesus." Nothing in this article can be conceded or given up, even if heaven and earth or whatever is transitory passed away. As St. Peter says in Acts 4[:12]: "There is no other name ... given among mortals by which we must be saved." "And by his bruises we are healed" (Isa. 53[:5]).[31] (SA 2, 1:1–5, in *BC*, 301)

The well-known phrase *faith alone* makes an appearance here. We are justified by faith alone. In context, the rejected antithesis to faith, as that which justifies, is "works prescribed by the law." Luther teaches that we are justified by "faith alone" and are not justified in whole or in part by such works. However, he does *not* teach that being justified by "faith alone" means that we are not justified by the gospel of Christ

---

[31]Emphasis added.

crucified for sinners to which a justifying faith clings, or that we are not saved by the objective justification of "all" that exists in the gospel and is received by means of faith.

Faith alone justifies before God, precisely because it believes, grasps, and obtains the objective, justifying truth of Christ. And as Luther explains it here, that truth includes the fact that Jesus Christ "was handed over to death for our trespasses and was raised for our justification"; the fact that Jesus Christ is "the Lamb of God, who takes away the sin of the world"; the fact that the Lord has laid on Jesus Christ "the iniquity of us all"; and the fact that all who have sinned "are now justified without merit" by God's grace "through the redemption that is in Christ Jesus," by his blood. A Christian's faith does not make any of this to be true. It is true because *God* made it to be true—in and through the perfect life of his Son, in and through the substitutionary death of his Son, and in and through the victorious resurrection of his Son. This truth does not exist *because of* faith, but it does exist *for the sake of* faith and *for the benefit of* faith. And God imputes this truth to those who do believe it.

In a more extensive sermonic commentary on one of the verses that he mentions in the Smalcald Articles, Luther notes that the proclamation of John the Baptist with respect to Jesus, "Behold, the Lamb of God!" (John 1:29), is "an extraordinarily free and comforting sermon on Christ, our Savior." The Son of God "assumes not only my sins but also those of the whole world, from Adam down to the very last mortal. These sins He takes upon Himself; for these He is willing to suffer and die . . . " And how, according to Luther, is this truth to be applied in view of the distinction between law and gospel that governs the church's proclamation?

JUSTIFICATION: OBJECTIVE AND SUBJECTIVE

As far as the law is concerned, Luther states that the reason why it was necessary for the *world's* sins to be assumed and taken upon himself by the Lamb of God is because "The entire world . . . is under the dominion of sin and completely discredited before God." Therefore, "Anyone who wishes to be saved must know that all his sins have been placed on the back of this Lamb!" As the gospel in this verse is then developed by Luther, he paraphrases the Baptist's words and draws out their meaning,

> Therefore John points this Lamb out to his disciples, saying: "Do you want to know where the sins of the world are placed for forgiveness? Then don't resort to the Law of Moses or betake yourselves to the devil; there, to be sure, you will find sins, but sins to terrify you and damn you. But *if you really want to find a place where the sins of the world are exterminated and deleted, then cast your gaze upon the cross.*[32] The Lord placed all our sins on the back of this Lamb . . . "

Luther had already explained in this sermon that the reason why Jesus was willing to suffer and die under the weight of the world's sins in this way was so that "our sins may be expunged and we may attain eternal life and blessedness." Now, he explains *how* our sins are personally expunged from our lives in God's sight and how we personally attain eternal life and blessedness. This is by means of faith, which receives and rests in Christ, and not by means of works or human religious efforts of any kind. He declares to his listeners:

---

[32]Emphasis added.

Therefore a Christian must cling simply to this verse and let no one rob him of it. For there is no other comfort either in heaven or on earth to fortify us against all attacks and temptations, especially in the agony of death . . . the pope has taught that the Christian must be concerned with bearing his own sin, atoning for it with alms and the like . . . But if what he teaches is true, then I, not Christ, am yoked and burdened with my sin. And then I would necessarily be lost and damned. But Christ does bear the sin—not only mine and yours or that of any other individual, or only of one kingdom or country, but the sin of the entire world. And you, too, are a part of the world.[33]

Luther's language is very vivid and evocative. In the *objective* sense of forgiveness, in Christ the sins of the world are "exterminated and deleted." In the *subjective* sense of forgiveness, the believer who clings to Christ in the gospel has the comfort and assurance that this extermination and deletion of sin is reckoned to him and that his own sins are therefore "expunged."

Luther touches on yet another of the verses that he had cited in the Smalcald Articles from the prophet Isaiah when he comments on the statement in the Epistle to the Hebrews that Jesus, in his death on the cross, had "made purification for sins" (1:3). Luther explains that it is not we who make purification of our own sins by our penances or good works but that *Jesus* makes this purification for us,

---

[33] Martin Luther, "Sermons on the Gospel of St. John," in *LW* 22:161–64 (Saint Louis, MO: Concordia Publishing House, 1957). Emphasis added.

JUSTIFICATION: OBJECTIVE AND SUBJECTIVE

in our stead. According to Luther, in saying that it is *Christ* who makes this purification, the author of the Epistle to the Hebrews

> makes useless absolutely all the righteousnesses and deeds of penitence of men. But he praises the exceedingly great mercy of God, namely, that "He made purification for sins," not through us but through Himself, not for the sins of others but for our sins. Therefore we should despair of our penitence, of our purification from sins; for *before we repent, our sins have already been forgiven*. Indeed, first His very purification, on the contrary, also produces penitence in us, just as His righteousness produces our righteousness. This is what Is. 53:6 says: "All we like sheep have gone astray, we have turned every one to his own way, and the Lord has laid on Him the iniquity of us all."[34]

The objective forgiveness of humanity's sins in Christ is not a remote or detached truth as far as the conscience of the individual Christian is concerned. Even though it involves all the people for whom Christ died—which is everyone—it is pondered by each believer in a very personal way. Luther gives evangelical direction to our meditation and reflection in this respect by telling us that Jesus made purification "not for the sins of others but for *our* sins." Each of us, in our personal repentance and faith, is able to say with relief and joy that purification was made by *my* Savior for *my* sins. A conscience that is properly comforted by the gospel no longer fears, therefore,

---

[34] Martin Luther, "Lectures on Hebrews," in *LW* 29:112-13 (Saint Louis, MO: Concordia Publishing House, 1968). Emphasis added.

that this purification was probably made for the sins of others, who are more worthy, and not for my sins.

But also, since this purification was accomplished *through Christ,* in the realm of sacred history, and not *through us,* in the realm of our religious experience, we appreciate the significance of the fact that "before we repent, our sins have already been forgiven." To the conscience of someone who is penitent and who is very much aware of his inability to produce anything that could earn God's favor, this assurance instills within him a certain confidence that his sins are truly forgiven. His forgiveness is not based on anything that is in him. It is based on the purification that Christ accomplished for everyone, and consequently *also* for him, long before he repented or believed.

In the objective sense, our sins were not just *potentially* forgiven before we repented. On the basis of Hebrews 1:3 and Isaiah 53:6, Luther teaches that "before we repent, our sins have already been forgiven." And if we might be tempted to think that it is our *penitence* that earns or produces our personal forgiveness or personal purification, Luther would remind us that the purification for sin that was accomplished by Christ is actually *what produces our penitence* and that this purification for sin is likewise what produces the faith that receives the forgiveness which Christ established and brought into existence for us, by his atoning death.

In his Smalcald Articles presentation, Luther cites a portion of another passage from the Epistle to the Romans which is often cited in discussions of objective and subjective justification, in which St. Paul teaches that righteousness "will be counted to us who believe in him who raised from the dead Jesus our Lord, who was delivered up for our trespasses and raised for our justification" (Rom. 4:24–25

ESV). This passage is also used by Luther in one of his Easter sermons, in which he develops his thoughts about the death and resurrection of Christ by means of a comparison of two contrasting "pictures" that he verbally paints for the mind's eye of his listeners—a "picture" of the events of Good Friday, which portrays the soteriological significance of that day; and a "picture" of the events of Easter Sunday, which portrays the soteriological significance of *that* day. He begins by saying that the first picture

> is sombre, full of distress, misery, and woes; it is the scene of blood presented to us on Good Friday—Christ crucified between murderers and dying with excruciating pain. This scene we must contemplate with much earnestness, . . . realize that it all happened on account of our sins, yea, that Christ as the true High Priest sacrificed Himself for us and paid with His death our debts. . . . Therefore, as often as we remember or view this doleful, bloody scene, we ought to bear in mind that we have before us our sins and the terrible wrath of God against them, a wrath so dire that no creature could endure it, that all atonement became impossible except the one made by the sacrifice and death of the Son of God.

But then, as Luther moves on to a consideration of what happened *after* the Lord's suffering and death—under the great weight and judgment of our sins—he says that now "this picture of sorrow is changed." Indeed, before three full days had gone by, our Lord and Saviour presents to us another picture, beautiful, full of life, lovely and cheerful, in order that we might have the sure consolation that not only *our sins were annihilated in the death of Christ*, but that *by His resurrection a new eternal righteousness and life was obtained*, as St. Paul says, Rom. 4: "Christ was delivered for our offences, and was raised again for our justification." And 1 Co. 15: "If Christ be not raised, your faith is vain; ye are yet in your sins. Then they also which are fallen asleep in Christ are perished. If in this life only we have hope in Christ, we are of all men most miserable." As in the former scene we saw the burden of our sin upon Him and bringing Him to the cross, so in this other scene of the resurrection *we witness no longer sin, pain and sorrow, but only righteousness, joy and happiness*. It is the victory of life over death—a life everlasting, with which this temporal existence on earth cannot be compared. Of this we have reason to rejoice.

As Luther then reflects more deeply and practically on these two contrasting pictures of Christ, he states:

> Merely to view the former scene would be terrible, but when we view it in connection with the glad event of the resurrection, and when we bear in mind why our Lord suffered thus, we will derive from such a contemplation much benefit and consolation. It will become apparent to us how inexpressibly great the love of God toward us poor sinners was, as He had compassion on our misery, even to such an

amazing extent that He did not spare His beloved and only Child, but gave Him up for us, to bear upon the cross and in death the burden of our transgressions, which were too heavy for us and would have crushed us to the earth. This load was taken from us and placed by God Himself upon His Son, who, as God from eternity, could alone bear the heavy weight of sin. Upon Him we now find our burden. Let us leave it there, for there is no one else to be found who could better relieve us of it.

The other scene presents to us Christ no longer in woe and misery, weighed down with the ponderous mass of our sins, which God has laid upon Him, but beautiful, glorious and rejoicing; for *all the sins have disappeared from Him*. From this we have a right to conclude: *If our sins, on account of the sufferings of Christ, lie no longer upon us, but are taken from our shoulders by God Himself and placed upon His Son, and if on Easter, after the resurrection, they are no more to be seen, where then are they?* Micah truly says: *They are sunk into the depth of the sea, and no devil nor any body else shall find them again* (Mic. 7:18–19).

After this recounting of the objective realities that have been established for those for whom Jesus died and rose again—established *in his death and resurrection*—Luther goes on to discuss the importance and role of faith as that which alone receives the benefit of our Savior's death and resurrection on our behalf. Where there is no faith, there is no such reception; and the benefits of the

Lord's death and resurrection are not personally applied or enjoyed. Luther says:

> This article of our faith is glorious and blessed; whoever holds it not is no Christian ... If we desire to be true Christians it is necessary for us firmly to establish in our hearts through faith this article, that Christ, who bore our sins upon the cross and died in payment for them, arose again from the dead for our justification. The more firmly we believe this, the more will our hearts rejoice and be comforted. For it is impossible not to be glad when we see Christ alive, a pure and beautiful being, who before, on account of our sins, was wretched and pitiable in death and in the grave. We are now convinced that our transgressions are removed and forever put away.[35]

Further on in the sermon, Luther summarizes these points once again and compares what happened to Jesus in his death and resurrection, for us and on our behalf, and what happens to us now, in our personal justification and forgiveness, as we hear and believe the Easter gospel:

> In the former scene of suffering and death we witnessed our sin, our sentence of condemnation and death resting heavily upon Christ, making Him a distressed, pitiable Man; now, on Easter, we have the other scene unalloyed with sin; no curse, no frown, no death is visible; it is all life, mercy, happiness and

---

[35] Martin Luther, "First Easter-Sermon," in *Dr. Martin Luther's House-Postil*, 2nd ed., vol. 2 (Columbus, OH: J. A. Schulze, 1884), pp. 268–71. Emphases added.

righteousness in Christ. This picture can and should cheer our hearts. We should regard it with no other feeling but that today God brings us also to life with Christ. We should firmly believe that as we see no sin nor death nor condemnation in Christ, so God will also, for Christ's sake, consider us free from these if we faithfully rely upon His Son and depend upon His resurrection. Such a blessing we derive from faith.[36]

These expositions of the passages Luther quotes in the Smalcald Articles help us to know more fully what these passages meant to Luther, and therefore, to see more clearly what Luther was intending to teach in the Smalcald Articles. And confessional Lutheran pastors who subscribe to the Smalcald Articles as an official symbolical book of their church, and as a testimony of their own beliefs, can accordingly be guided by these expositions in understanding with greater insight what *they* are expected to confess and teach regarding our redemption by God, our reconciliation with God, and our justification before God.

We should not think that this way of teaching about justification and forgiveness was invented by Luther. The fathers of the ancient church who had a better-than-average understanding of justification by faith, also had a better-than-average understanding of objective and subjective justification! In explaining the meaning of St. Paul's teaching that "all have sinned and fall short of the glory of God, and are justified by his grace as a gift, through the redemption that is in Christ Jesus" (Rom. 3:23–24 ESV), St. John Chrysostom employs the

---

[36]Ibid., 2:276.

imagery of a king delivering a reprieve to a body of imprisoned criminals and setting them free from their chains, to illustrate the way in which God, in Christ, has pardoned and liberated the human race. He states:

> All human nature was taken in the foulest evils. "All have sinned," says Paul [Rom. 3:23]. They were locked, as it were, in a prison by the curse of their transgression of the Law. The sentence of the judge was going to be passed against them. A letter from the King came down from heaven. Rather, the King himself came. Without examination, without exacting an account, he set all men free from the chains of their sins. All, then, who run to Christ are saved by his grace and profit from his gift. But those who wish to find justification from the Law will also fall from grace. They will not be able to enjoy the King's loving-kindness because they are striving to gain salvation by their own efforts; they will draw down on themselves the curse of the Law because by the works of the Law no flesh will find justification.[37]

Chrysostom describes the justification and forgiveness that God established in Christ for all sinners, in terms of the divine king setting "all men" free from the chains of their sins. This objective truth then becomes the basis upon which individual sinners are now invited to

---

[37]St. John Chrysostom, Discourse II 1:7–2:1, in *Discourses Against Judaizing Christians: The Fathers of the Church*, trans. Paul W. Harkins, vol. 68 (Washington, DC: Catholic University of America Press, 1979), pp. 38–39.

JUSTIFICATION: OBJECTIVE AND SUBJECTIVE

"run to Christ," by faith, to profit personally from the pardon that had been issued to humanity.

In a truly remarkable letter that St. Ambrose of Milan penned to a layman named Irenaeus (a portion of which is quoted in the Apology of the Augsburg Confession), St. Ambrose discusses original sin and its effects, natural law and the revealed Mosaic law, the distinction between law and gospel, the objective forgiveness of all men in Christ, the evangelical and saving character of Baptism, and the personal justification of a baptized Christian by faith. Irenaeus had asked for an explanation of the following words from St. Paul's Epistle to the Romans: "For the Law works wrath; for where there is no Law, neither is there transgression" (4:15). As a part of his response, Ambrose said this:

> The Law of Moses ... entered ... into the place of the natural law. ... since deception had banished that [natural] law and nearly blotted it out of the human breast, pride reigned and disobedience was rampant. Therefore, that other [Law of Moses] took its place so that by its written expression it might challenge us and shut our mouth, in order to make the whole world subject to God. The world, however, became subject to him through the Law, because all are brought to trial by the prescript of the Law, and no one is justified by the works of the Law; in other words, because the knowledge of sin comes from the Law, but guilt is not remitted, the Law, therefore, which has made all men sinners, seems to have caused harm. But, when the Lord Jesus came he forgave all men the sin they could not escape, and canceled the decree against us by

shedding his blood [Col. 2:14]. This is what he says: "By the Law sin abounded, but grace abounded by Jesus" [Rom. 5:20], since after the whole world became subject he took away the sins of the whole world, as John bears witness, saying: "Behold the Lamb of God, who takes away the sin of the world!" [John 1:29] Let no one glory, then, in his own works, since no one is justified by his deeds, but one who is just has received a gift, being justified by Baptism. It is faith, therefore, which sets us free by the blood of Christ, for he is blessed whose sin is forgiven and to whom pardon is granted [Ps. 32:1].[38]

Ambrose does not treat the general forgiveness or justification of "all men" and of "the whole world" in isolation from the personal forgiveness or justification of the one who has received the gift of the Lord's justification in Baptism and who by faith has been individually set free from sin through the blood of Christ. The personal and individual aspect of justification always presupposes the objective and general aspect of justification, and always builds on it. And the proclamation of the objective and general aspect of justification—when it is proclaimed rightly and for the right reason—always serves, promotes, and feeds into the personal or individual aspect of justification. The significance of what Jesus accomplished for all men, and for the whole world, is the content of what is preached for the sake of an individual's justifying faith. These intimately related

---

[38]St. Ambrose, Epistle 73 "To Irenaeus," in *Letters 1–91: The Fathers of the Church*, trans. Mary Melchior Beyenka, vol. 26 (Washington, DC: Catholic University of America Press, 1954), pp. 464, 467–68 and as quoted (in part) in *Ap. AC* 4:103, in *BC*, 137–38. The above translated text is conflated from both sources.

truths of the gospel can never be separated, even though they can and should be distinguished, as St. Ambrose does distinguish them.

The confusion and controversy that have so often surrounded the teaching on objective and subjective justification—in the nineteenth century, in the twentieth century, and in our own time—is very puzzling and discouraging. From what I have seen, some of the confusion arises from the weak and misleading expressions that have occasionally been used by would-be teachers and defenders of objective justification. Jon D. Buchholz offers some helpful counsel in this respect:

> Some of the problems about justification that have arisen in Lutheran circles are the result of ignorant, careless, or otherwise imprecise communication. When we are speaking about universal justification, we must use universal terms; when speaking about individual justification, we must use individual terms. We should be careful that we do not mix metaphors in such a way that it becomes unclear whether we are speaking universally or individually. We must not extend metaphors beyond the scope of their illustration. We must always properly distinguish between law and gospel, both in their teaching and in their proper application. We cannot use passages that treat objective justification to prove or disprove subjective justification, and we cannot use passages that treat subjective justification to prove or disprove objective justification. We cannot become one-dimensional in our teaching, so that we ignore either the objective or the subjective side of the whole doctrine of justification. Finally,

we must recognize that some terms are used universally, some terms are used exclusively for individuals, and some terms are used in both the general and the particular sense.

Buchholz then offers this specific advice:

> I suggest that most problems articulating the doctrine with precision can be avoided if we maintain three distinctions: (1) The forgiveness of sins was completed and won at the cross and empty tomb. (2) The forgiveness of sins is distributed in the means of grace and received by faith. (3) The forgiveness of sins is only *en Christō*, in Christ.[39]

Another reason for the confusion that abounds concerning the teaching on objective and subjective justification is the failure of many of those who criticize it to make sure they actually understand what they are criticizing. I have seldom heard fully accurate descriptions of the doctrine—as taught correctly—from those who reject it. In my experience, the most common mistakes of the critics are that they fail to notice, in this teaching, that the only individual *as an individual* who is justified in the objective sense is *Jesus;* and that justification in the objective sense has *not* been *received* by the world, the human race, all men, or whatever the universal term may be. Any proper discussion of the justification that is *received* is a discussion of the *subjective* aspect of justification.

---

[39]Jon D. Buchholz, "Jesus Canceled Your Debt!," 21–22.

JUSTIFICATION: OBJECTIVE AND SUBJECTIVE

It must also be conceded that in Lutheran history, the term *justification* in particular was used by many Lutheran theologians only according to its subjective meaning. Those theologians used other expressions to describe the objective aspect of justification, yet without denying the reality of what the term *objective justification* is intended to convey. When differences among teachers are differences only in terminology and not in substance, this is not divisive. We are "not to quarrel about words" (2 Tim. 2:14 ESV).

Martin Chemnitz, for example, wrote that God's transfer of the law to Christ—whose fulfillment of the law was "by satisfaction and obedience for the whole human race" and whose "satisfaction is the expiation for the sins of the whole world"—is "a matter which *belongs to* the article of justification."[40] But he did not say that this saving work of Christ constitutes, in an *objective* sense, a "justification" itself of "the whole human race" and of "the whole world." Yet Chemnitz *does indeed* teach the *doctrine* of objective justification, even though he does not use the *term*. He writes in his *Loci Theologici*, "Regarding Our Redemption" that God

> demonstrated His love toward us, whereby in the fulness of time He sent forth His only-begotten Son and delivered Him up for all, Rom. 5:8; 1 John 4:9. Luke 1:78 and 54: "through the bowels of His mercy . . . in remembrance of His mercy." John 3:16: God accepted the sacrifice of His Son as satisfaction and propitiation for the sins of the whole world. 1 John 4:10 and 1

---

[40]Martin Chemnitz, *Examination of the Council of Trent*, trans. Fred Kramer, pt. 1 (Saint Louis, MO: Concordia Publishing House, 1971), 499. Emphasis added.

Cor. 1:30: He was made for us by God our redemption, righteousness, etc. 2 Cor. 5:19: *"God was in Christ reconciling the world unto Himself."*[41]

It is of great significance that Chemnitz includes 2 Corinthians 5:19 in this section of his *Loci*, "Regarding Our Redemption," rather than in the section that immediately follows, "Regarding the Distribution or Application of This to the Believer." Chemnitz likewise does not hesitate to cite with approval St. Gregory of Nazianzus "in the oration for the sacred Easter festival, where he says: 'O Easter, great and holy, and *the cleansing of the whole world!*'"[42]

Francis Pieper observes that "Scripture and the Confessions . . . know of only one object of justifying faith and use the terms 'Christ,' 'Christ's righteousness,' 'Christ's obedience,' 'Christ's suffering,' 'Christ's merit,' 'forgiveness,' 'justification,' etc., *promiscue*, or as synonyms . . . "[43] Pieper himself employs the terms *objective justification* and *objective reconciliation* as functionally synonymous.[44] Might it be easier for all Confessional Lutherans of good will to come to an agreement on "objective reconciliation" and then move from there to a mutual recognition that "objective justification" really means the same thing? Perhaps we can all also listen, calmly and carefully, to Marquart's constructive suggestions for how a common

---

[41] Martin Chemnitz, *Loci Theologici*, trans. J. A. O. Preus, vol. 2 (Saint Louis, MO: Concordia Publishing House, 1989), 548–49. Emphasis added.

[42] Martin Chemnitz, *Examination of the Council of Trent*, trans. Fred Kramer, pt. 3 (Saint Louis, MO: Concordia Publishing House, 1986), 462. Emphasis added.

[43] Francis Pieper, *Christian Dogmatics*, vol. 2 (Saint Louis, MO: Concordia Publishing House, 1951), 539.

[44] Ibid., 321–22, 347–51.

JUSTIFICATION: OBJECTIVE AND SUBJECTIVE

understanding could be reached by all those who sincerely want to be Confessional Lutherans:

> A contemporary clarification of justification would have to begin with what the Formula of Concord calls "the only essential and necessary elements of justification," that is, (1) the grace of God, (2) the merit of Christ, (3) the Gospel which alone offers and distributes these treasures, and (4) faith which alone receives or appropriates them (SD III.25). The first three items define the universal/general dimension of justification (forgiveness as obtained for all mankind on the cross, proclaimed in the resurrection [see Rom. 4:25 and 1 Tim. 3:16] and offered to all in the means of grace), and the fourth, the individual/personal dimension. No one actually *has* forgiveness unless and until he receives it by faith. This distinction between forgiveness as obtained for and offered to all, and that same forgiveness as actually received and possessed, is often described . . . with the words "objective" and "subjective." . . . The right teaching here must defend the fullness of our Lord's saving work against the denial of *sola gratia* (grace alone) by Rome on the one hand and against the denial of *universalis gratia* (universal grace) and the means of grace by Geneva on the other. Only the Church of the Augsburg Confession teaches the article of justification in its evangelical

truth and plenitude, that is, both grace alone and universal grace, and therefore also the means of grace![45]

---

[45]Kurt E. Marquart, "Augsburg Revisited," in *2001: A Justification Odyssey*, ed. John A. Maxfield (Saint Louis, MO: The Luther Academy, 2002), pp. 173–74. Emphasis in original.

JUSTIFICATION: OBJECTIVE AND SUBJECTIVE

Obedientia Christi Activa: The Imputation of Christ's Active Obedience in the Lutheran Tradition and Scripture

By Jordan Cooper

The doctrine of justification by grace alone through faith alone on account of Christ alone has often been labeled the *articulus stantis et cadentis ecclesiae* ("the article upon which the church stands or falls") in the Lutheran tradition. Yet, though there is broad agreement as to the centrality of this doctrine, agreement regarding some of the particulars of the teaching has not been quite so uniform. Controversies surrounding the nature of justification have permeated the Lutheran Church from its inception. Soon after the death of Luther, a disciple of his named Andreas Osiander proposed that justification is the result of the believer's reception of Christ's indwelling divine nature, rather than an act of forensic imputation. This resulted in a fierce debate that was concluded by the publication of the Formula of Concord in 1580. Even so, in the following years, it was clear that the issue of justification was far from settled. A variety of other controversies surrounding the teaching have arisen since.

In recent decades, one of the primary facets of the historic Reformation teaching of justification that has been challenged is the doctrine of the imputation of Christ's active obedience. This is the contention that the righteousness merited by Christ for his people consists in a twofold structure. First is Christ's passive obedience, or his paying the penalty for sin on the cross through his vicarious suffering and death.¹ Second is Christ's active obedience, which consists in his fulfilling the law throughout his earthly life in order to gain a positive righteousness that is imputed to his people through faith. Though perhaps not explicitly stated in the writings of Martin Luther himself on this subject, the imputation of Christ's active obedience is confessed in the Formula of Concord:

> Therefore, his obedience consists not only in his suffering and death but also in the fact that he freely put himself in our place under the law and fulfilled the law with this obedience and reckoned it to us as righteousness. As a result of his total obedience—which he performed on our behalf for God in his deeds and suffering, in life and death—God forgives our sin, considers us upright and righteous, and grants us eternal salvation. (FC SD 3:15)

Though no extensive debate existed on this issue during the sixteenth century, the Brandenburg theologian George Karg rejected the imputation of Christ's active obedience.² He argued that since obedience to law is simply an obligation for God's creatures, one could not gain any positive merit through such obedience.³ The Formula settled the question for the immediate years following the

---

[1] Though, I would not limit Christ's passive obedience to his final hours. His taking the place of sinners through self-identification is evident in other places, such as his reception of a baptism of repentance even though he needed no repentance (Matt. 3:13–17).
[2] Karg retracted this belief after being removed from his teaching position and was consequently reinstated.
[3] This same argument was put forward by Anselm in *Cur Deus Homo*.

Reformation, yet it has been under extensive scrutiny since the nineteenth century.

Theologians of disparate perspectives have rejected the doctrine of the imputation of Christ's active obedience in recent years. Modernist theologians in the late nineteenth and early twentieth centuries tended to reject the doctrine of Christ's active obedience for moral reasons.[4] It was said that the moral character of the gospel was lost through a reliance on Christ's own holiness as imputed to humanity. One of the prominent contemporary opponents of the imputation of Christ's active obedience is the proponents of the so-called New Perspective on Paul—most significantly, N.T. Wright. In this view, the imputation of Christ's active obedience as a doctrine was developed through an acontextual reading of medieval debates about merit into the arguments of the Pauline epistles. It is claimed that this doctrine is not explicitly taught in Paul, nor was it something that was an aspect of his Jewish worldview through which his theology developed. Within the Reformed tradition, there are certain proponents of (what was at least once labeled) the Federal Vision movement who reject the imputation of Christ's active obedience on the basis of a modified covenant theology, often referred to as Monocovenantalism.[5] These writers view the active obedience of

---

[4]This is reflected, for example, in Harnack's treatise *What Is Christianity?* wherein he argues that the religion of Paul as misinterpreted by the Reformers lost the moral center of Jesus's own gospel (which is about God the Father) for a gospel about Jesus. Harnack argues, in contrast to the Reformers, that central tenants of Christianity are the Fatherhood of God and the brotherhood of man.

[5]See, for example, Norman Shepherd's article "The Imputation of Christ's Active Obedience," in Andrew P. Sandlin, *A Faith That Is Never Alone:*

Christ as necessary in that Jesus, in order to be qualified as the spotless lamb, must have lived a life devoid of sin and, thus, of perfect obedience; this obedience, however, is not imputed to his people. Along with this, several of these authors contest the use of language of merit altogether as a valid theological category. In Baptist theology, some in the New Covenant Theology movement have also rejected the doctrine of active obedience due to their emphasis on the discontinuity of the old and new covenants, arguing that the Mosaic law has been completely abolished. In this perspective, the law is invalid for the new covenant member, and thus there is no need for Christ to fulfill the law on behalf of believers.

The rejection of the doctrine of active obedience in contemporary Lutheranism is most important for this paper. For those who adopt a *quia* subscription to the confessional documents, this issue is settled due to its presence in the Formula of Concord.[6] However, theologians of other Lutheran traditions who do not accept the authority of the Formula of Concord have deviated from this teaching. One influential theologian who has done this is Gerhard O. Forde. Forde's career was centered on the doctrine of justification by faith as he perceived it in the early writings of Luther. He argues that justification by faith alone must once again become the central doctrine of Lutheranism and be boldly proclaimed from Lutheran pulpits. Forde does not, however, adopt the traditional scholastic approach to justification but proposes a view that he argues is

---

A Response to Westminster Seminary California (La Grange, CA: Kerygma, 2007), pp. 249-278.

[6]The *quia* position denotes that the *Book of Concord* is to be believed because it agrees with Scripture, rather than insofar as (*quatenus*) it does.

consistent with Luther's own theology as opposed to the later confessional documents.[7]

Gerhard Forde's View of Justification

Gerhard Forde's doctrine of justification is articulated in contrast to traditional approaches to imputation in his book *Where God Meets Man*. Forde argues in this volume that all theology has tended to adopt either a ladder scheme of salvation or an eschatological approach to justification. He rejects the former in favor of the latter. The ladder scheme is a theology of merit. In Forde's view, this characterizes both Roman Catholic theology and Protestant scholastic teaching. For both, there is a ladder to heaven that is characterized by one's merit, or obedience to the law. In the Roman Catholic scheme, this ladder is climbed through the merit of Christ, the saints, and one's own good works. The Protestants have unfortunately (in Forde's view) adopted a similar system.

> We begin by assuming the law is a ladder to heaven. Then we go on to say, "Of course, no one can climb the ladder, because we are all weakened by sin. We are therefore guilty and lost." And this is where "the gospel" is to enter the picture. What we need is someone to pay our debt to God and to climb the ladder for us. This, supposedly, is what Jesus has done. As our

---

[7] I critique his approach in depth in Jordan Cooper, *Lex Aeterna: A Defense of the Orthodox Lutheran Doctrine of God's Law and Critique of Gerhard Forde* (Eugene, OR: Wipf and Stock, 2018).

ACTIVE OBEDIENCE OF CHRIST

> "substitute" he has paid of God and climbed the ladder for us. All we have to do is "believe" it.[8]

In this perspective, one cannot affirm either substitutionary atonement or the imputation of Christ's active obedience. Both of these doctrines, which developed through the work of Melanchthon and Chemnitz, do not depart significantly from the Roman Catholic soteriological paradigm, because they both depend on the conviction that the law needs to be fulfilled for God's justice to be satisfied. This destroys the eschatological nature of the gospel, which breaks free from the constraints of God's law. Forde purports,

> We have, in fact, interpreted the gospel merely as something that makes the ladder scheme work. The gospel comes to make up for the deficiencies of the law. The gospel does not come as anything really new. It is not the breaking in of a radically new age with an entirely new outlook. It is simply a "repair job." It merely fixes up the old where it had broken down. It is an attempt to put new wine in old wine skins, or a new patch on an old garment. When we do this, the gospel always comes off as second best. It is trapped in the understanding of law which we have ourselves concocted.[9]

When arguing for such a view of the gospel, in which Christ dies as a substitute for one's failure to obey the law and lives righteously under

---

[8]Gerhard Forde, *Where God Meets Man* (Minneapolis, MN: Augsburg, 1972), 10.
[9]Ibid., 11.

the law in order that his obedience might be imputed to his people, "The gospel itself simply becomes another kind of law."[10]

Forde argues that this destroys the nature of forgiveness. He asks, "If God has been paid, how can one say that he really forgives? If a debt is paid, one can hardly say it is forgiven. Nor could one call God's action mercy."[11] He assumes that God's justice should not and does not require payment for sin because forgiveness has to be given without conditions. While the law is based on conditions, the gospel is free and unbound to law. An important aspect of Forde's scheme of law is the manner in which the term *law* is defined. For Forde, "The law is not defined only as a specific set of demands as such, but rather in terms of what it does to you."[12] Rather than speaking of law as Torah, a specific set of commands that adhere to God's moral nature, Forde opts for an existential understanding of the law. The law, as well as the gospel, is not defined by its content but by its effect on the hearer. He argues that "The gospel too, is defined primarily by what it does: the gospel comforts because it puts an end to the voice of the law."[13] Theological attempts to define the gospel by Christ's active and passive obedience are what Forde labels "spectator theology." They depend on an assumption that the gospel is a theory with a set of truths that one must adhere to rather than the doing of God. He argues,

---

[10]Ibid., 11.
[11]Ibid., 12.
[12]Ibid., 15.
[13]Ibid., 16.

ACTIVE OBEDIENCE OF CHRIST

> When [a theology of glory] is applied to the event of the cross itself, this kind of thinking leads back to the theology of the ladder. The law is the way of salvation, a ladder to heaven. Because we have failed and are too weak to climb it, Jesus becomes our substitute. By his perfect life he climbs the ladder and by his death he pays for our failure. In terms of dogmatic theology, Jesus "vicariously satisfied" the demands of the law. He paid the bill, so to speak, which we couldn't pay. Such theology is a spectator theology. It is the result of an attempt to fit the cross into a system of meaning which one already has and which remains standing as an eternal scheme indicating what would have to be done to placate God.[14]

The ideas of both substitutionary atonement and the imputation of active obedience are dependent upon a theology of glory, rather than a theology of the cross. This harkens back to Luther's Heidelberg Disputation of 1515, which is highly influential for Forde's own theology. Interestingly, Forde admits that Luther did "use language which sounds like vicarious satisfaction language"[15] but then makes the statement that "Luther vehemently rejects the idea that God is one who can be bargained with in commercial fashion or satisfied in the sense that amends may be made to him."[16] Forde gives no citations from Luther to defend this statement. One would think that one needs some strong evidence to substantiate the idea that Luther would reject substitution when he himself utilized such language.

---

[14]Ibid., 34.
[15]Ibid., 41.
[16]Ibid., 41–42.

Rather than substitution, or the imputation of merit, Forde purports that justification is primarily to be defined as a death and resurrection. He states that "'Full and complete justification' is equated with death and resurrection, not with a legal scheme as such."[17] Again, in another place, Forde argues that justification "means precisely not some sort of legal transaction but, according to the New Testament, a death and a resurrection."[18] Forde does admit that one can, in some sense, talk about justification as forensic and legal. He purports that "Righteousness comes just by divine pronouncement, by divine 'imputation' as Luther liked to put it."[19] Justification is "a re-creative act of God, something he does precisely by speaking unconditionally."[20] Forde certainly is willing to speak of imputation. God imputes the sinner righteous by faith, but that is not by the imputation of Christ's merit to the sinner. It is rather a free forensic declaration that creates new life, so that "justification and death-life are complimentary."[21] He even argues that "The more forensic it is the more effective it is!"[22] Forde's claims here merit a thorough Biblical response, which is the task of the remainder of this article.

Biblical Evidence

Although Forde's argument against the imputation of Christ's active obedience rests largely upon historical arguments from Luther's

---

[17]Gerhard Forde, *Justification by Faith: A Matter of Life and Death* (Mifflintown, PA: Sigler, 1991), 16.
[18]Ibid., 10.
[19]Ibid., 29.
[20]Ibid., 30.
[21]Ibid., 36.
[22]Ibid., 36.

writings, the primary source in defining doctrine is Scripture rather than Luther's own theology. It is important to emphasize that the Lutheran Church does not subscribe to Luther's personal corpus as its theological foundation. Rather, as heir of the Reformation, the church adopts the *sola scriptura* principle and the Lutheran confessional documents as correct interpretations of holy writ. Even if Forde is correct about Luther's doctrine of justification (and I contend strongly that he is not), this does not have any direct bearing upon the theology of the church that has his name.

In my previous study of Luther, I have not found convincing evidence that Luther did indeed adopt the concept of the imputation of Christ's obedience under the law.[23] Luther seems to connect Christ's righteousness largely with his death and resurrection rather than his active obedience per se.[24] That, however, does not necessitate a rejection of the idea. Although Forde is correct to emphasize the language of death and resurrection in justification and properly asserts that salvation should not be limited to strictly legal metaphors, it is apparent through biblical study that the historical formulation of Christ's active and passive obedience is a necessary and beneficial element of Christian theology. It may be a valid criticism that some heirs of the Reformation have overemphasized the centrality of Christ's active obedience in justification while neglecting the centrality of the resurrection in God's justifying act.[25] It is also true

---

[23] I discuss this in Jordan Cooper, *The Righteousness of One: An Evaluation of Early Patristic Soteriology in Light of the New Perspective on Paul* (Eugene, OR: Wipf and Stock, 2013), 40–67.

[24] Though, occasional statements of the reformer regarding Christ's merit may strongly imply an imputation of active obedience.

[25] It is hard to cite a particular source here, especially as this is a

that Protestantism in general has tended to place vicarious satisfaction in a more central role than did Luther or Paul, who emphasized a *Christus Victor* approach alongside of vicarious satisfaction. Nonetheless, the veracity of both the imputation of Christ's active obedience and his vicarious suffering should not be questioned due to an imbalance of some of their proponents. In the next section, it is demonstrated that while some common proof texts may not explicitly teach the imputation of Christ's active obedience for justification, the concept itself is present throughout the New Testament, especially in a Christology that recognizes Christ as the faithful Israel whose obedience earns the eschatological Promised Land.

Romans 5

Much of the exegetical discussion regarding Christ's active obedience centers on Paul's contrast between Adam and Christ in Romans 5. Brian Vickers, in fact, claims that "It is not an exaggeration to say that the imputation of Christ's righteousness hangs on the interpretation of Romans 5:12–21."[26] Of particular debate is the following section:

> And the free gift is not like the result of that one man's sin. For the judgment following one trespass brought condemnation, but the free gift following many trespasses brought justification. For it, because of one man's trespass,

---

matter of emphasis. I tend to notice it in practical ministry settings, particularly in preaching. The resurrection has, unfortunately, been neglected in its central role here in some preaching on justification.

[26] Brian Vickers, *Jesus' Blood and Righteousness: Paul's Theology of Imputation* (Wheaton, IL: Crossway, 2006), 199.

death reigned through that one man, much more will those who receive the abundance of grace and the free gift of righteousness reign in life through the one man Jesus Christ. Therefore, as one trespass led to condemnation for all men, so one act of righteousness leads to justification and life for all men. For as by the one man's disobedience the many were made sinners, so by the one man's obedience the many will be made righteous. (Rom. 5:16–19)

In this text, Paul contrasts the condemnatory actions of Adam in the garden and the redemptive work of Christ. Something that Adam did brought condemnation and the making of sinners, and some act of obedience on the part of Christ resulted in many being made righteous. What needs to be determined is what "one act" Paul refers to in this text.

Reformed theologian David VanDrunen gives a classic Calvinistic exposition of this text in defense of active obedience in his essay "To Obey Is Better Than Sacrifice."[27] VanDrunen explains that his exposition of this text is rooted in his understanding of covenant theology. In traditional Reformed covenant theology, a distinction is made between the covenant of grace and the covenant of works.[28] The

---

[27]David VanDrunen, "To Obey Is Better Than Sacrifice," in *By Faith Alone: Answering the Challenges to the Doctrine of Justification*, ed. Gary L. W. Johnson and Guy P. Waters (Wheaton, IL: Crossway, 2006), pp. 127–146.

[28]For a brief exposition of this theological approach, see Michael S. Horton, "Covenant and Justification: Engaging N.T. Wright and John Piper," in *Justified: Modern Reformation Essays on the Doctrine of Justification* (Escondido, CA: Modern Reformation, 2010), pp. 11–32. For a more detailed look at this view, see Michael S. Horton, *Introducing Covenant Theology* (Grand Rapids, MI: Baker, 2009).

covenant of works is an agreement with conditions. God gives blessings to those he covenants with based on the merits of those individuals. The Adamic administration is the primary instantiation of the covenant of works, wherein God promised Adam life based on his obedience. There is no grace in this covenant, only merit and reward.[29] Adam served as a federal head of the human race, vicariously representing the entirety of humanity. The first man was placed on a probationary period in the covenant of works. If he obeyed the law, Adam would be confirmed in righteousness, and the future human race would be confirmed along with him; if he disobeyed, he would be punished with physical and spiritual death, and his descendants would be both imputed as guilty and born inherently sinful due to the act of Adam as their representative. In this scheme, Christ, as the second Adam, was also placed in the covenant of works. Like Adam, Christ was required to obey the law perfectly so that those whom he represented (the elect) would be imputed righteous. In this scheme, there is both an alien guilt (Adam's) and an alien righteousness (Christ's). It is this parallel between Adam and Christ in the covenant of works that then frames the doctrine of active obedience. White and Beisner argue,

> [T]he relationship of Adam's seed (the whole human race naturally born) to God in the covenant of works was like the redemption of Christ's seed (the elect) to God in the covenants of redemption and grace. For both Adam's seed and Christ's seed, the inheritance of eternal life is conditioned on the

---

[29]Though, there is some contention surrounding the role of grace in Reformed federal theology.

obedience of their representative and is, therefore, procured vicariously for the seed by the meritorious works of another. The crucial difference between the two seeds is, of course, that Adam failed to fulfill the condition for his seed and thus failed, as their representative, to merit eternal life for them, while Christ fulfilled the covenantal condition for his seed and thus did, as their representative, merit eternal life for them and pay the penalty for which they were liable due to Adam's (and their own) demerit.[30]

Since the Adamic administration is primarily one of merit, the actions of Christ are defined in that same way, which is why Reformed theology has often placed Christ's active obedience in a more central role than Lutherans have.[31]

It is in this context that VanDrunen exposits Romans 5. He argues that "Paul's concern in this pericope is with justification and the covenant of works."[32] In the beginning of the above text in Paul, starting in verse 16, Paul contrasts righteousness and condemnation. This, for VanDrunen, is necessarily covenantal because "the references to Adam, transgression, the disobedience of the one, and death draws readers to the covenant of works at creation."[33] Because

---

[30] R. Fowler White and E. Calvin Beisner, "Covenant, Inheritance, and Typology," in Johnson and Waters, eds., *By Faith Alone*, pp. 154–155.

[31] There have been differences, historically, on this question. The Westminster Confession does not explicitly identify the righteousness of Christ as inclusive of his active obedience for this reason. However, for those who adhere strictly to the bicovenantal system, active obedience is highly emphasized.

[32] VanDrunen, "To Obey," 142.

[33] Ibid., 142.

verse 17 begins with γάρ ("for"), VanDrunen argues that "Verse 17 explains what the justification mentioned in 5:16 entails."[34] In other words, justification involves the granting of the "free gift of righteousness." It is this free gift of righteousness that is then connected to the obedience of Christ in contrast to Adam. VanDrunen summarizes: "Paul asserts that a gift brings justification (5:16), this gift is a gift of righteousness (5:17), this gift of righteousness focuses upon one righteous act (5:18), and this righteous act is the obedience of the one man, Jesus Christ (5:19)."[35]

The problem faced by VanDrunen and other proponents of active obedience as a referent in this passage is with the phrase ἑνός δικαιώματος ("one act of righteousness"). The contrast made by Paul is not between Adam's entire life of obedience and Christ's entire life of obedience but is between one act of Adam and one act of Christ. VanDrunen offers a number of counterarguments in defense of one act of righteousness being a referent to Christ's entire life of obedience. He first counters the argument that the phrase *one act* cannot refer to multiple acts with the question "Was the crucifixion really one act of Christ? Insofar as Christ submitted himself to this fate and interacted with his Father and those around him, the crucifixion itself was a series of actions rather than a single act."[36] In VanDrunen's view, if this text references either Christ's active or passive obedience, it has to be referencing multiple acts rather than a single one.

This argument remains unconvincing for a number of reasons. First, any action can be divided up into several acts. For example,

---

[34]Ibid., 142.
[35]Ibid., 143.
[36]Ibid., 143.

when Adam ate of the tree, he first had to listen to Eve, and then he thought about the act before he performed it, he moved his hand toward the fruit, he put the fruit in his mouth, he bit and chewed it, and he also swallowed it. Just because one act can be divided in a certain manner of thinking into several different actions does not mean that speaking of "one act" is an elastic concept that can refer to any length of time or number of actions. In the same manner that Adam's act of eating the forbidden fruit can be said to be a single action, so can the crucifixion when viewed broadly. It is a common manner of speaking to associate a number of actions performed toward the same end in a finite period of time as "one act." For example, it would be common for one to refer to the September 11 terrorist attacks which devastated the United States as a horrible singular act of violence, even though the action involved a number of different steps. If one were to speak of one terrible act that the terrorists responsible performed, would anyone assume that this could be a reference to all of the evil actions that these evil figures performed, including their education, training, and previous acts of violence? It is common parlance to refer to a number of connected actions within a short time span that are performed toward a common end as one act, but not every action performed by an individual for thirty-three years. Unless some precedent for understanding multiple years' worth of actions as a single event can be found in other literature, this is not a tenable argument.

The second problem with this argument is that the parallel does not fit. Unless one has a preconceived covenant-of-works/covenant-of-grace grid through which this text is understood, there is no parallel between one act of disobedience on the part of

Adam and thousands of actions of obedience performed by Christ. The parallel Paul makes is between ἑνός δικαιώματος ("one act of righteousness") and ἑνός παραπτώματος ("one trespass"). If one action of Adam is discussed here, then so is one action of Christ. This is how this text was understood in the Patristic period. John Chrysostom, for example, when discussing Romans 5, states:

> Now this is why Adam is a type of Christ. How a type? it will be said. Why in that, as the former became to those who were sprung from him, although they had not eaten of the tree, the cause of that death which by his eating was introduced; thus also did Christ become to those who sprung from Him, even though they had not wrought righteousness, the Provider of that righteousness which is through His Cross He graciously bestowed on us all.[37]

Chrysostom speaks here of righteousness that is bestowed, which is provided by Christ, but he connects it not with Christ's active obedience, but with his death on the cross. This is similar to how Irenaeus interprets this passage. Though Irenaeus emphasizes the importance of Christ's righteous life in other contexts, he does not connect this to Romans 5. Instead, he writes, "As by means of a tree we were made debtors to God, [so also] by means of a tree we may obtain the remission of our debt."[30] Prior to the development of

---

[37]Chrysostom, "The Epistle to the Romans" 10:13, in *Nicene and Post-Nicene Fathers*, vol. 11 (Peabody, MA: Hendrickson, 2004), p. 402.
[38]Irenaeus, "Against Heresies" 5:17.3, in *Ante-Nicene Fathers*, vol. 1 (Peabody, MA: Hendrickson, 2004), p. 545.

Protestant scholastic categories, Pauline interpreters did not view Romans 5 as a reference to Christ's obedient life.[39]

Finally, there are references to Christ's redemptive work in the immediate context, but none of those references refer to his obedience to the law. In verse 9 of chapter 5, Paul connects righteousness specifically with Christ's death. He argues, "Now, having been justified by his blood (δικαιωθέντες νῦν ἐν τῷ αἵματι αὐτοῦ σωθησόμεθα) we will be saved by the wrath of God through him." He then continues his argument, writing, "For if while we were enemies we were reconciled to God by the death of his Son, much more, now that we are reconciled, shall we be saved by his life" (Rom. 5:9-10). Paul parallels the concept of reconciliation (καταλλαγέντες) and justification (δικαιωθέντες) and attributes both to the death of Christ. Paul then references Christ's life of mediation as the means by which final salvation will be received (5:11). The discussion of Christ as the second Adam begins in verse 12 and is not a separate discussion, as is demonstrated by the use of Διὰ τοῦτο ("therefore") prior to describing the effects of sin. The only conceivable way in which these two discussions can be connected is if the righteous act of Jesus in verse 19 is connected with his righteous act in verses 9 and 10, which is his death on the cross, not his obedience to the law.

Reading the Justification Texts Synoptically

It may seem that if Romans 5 does not teach the imputation of Christ's active obedience, which Vickers calls "the best ground for asserting that Christ's righteousness, his positive obedience, is imputed to

---

[39] At least, not anywhere that I have been able to locate.

believers,"⁴⁰ then there no longer remains any valid theological or exegetical reason to adopt the conviction that Christ's active obedience to the law is imputed to believers. However, though I am not convinced that the text often used to defend the concept of active obedience teaches the concept, I remain committed to the veracity of the doctrine and its importance for the Christian's faith, life, and preaching. Here, an argument is presented which gives credence to the doctrine of the imputation of Christ's active obedience apart from Romans 5.

Prior to defending active obedience, something must be said of the teaching of the imputation of Christ's obedience in general. Throughout his epistles, Paul continuously speaks of a righteousness being counted to the believer by faith. Brian Vickers helpfully demonstrates that the texts speaking of imputation need to be read synoptically. In other words, though no one text explicitly states that through faith Christ's righteousness is imputed, this is clearly a Pauline concept when the various justification texts are read together. There are three groups of texts in Paul discussed here.

First, there are several texts that speak of a righteousness that comes "from God." In Romans 3, for example, Paul speaks of "the righteousness of God [which] has been manifested apart from the law, although the Law and the Prophets bear witness to it—the righteousness of God through faith in Jesus Christ for all who believe" (Rom. 3.21–22). This is a righteousness that belongs to God but is given εἰς πάντας τοὺς πιστεύοντας ("to all who believe"). In this text, Paul deals with the thesis statement of his epistle, expressed in

---

⁴⁰Vickers, *Blood and Righteousness*, 227.

chapter 1: "For I am not ashamed of the gospel, for it is the power of God for salvation to everyone who believes, to the Jew first and also to the Greek. For in it the righteousness of God is revealed from faith for faith, as it is written, 'The righteous shall live by faith'" (Rom. 1:16–17). In Paul's Second Epistle to the Corinthians, Paul again references the righteousness of God as something given to believers: "For our sake he made him to be sin who knew no sin, so that in him we might become the righteousness of God" (2 Cor. 5:21). In these verses, it is apparent that there is a righteousness of God that believers somehow receive.

The second set of texts references the imputation of righteousness through faith. Speaking of Abraham's faith, Paul writes: "And to the one who does not work but believes in him who justifies the ungodly, his faith is counted as righteousness" (Rom. 4:5). There are similar texts in Galatians 3:6, Romans 4:9, and Romans 4:22–24. Some interpreters, such as Robert Gundry, argue that Romans 4 teaches that faith is counted as righteous not because it receives Christ's righteousness but because faith, though not a work, is itself counted as righteousness. He argues that "None of these texts say that Christ's righteousness was counted. With the exception of Romans 4:6 . . . they say that Abraham's faith is counted, so that righteousness comes into view not as what is counted but as what God counts faith to be."[41] This argument hinges upon the language of imputing (λογίζεται) faith for (εἰς) righteousness. The language of these particular texts cannot be used definitively to argue that faith itself is

---

[41]Robert H. Gundry, "The Nonimputation of Christ's Righteousness," in Mark Husbands and Daniel J. Treier, *Justification: What's at Stake in the Current Debates?* (Downers Grove, IL: IVP, 2004), p. 18.

regarded as righteous because, as D.A. Carson demonstrates, there is grammatical precedent for something to be "imputed or reckoned as something else."[42] The problem with Gundry's argument is that he attempts to make his case from one particular grammatical construction instead of reading these verses within the context of Paul's overall theology.

The final set of texts that need to be examined in Paul's theology includes those which connected the righteousness of God with Christ. In Philippians, Paul writes, "For his sake I have suffered the loss of all things and count them as rubbish, in order that I may gain Christ and be found in him, not having a righteousness of my own that comes from the law, but that which comes through faith in Christ, the righteousness from God that depends on faith" (Phil. 3:8–9). What is important about this text is that Paul connects receiving the righteousness of God with being ἐν αὐτῷ ("in him [Christ]") and is also with his desire that Χριστόν κερδήσω ("I may gain Christ"). He reiterates the same point in 2 Corinthians 5:21: "For our sake he made him to be sin who knew no sin, so that in him we might become the righteousness of God."[43] Again, it is only "in Christ" that one becomes the righteousness of God. There is one text in which Paul specifically connects saving righteousness with that of Christ. In 1 Corinthians, Paul writes that Christ "became to us wisdom from God, righteousness and sanctification and redemption" (2 Cor. 5:21). When read together, these three texts produce the inevitable conclusion that:

---

[42]D.A. Carson, "The Vindication of Imputation," in Husbands and Treier, *Justification*, p. 58.
[43]Emphasis added.

ACTIVE OBEDIENCE OF CHRIST

1. A righteousness is delivered from God for salvation.
2. Faith is credited, or imputed, as righteousness.
3. God's righteousness is only received "in Christ" and is in one place identified with Christ explicitly.

When these verses are harmonized, it is clear that through faith the one who believes receives the righteousness of Christ as a gift. One need not identify one singular proof text which says as much. With the establishment of the validity of the imputed righteousness of Christ as a Pauline teaching, the question now arises as to the content of that righteousness. Is it Christ's death alone, or is it a righteousness that encapsulates his entire redemptive activity, from his birth through his resurrection from the dead? It is my argument that broader theological considerations make it apparent that this righteousness is holistic and, as such, has reference to Christ's fulfillment of the divine law.

A Biblical-Theological Approach to Active Obedience

The work of Christ needs to be approached in its broader theological context. The manner in which this should be done is not by imposing a "covenant-of-works/covenant-of-grace" scheme upon the biblical text but is by the use of categories clearly defined and expounded in Scripture.[44] That is done here through the consistent New Testament parallel between Christ and Israel, in which Jesus actively obeys the divine laws that Israel consistently disobeyed, resulting in divine punishment.

---

[44]Recognizing, of course, that the Reformed federal theologians believe this to be explicit in the text. I am not convinced of such a scheme.

One outspoken critic of the doctrine of active obedience is Reformed theologian Norman Shepherd. He argues that the broader biblical context of Christ's threefold office is incommensurate with the doctrine of Christ's active obedience. Shepherd writes,

> The Old Testament prepares us for understanding the threefold office of Christ as prophet, priest, and king in the work of the prophets, the priests, and the kings of the old economy. Throughout his public ministry Jesus served as a prophet announcing the coming of the kingdom of God and calling sinners to repentance. At the end of his ministry he offered himself as priest on the cross as a sacrifice for the sins of his people. After his resurrection he ascended into heaven to rule as king over his people and to build his church. In performing a lifetime of perfect and personal obedience, Christ is not doing the kind of official work assigned to prophets, priests, or kings as described in the Old Testament. However, in giving his life as a sacrifice for sin (passive obedience), Jesus is clearly doing the work of a priest as the Book of Hebrews makes abundantly obvious. The imputation of active obedience does not correlate with the way Scripture presents Christ to us as our prophet, priest, and king.[45]

The problem with Shepherd's proposal is that he negates what is perhaps the primary typological category of the Old Testament—that Christ not only fulfills the threefold offices given to Israel, but that

---

[45]Shepherd, "The Imputation," 266–267.

ACTIVE OBEDIENCE OF CHRIST

Jesus is Israel itself. If it is understood that Jesus does, in fact, fulfill the role of Israel, then there is ample place for Christ as the faithful Son who obeys on behalf of his people.

Two points, then, need to be substantiated for it to be proven that Jesus, as Israel, needed to be faithful to God's law in order that eternal life might be given to his people. First, it needs to be shown that Jesus is the fulfillment and embodiment of Israel. Second, it needs to be demonstrated that Israel was required to keep the law in order to be given the Abrahamic blessings. The first point can be shown in a number of texts. Old Testament scholar Tremper Longman argues that the pattern of Jesus's life follows that of Israel. He states, "As the embodiment of the faithful remnant, he would undergo divine judgment for sin (on the cross), endure an exile (three days forsaken by God in the grave), and experience a restoration (resurrection) to life as the foundation of a new Israel, inheriting the promises of God afresh."[46] It is to be remembered that there was no idea in the Jewish faith that a messiah would be resurrected from the dead, but instead that Israel would experience resurrection at once. In rising from the dead alone, Jesus showed himself as the fulfillment of the hopes for a restoration of Israel.

Matthew's Gospel is particularly insightful on this point. David Scaer demonstrates that Matthew's Gospel is divided into five discourses, mirroring the five books of the Torah.[47] Jesus portrays himself as a new and better Moses by delivering the law on a mountain

---

[46] Tremper Longman III and Raymond B. Dillard, "Isaiah," in *An Introduction to the Old Testament* (Grand Rapids, MI: Zondervan, 2006), p. 315.
[47] David P. Scaer, *Discourses in Matthew: Jesus Teaches the Church* (St. Louis, MO: Concordia, 2004).

through the Sermon on the Mount. This is also apparent in the utilization of texts about Israel in reference to Jesus. Matthew cites the prophet Hosea as a reference to Christ's birth, writing, "This was to fulfill what the Lord had spoken by the prophet, 'Out of Egypt I called my son'" (Matt. 2:15). If one examines the text in Hosea, it is apparent that this verse references the nation of Israel. The full verse states, "When Israel was a child, I loved him, and out of Egypt I called my son" (Hosea 11:1). If one admits to the inspiration of the biblical authors and the fact that Matthew is not simply misquoting Hosea out of context, it is clear that Matthew means to identify Jesus with Israel. The nation of Israel was taken out of Egypt and into the Promised Land, and this was recapitulated in the birth of Christ.

Another testimony to the conviction that Jesus is Israel comes from Paul. He writes, "Now the promises were made to Abraham and to his offspring. It does not say, 'And to offsprings,' referring to many, but referring to one, 'And to your offspring,' who is Christ" (Gal. 3:16). The Abrahamic promise is the foundation for the blessings given to Israel throughout the Old Testament. Paul's point is that the true seed of Abraham is not the physical nation of Israel identified with the Mosaic administration, but ultimately is Christ himself. Those who inherit the promise of Abraham are adopted as members of spiritual Israel through incorporation into Christ, who is the true Israel. This is why Paul argues: "And if you are Christ's, then you are Abraham's offspring, heirs according to promise" (Gal. 3:29). When placing the texts from Matthew's Gospel and Paul's Epistles together, it becomes apparent that it was the belief of the early apostles that Jesus himself is Israel.

ACTIVE OBEDIENCE OF CHRIST

The second point remains to be proven. It must be shown that the Abrahamic promises were in some sense dependent upon the obedience of Israel. In Exodus 19, God tells Moses, "Now therefore, if you will indeed obey my voice and keep my covenant, you shall be my treasured possession among all peoples, for all the earth is mine; and you shall be to me a kingdom of priests and a holy nation" (Exod. 19:5). The promises of being a "holy nation" and a "kingdom of priests" are identified with obedience and covenant keeping of Israel. The New Testament identifies those who belong to Christ as both a holy nation and a kingdom of priests, demonstrating that the conditions had been fulfilled; Israel was obedient and kept the covenant.

After the conditions are laid out, the people of Israel agree to keep God's commandments. The people of Israel confess, "All that is spoken we will do" (Exod. 19:8). The conditionality of the Mosaic administration is expressed explicitly in Deuteronomy 11, which states,

> You shall therefore keep the whole commandment that I command you today, that you may be strong, and go in and take possession of the land that you are going over to possess, and that you may live long in the land that the LORD swore to your fathers to give to them and to their offspring, a land flowing with milk and honey . . . And if you will indeed obey my commandments that I command you today, to love the LORD your God, and to serve him with all your heart and with all your soul, he will give the rain for your land in its season, the early rain and the later rain, that you may gather in your grain and your wine and your oil. And he

will give grass in your fields for your livestock, and you shall eat and be full. Take care lest your heart be deceived, and you turn aside and serve other gods and worship them; then the anger of the LORD will be kindled against you, and he will shut up the heavens, so that there will be no rain, and the land will yield no fruit, and you will perish quickly off the good land that the LORD is giving you. (Deut. 11:8–17)

The inheritance of the land promised to Abraham is in some sense dependent upon the people of Israel's fulfillment of the law. If they obeyed the covenant stipulations, they would be blessed; if they disobeyed, they would be punished. The remainder of Israel's story in the Old Testament is consistent with this perspective, as the disobedience of the first generation of Israelites, including Moses, negated their entrance into the land. Similarly, the continued disobedience of Judah and Israel resulted in exile.

Jesus, as the true Israel, therefore necessarily had to obey God's law in order to gain the Abrahamic inheritance and receive the heavenly land due God's people. In Jesus, the entire story of Israel is recapitulated, including his birth in Egypt, tempting in the wilderness, and exile at the cross. The difference, however, between Jesus and physical Israel is that Jesus obeyed where Israel disobeyed. While Israel failed to follow the covenant stipulations given through the law, Jesus obeyed them. And through his obedience to these stipulations, Christ overcame the curse of exile that was due to Israel's disobedience. When viewed in this manner, Christ's active obedience to the law (his role as faithful Israel), death (his taking the curse of exile due to disobedience upon himself), and resurrection (the fulfillment of the Abrahamic promise and end to the exile due to Christ's role as obedient Israel) form a compact and consistent unity with one another. Through faith, believers are incorporated into Christ and share in the blessings he won as the obedient seed of Abraham.

Conclusion

Now is a time when it is crucial to engage in the historic discussion about Christ's active obedience. We need not revert to proof texting to demonstrate the veracity of this claim. It has been shown in this essay that the classic defense of Christ's active obedience in view of Romans 5 is, at the very least, not a clear reference to Christ's fulfillment of the law and is thus insufficient as a sole basis for the conviction that Christ's law keeping is imputed to his people. However, rather than rejecting the doctrine, as do Forde and many other interpreters, this doctrine should be proclaimed even more clearly on its biblical grounds, because it is not present merely in one section of Romans but carries through the narrative of Israel and its fulfillment in the obedient Messiah. Jesus is the embodiment of Israel, and he was the perfectly faithful and righteous Son who, through his obedience, won entrance into the Promised Land for his people. When this is recaptured, God's people can cling not only to Christ's death as the grounds of their forgiveness but also to his life as the grounds for the righteousness needed to avail before God the Father. Let us then proclaim with the great hymn writer Edward Mote that our hope is built on nothing less than Jesus's blood and righteousness.

Oswald Bayer and the Theology of Promise
By David P. Scaer

Theologians advancing the late Gerhard Forde's theology of the cross have found a fellow traveler in University of Tübingen emeritus professor and prominent Luther scholar Oswald Bayer, whose writings appear regularly along with theirs in the *Lutheran Quarterly* journal and its monographs.[1] Helpful in understanding Bayer's theology of promise is the speech-act theory of John L. Austin. Speech-act theory divides words into two categories: constative and performative. Constative utterances correspond to, and provide information about, past events. Performative utterances create relations that did not previously exist. Performative speech "does not refer to a preexisting situation whose existence the sentence merely reveals. Rather, it constitutes and creates a relationship and incorporates features that are both personal and objective."[2] In submitting the writings of Luther to this theory of performative speech, Bayer hopes to open a previously unrecognized dimension in the reformer's theology.

---

[1] Virgil Thompson, ed., *Justification Is for Preaching: Essays by Oswald Bayer, Gerhard O. Forde, and Others* (Lutheran Quarterly Books, 2012). Among the other contributors are Robert Kolb and Steven Paulson. Oswald Bayer's *Living by Faith* is already available, and forthcoming is his *Promissio: The Story of the Reformation Turn in Luther's Theology.* Fortress Press provides publishing services for *Lutheran Quarterly.* Articles by Bayer published in *Lutheran Quarterly* include "Justification," in 34, no. 3 (2010): pp. 337–340; "God's Hiddenness," in 38, no. 3 (2014): pp. 266–279; "Trust," in 39, no. 3 (2015): pp. 249–261; and "The Relationship between Theology and Nature Sciences," in 31, no. 2 (2017): pp. 150–171.

[2] Oswald Bayer, *Theology the Lutheran Way*, ed. and trans. Jeffrey G. Silcock (Grand Rapids, MI / Cambridge, UK: Wm. B. Eerdmans, 2007), 126–128.

BAYER AND THE THEOLOGY OF THE PROMISE

Bayer's Doctrine of Justification

Bayer sees his primary contribution to theology in making justification the reigning theological principle in every doctrine, including prolegomena.[3] This differs from classical Lutheran dogmatics, which holds to the inspired Scripture as the foundation of theology. Bayer's program shares similarities with Karl Barth's approach. To counter the classical nineteenth-century liberalism that placed the individual self—what Schleiermacher called "Christian self-consciousness" and what his Lutheran followers called the "theological I"—as the source of theology, Barth made the encounter (German: *Begnung*) between the believer and the word of God the criterion of theology. Bayer distances himself from Barth in significant ways, but by placing the crucial moment in the believer's acceptance of the promise, he demonstrates continuity with Barth. For Bayer, the believer's justification is the revelatory moment—a concept underlying all of Bayer's theology. The proclaimed or preached word is the word of God in the primary sense because it creates what it promises. Bayer uses the Latin term *promissio* for his proposal throughout his writings. Now a widely recognized and celebrated Reformation scholar, Bayer proposes that Luther's concept of justification should be understood as a performative word; it performs the justification it promises. In order to bolster his thesis,

---

[3]See Bayer, *Theology the Lutheran Way*, 138. "Our thesis is that the gospel, understood as a particular speech act, is itself the ground of faith. Since the 'essence of Christianity' is a speech act, it must be illuminated, not primarily by an analysis of existence, but by an analysis of language." This Bayer takes over from the linguistic philosophy of John L. Austin and Martin Heidegger.

Bayer depends on selected early writings of Luther, which he interprets in accord with Austin's speech-act theory.

Titles of his books and articles and his frequent use of such terms as *word*, *justification*, and *promise* and its cognates show that he portrays himself as standing in the classical Lutheran theological tradition. Along with using traditional Lutheran terminology, Bayer consistently describes the speech-act philosophy of Austin as well as the linguistic philosophy of Ludwig Wittgenstein, through which he reads Luther. In some ways, Bayer's use of such sources in his theology is not new. The use of philosophy in the formation theology has occurred since the apostolic age. Eighteenth-century rationalism, Friedrich D. E. Schleiermacher, J.C.K. von Hoffmann, and Karl Barth all claimed that they had located the kernel of Luther's theology that would provide an authentic understanding of his thought, in contrast to the older confessional approach. Rudolph Bultmann, for example, understood justification in terms of Martin Heidegger's existentialism. Thus, recruiting Luther in proposing new theological insights has been a common tactic of Lutheran theologians since the eighteenth century. In this way, what Bayer proposes is not novel, especially with regard to justification—the central theme of his program.

Luther's doctrine of justification was already misunderstood during his lifetime, as was addressed in the Formula of Concord. Rather than the 2017 Reformation quincentennial marking an era of agreement among Lutherans, things remain diffuse—perhaps even more than in previous centuries. Bishop Hans Lilje, a former President of the Lutheran World Federation, noted that Lutherans were unable to come even close to agreement on the central article of justification at their 1963 Helsinki convention.⁴ This would matter little were justification a subsidiary teaching. To the contrary, Lutherans are recognized by the broader church precisely by their formulation of this doctrine, which Bayer has taken over to advance his own theological proposal. In making justification *the* overarching principle in theology, Bayer intends to be understood as standing in the authentic Lutheran theological tradition, but it must be asked whether he really does.

Bayer defines justification as the certainty of salvation, which is both the origin and goal of all theology, including the doctrine of creation.⁵ He argues that self-justification is the overarching reality of all human existence. Regardless of what a person knows about the gospel, self-justification is a universal personal reality, for both Christians and unbelievers. All people inherently want to justify themselves.⁶ In this formulation, justification no longer refers to God forgiving the sinner in response to Christ offering himself as a sacrifice for sin, but it instead references personal awareness that one is forgiven—an essential theme in Bayer's conception of the theology of the cross. Justification is the primary doctrine under which the others are subsumed, resulting in Bayer's claim that the person who does not

---

⁴David P. Scaer, *The Lutheran World Federation Today* (Saint Louis, MO: Concordia Publishing House, 1971), 15.

⁵Steven D. Paulson shows how creation can be understood as an act of justification by explaining that "This creation is not a one time act, but a daily matter—moment by moment—God speaking creation continually by means of the very creation." Steven D. Paulson, foreword to Joshua C. Miller, *Hanging by a Promise: The Hidden God in the Theology of Oswald Bayer* (Eugene, OR: Pickwick Publications, 2015), xi.

⁶Bayer lays out this program as trust or faith as an overarching reality in his article "Trust." The original temptation "is not to trust God's promise to grant [Adam] all good and to rescue him in every need" (255).

know that they are justified has no knowledge of God.[7] For Bayer, all doctrine and practice are normed by justification. The performative word that enacts the promise of forgiveness is the basis of religious truth and certainty.

Bayer presents his proposal within the context of philosophies that he rejects. Citing Immanuel Kant, he argues for the dismantling of the rationalism of the eighteenth-century Enlightenment—particularly, the notion that the mind or the intellect can grasp and interpret the physical world. With external proofs for religion discredited, Kant substituted moral imperatives, which are a universal human possession. Friedrich D. E. Schleiermacher built on Kant's subjectivism by proposing that consciousness, as it has progressed, is the source of religious truth. This philosophical paradigm reigned in European Protestant theology until the rise of neoorthodoxy at the end of World War I. During this time, G.W F. Hegel held that history was self-revelatory and was progressing along a scheme of a thesis, which requires an antithesis, which is then resolved in a synthesis. Bayer attempts to steer a middle way between Schleiermacher's subjectivism (the idea that truth arises from within the self) and Hegel's objectivism (the idea that what can be seen can be grasped by the mind). Between these two options, Bayer places the word with its promises as the object of faith that resolves a person's desire for self-justification. This word that justifies does not derive its reality and efficacy from the past, but from the present speech act. Were it based in the past, it would be a constative word and not a performative word. The promise, or the word that justifies, is a

---

[7] See Bayer, "Trust."

performative word, and faith is directed to this word that performs what God promises.

Bayer does not portray himself as an innovator but as a faithful interpreter of the reformer. This is evident in the title of his massive *Promissio: Geschichte der Reformatischen Wende in Luthers Theologie* ("*Promise: History of the Reformation Turning Point in Luther's Theology*"). The first section of this work was presented as his doctoral dissertation in 1967 and the second as his *Habilitation*, an advanced dissertation, in 1969 to the University of Bonn.[8] For the moment, we will table the question of whether Austin's speech-act theory is a valid method of interpreting when and how the reformer came to his mature understanding of justification by faith. Regarding the date of Luther's Reformation discovery, there is disagreement among scholars. A date around 1512 for Luther's discovery of the doctrine of justification would suggest he held to an Augustinian understanding, wherein justification occurs within the believer, which is in continuity with medieval Catholicism. Were this shift to have occurred at a later date, this would imply that Luther held to the forensic view, which differs from his earlier perspective, that God declares the sinner justified or righteous—a long preferred, but not universally held, option for Lutherans.

For Luther's discovery of justification, Bayer favors the spring of 1518, barely a half year after he posted the Ninety-Five Theses. Bayer argues that the turning points for Luther were his reflections upon and struggles with the medieval Catholic doctrine of penance (*Busssakrament*), which consisted of *contritio*, *confessio*, and

---

[8]Oswald Bayer, *Promissio: Geschichte der reformatischen Wende in Luthers Theologie* (Göttingen, Germany: Vandenhoeck & Ruprecht, 1971), 8.

satisfactio, or, in their English renderings, contrition (sorrow), confession (articulation of sins), and satisfaction (works assigned by the priest).[9] From that time forward, in Bayer's view, Luther saw the promise given in absolution (*promissio absolutionis*) and faith in that promise as foundational for all theology. In confronting the medieval doctrine of penance, Luther came to his Reformation breakthrough regarding justification through faith alone. He no longer held to his prior Augustinian view of justification—that in absolving the penitent, the priest merely recognized the penitent's sorrow over their sin. Now, for Luther, absolution was seen as "a declarative act, or to use Austin's language, a constative speech act, in that: the priest sees the remorse, takes it as a sign of divine justification that has already occurred in the penitent, without that person knowing it."[10] According to the Augustinian model, absolution does not bring about a new state of affairs but only recognizes an already-present reality. Beginning in 1518, in Bayer's view, Luther saw absolution as a performative speech act that justifies by "bring[ing] about a state of affairs, by creating a relationship between the one in whose name it is spoken and the one to whom it is spoken and who believe the promise. Such a speech act establishes communication, liberates and gives certainty. Luther calls it '*verbus efficax*' an active and effective word. In Austin's terminology, it is a performative speech act."[11]

Justifying faith arises by trusting in the word as promise, or *promissio*—a word that has come to dominate Bayer's entire

---

[9] Bayer, *Promissio*, 165.
[10] Bayer, *Theology the Lutheran Way*, 129.
[11] Bayer, *Theology the Lutheran Way*, 130.

theological program.¹² Bayer can speak of the subjective and objective elements of justification, terms familiar to readers of Francis Pieper's *Christian Dogmatics*, but for Bayer, objectivity rests in the promise, in the orally spoken word, and not in anything or anyone beyond or outside of that proclamation. Trygve Wyller describes Bayer's understanding of faith in this way: *"Glaube ist Vertrauen auf die promissio als Sprachhandlung"* ("Faith is trust in the promise as a speech act").¹³ When Bayer speaks of justification as *extra nos*, he does not refer to an event which took place in history—what the Lutheran Orthodox called objective justification—but what takes place when someone believes the word or promise. This is so essential to this theological program that Bayer speaks for himself here: "In contradistinction to every metaphysical construct of the doctrine of God, God's truth and will therefore are not abstract properties but are a concrete promise, made orally and publicly, to a particular person in a particular situation. 'God' is the one whose promise to us in the oral word is such that we can depend on him. God's truth lies in his faithfulness to the word that he speaks."¹⁴

Summons to believe the word in Bayer's proposal can be deceptively attractive to those who are accustomed to preachers summoning their hearers to believe the word by human will or effort. For Bayer, this is not an invitation to believe in a *something* behind the

---

¹²Trygve Wyller, *Glaube und Autonome Welt*, 94. See 93–101, a section that Wyller titled "Promissio: Oswald Bayer as Luther-Forscher," in which Wyller notes that *"Bayers Ausgangspunkt in der Kategorie der promissio [ist] notwendig. Sie ist der Eckstein seines gegenwaertigen systematicische-theologischen Denkens. Bayers Beschaeftigung Lutherstudien der sechziger Jahre"* (93).

¹³Ibid., 94.

¹⁴Bayer, *Theology the Lutheran Way*, 130–131.

word, such as the resurrection as an event in history or a God who stands outside of the word, but to believe in the word as proclamation, whether written or oral. For Bayer, the theological task is not to peer behind the text "to a specific concept of human existence," as proposed by theologians from Schleiermacher to Bultmann, nor does faith "cling to the letters in a kind of biblistic legalism as in theological positivism."[15] Here Bayer does not delineate who he has in mind, but it is likely that those who take "constative" approaches are those who believe that what the Bible reports as historical events really happened. For Bible passages to be effective, they must be converted into performative words called "speech actions."[16] For Bayer, formative, constitutive, and declarative acts correspond to Luther's "blessings of a promise, or faith, and of a gift."[17] For Bayer, the phrases *word of absolution*, *absolve*, and *absolving* are speech acts.

Augustine, Bayer points out, distinguishes between the thing signified, the *res*, and the sign or signification of the thing, the *signum*. Bayer holds that "Luther overcame the distinction, and in doing so shares something in common with the linguistic analysis of the later Wittengenstein."[18] For Luther, the "thing" and the "sign" become one. Bayer further writes, "The speech act with the promise of forgiveness in the name of Jesus is not an 'appearance' but the 'essence' itself." Bayer holds that for both Luther and Wittgenstein, "*Essence* is

---

[15] Ibid., 131.
[16] Ibid. "In fact, theology is guided only by particular sentences, particular speech acts, none of which is derived from some principle behind the text. For the Bible itself is full of promises and sentences that can be easily converted into particular kinds of sentences and speech actions without doing violence to the texts" (131).
[17] Ibid., 269, n. 211.
[18] Ibid., 137.

expressed by grammar."[19] While Bultmann (among others) "locates the original source of life" in the "pre-linguistic realm," Luther begins "with the external word (*verbum externum*) in the sense of promise, understood as a speech act."[20] So for Bayer, "theology [is done] on the basis of linguistic analysis rather [than] the analysis of existence," and so "we will still preserve what existential interpretation considers important in its privileging of proclamation."[21] Like Bultmann, Bayer understands faith existentially—where rather than faith finding its object within oneself, it finds it in the word of promise, which is external to the believer. For Bayer, "there is the primary sphere of the performative speech acts, the sphere of the word and faith. On the other hand, there is the secondary but related sphere of constative speech acts, the sphere of theology (in the narrow sense) and its propositions."[22]

---

[19] Ibid., 137. Emphasis in original.
[20] Ibid., 138. The German equivalent is *leibliches Wort*, which, like Luther's *Anfechtung*, defies adequate English translation. See Thomas H. Trapp, "Keep a Low Profile! Observations of a Translator" or Oswald Bayer, *Promising Faith for a Ruptured Age*, ed. John T. Pless, Roland Ziegler, and Joshua Miller (Eugene, OR: Pickwick Publications, 2019), 231. *Leibliches Wort* might be translated literalistically to "bodily word" or "physical word" and is used by Bayer to give a substantive, concrete reality to the spoken word so it can be regarded a "thing" (Latin: *res*), an object of belief. As discussed elsewhere, Bayer eradicates the distinction between *res* and *signum* ("word"). With Bayer's permission, Trapp chose to translate *leibliches Wort* to "external word." This is not fully adequate, but it does respect Bayer's desire to treat the spoken word as if it were a physical substance, which it is not. If this were so, "the word was made flesh" would be redundant.
[21] Ibid., 138.
[22] Ibid., 171.

DAVID P. SCAER

The Relationship among Oswald Bayer, Gerhard Forde, and Steven Paulson

Forde's book titles, like *Theology Is for Proclamation* and the more telling *The Preached God*, point to an unintended theological consanguinity with Bayer, who later came into prominence. Not unsurprisingly, Bayer is not referenced in Forde's locus on Christology in *Christian Dogmatics*, edited by Robert Jenson and Carl Braaten. He is, however, frequently cited by Forde's contemporary disciples. Both Forde and Bayer hold that preaching justification is the goal and foundation of all theology.[23] Bayer, however, goes even further than Forde's version of the theology of the cross in holding that justification is determinative not only for theology, but for all reality.[24] For Bayer, the word of the promise is the foundation of theology. Similar to Steven Paulson, a popular disciple of Gerhard Forde, Bayer speaks of "a wondrous exchange or swap of human sin and divine righteousness."[25] As with Forde and his disciples, here the chief redemptive moment is not located in the historical acts of Christ at Golgotha, but in God speaking "for me" in the gospel through

---

[23]"The preaching of the justification of the sinner is the ground and center of the church." Bayer, "Justification," 337. See also Gerhard Forde, *Theology Is for Proclamation* (Minneapolis, MN: Fortress Press, 1990).

[24]Oswald Bayer, "The Doctrine of Justification and Ontology," *Neue Zeitschrift für Systematische Theologie und Religionsphilosophie* 43, no. 1 (2001): pp. 44–53. For example, "The doctrine of justification is not merely a single theological theme; rather concerns theology as a whole and has ontological significance."

[25]Bayer, "Justification," 338. This happens in the "event of Christ's atoning death and the gifts of himself bodily in the sermon, the Lord's Supper and baptism 'for you'—is the criterion of truth in the church" (338).

proclamation. Determinative phrases "for me" and "for you" locate the act of atonement in *preaching* when the sinner is justified by the word. Atonement is external in its connection to the preached word, and this is not because it takes place in a historical event apart from the believer. "This event of Christ's vicarious atoning death and the gift of himself bodily in the sermon, the Lord's Supper and baptism—'for you'—is the criterion of truth for the church."[26] This corresponds to Bayer's view that "The preaching of the justification of the sinner is the ground and center of the church"[27] and that all reality is to be understood within the context of justification.[28] Law, for Bayer, as it is for Steven Paulson, is identified not with the eternal will of God but with one's attempt at self-justification. Bayer describes "[j]ustification as an overarching reality in that all seek to justify themselves." Thus, Luther's question "How can I find a gracious God?" takes precedence over "the more radical question: 'Does God exist?'"[1] A solution to self-justification is resolved "by the word of the cross that brings liberation: As I am taken into the wondrous exchange where God takes, my place, I am free to look outside myself. I can step out of the context of blame and accusation, leave behind the struggle for mutual recognition and turn to God and the whole creation."[29] Since now "we experience the blessing of a life lived in the splendor of justification,"

---

[26]Ibid., 338.

[27]Ibid., 337.

[28]Oswald Bayer, *Living by Faith: Justification and Sanctification*, trans. Geoffrey W. Bromiley (Grand Rapids, MI / Cambridge, UK: Wm. B. Eerdmans, 2003). "The theme of justification is not one special theme, such that there might be a theme alongside it. It embraces the totality. All reality is involved in the justification debate" (9).

[1] Bayer, "Justification," 340.

[29]Ibid.," 340.

justification brings a sense of relief.[30] Release from the futile attempts at self-justification comes "by the word of the cross that brings liberation." Bayer uses the biblical example of Job as one whose unsuccessful attempts to justify himself demonstrate this search for self-justification.[31] Things possess their reality not in themselves but in the word. "What God says, God does. The reverse is also true. What does, God says; his doing is not ambiguous. God's work is God's speech."[32] This is easily recognized as speech-act theory—that things have their existence in their being spoken.[33] Speech acts for Bayer are not empirically verifiable, which is a fundamental principle for neoorthodoxy. Bayer notes that he applies the linguistic analysis of Wittengenstein and Austin rather than the existentialist interpretation of the Bible practiced by Rudolph Bultmann, which originated with the existentialist philosopher Martin Heidegger.[34] For Bayer, God's word is a promise not of what he will do in the future but of "the justifying Word of God in the promises at penance, baptism, and the Lord's Supper."[35] Like Calvin and Barth, Bayer reduces each of the means of grace to the lowest common denominator, and this is, for him, God's presence in the justifying word.[36] Bayer sees Christ's essential work taking place in the believer's experience of

---

[30] Ibid., 340.
[31] Bayer, *Living by Faith*, 1–8.
[32] Ibid., 43.
[33] This approach is attractive to those who find the ultimate reality in the church's worship. See Nicholas Wolterstorff, *The God We Worship: An Exploration of Liturgical Worship* (Grand Rapids, MI: Wm. B. Eerdmans, 2015).
[34] Bayer, *Theology the Lutheran Way*, 138.
[35] Bayer, *Living by Faith*, 51.
[36] David P. Scaer, *Baptism.* Confessional Lutheran Dogmatics. (Saint Louis, MI: Luther Academy, 1999), 175.

justification—a view essential to the theology of the cross set forth by Forde and by his students, such as Timothy Wengert, Steven Paulson, and James Nestingen.

An underlying theme for both these modern "theologians of the cross" and Bayer is the inability to get beneath or beyond the word, or the promise, to the historically concrete. *Everything* that God has to offer can be found in the preached or proclaimed word. Thus, in this way, the theology of the cross and Bayer have not advanced much beyond the neoorthodoxy-informed gospel reductionism of the Concordia Seminary, St. Louis faculty of the early 1970s. For both theological schools, the gospel is not derived from the events described in the Bible but by a particular manner of presentation. Rather than advancing their position with biblical arguments in the way the classical neoorthodox theologians (especially Barth) did, the theologians of the cross and Bayer chiefly reference Luther to give the appearance that theirs is an authentic Reformation theology. Justification is the overriding theological theme for both Bayer and the theologians of the cross with this important proviso: justification is understood as an existential moment in which the individual finds themself free from the law's accusations. The redemptive moment is not identified with Golgotha, in Christ offering himself as an eternal sacrifice to the Father, but it is instead found in the moment in which one believes the preached gospel or promise and is consequently relieved from the law's accusations. Justification, described as the chief article in the Lutheran confrontation with Rome, is existentially redefined and made the *only* article. In the new scheme, absolution is not only given sacramental status but made determinative for how baptism and the Lord's Supper are understood.³⁷

Resolving the dilemma in which the church has been placed by this redefinition of justification requires reflection upon how Lutherans should think of justification as the chief article. In Galatians justification is most central, but in 1 Corinthians Christ's resurrection is described as the most critical doctrine. "But if there is no resurrection of the dead, then Christ has not been raised; if Christ has not been raised, then our preaching is in vain and your faith is in vain" (1 Cor. 15:13-14). Justification by faith depends on preaching the resurrection, which, in turn, depends on Christ's resurrection. Bayer turns this around, claiming that "The preaching of the resurrection is the ground and center of the church."³⁸ This subtle shift makes preaching itself the church's foundation, rather than the historical event of the resurrection (upon which preaching depends). Bayer claims that Luther's great Reformation discovery was a linguistic one rather than a theological one, though it had theological consequences. Until Luther came along, Bayer writes,

> language [was] a system of signs that point to an object or state of affairs, or that express an exemption. In either case, the sign (*signum*), understood as a statement or expression, is

---

[37] To see how the theology of the cross's attention on justification has infected its entire system, see the posthumously published essays in Gerhard O. Forde, *The Preached God: Proclamation in Word and Sacrament*, ed. Mark C. Mattes and Steven D. Paulson (Grand Rapids, MI: Wm. B. Eerdmans, 2007). Titles of the chapters are telling; for instance, see "Whatever Happened to God? God Not Preached" (33–55) and consider that the chapter "Preaching the Sacraments" (89–115) is given in the section titled "Doing the Word."

[38] Bayer, "Justification," 337.

not the reality (*res*) itself. However, Luther's great hermeneutical insight, his Reformation discovery in the strict sense, was that the verbal sign (*signum*) is the reality itself. This new insight turned the ancient understanding of language on its head.[39]

To summarize Bayer's argument, Luther's great Reformation discovery of justification by faith is no longer a theological or hermeneutical one but a linguistic—or more accurately, a philosophical—one. Bayer enjoys increasing support and appreciation of his views. Whether they represent biblical and confessional standards is another matter.

---

[39]Bayer, *Theology the Lutheran Way*, 129.

Philipp Melanchthon's Use of Augustine in the Apology's Presentation of the Doctrine of Justification

by Eric Phillips

While I was researching to write this essay, two recent critiques came to my attention that accuse Philipp Melanchthon of misrepresenting Augustine's doctrine in the crucial fourth article of his Apology of the Augsburg Confession, "Of Justification." In the first of these, David C. Fink offers a scholarly and sympathetic reconstruction. "Melanchthon's own theology, as well as his understanding of Augustine, was continually evolving, especially in the first 10 to 15 years of his career as a public figure. Toward the end of this period, a significant gap opened up between Melanchthon's public, rhetorical use of Augustine and the trajectory of his own theology on the doctrine of justification by faith."[1] Fink says this gap began to show itself in 1531, when Melanchthon was composing the Apology. In a private correspondence with Johannes Brenz, whom he had asked to read a draft of his defense and who apparently had made some Augustinian suggestions (in a reply that is not extant), he criticizes "the fancy of Augustine [*imaginatione Augustini*] concerning the fulfillment of the Law,"[2] which he says had allowed later generations to "imagine that we are reckoned righteous because of this fulfilling of

---

[1] David C. Fink, "Bullshitting Augustine: Patristic Rhetoric and Theological Dialectic in Philipp Melanchthon's *Apologia* for the Augsburg Confession," in *Studia Patristica* (2017), p. 223.

[2] Ibid., 232. Fink is here quoting (and translating) from Philipp Melanchthon, *Texte 1151*, ed. Walter Thüringer, in *Melanchthons Briefwechsel: Kritische und Kommentierte Gesamtausgabe* (Stuttgart, 2003), pp. 108–110.

the Law."³ He explains that, for purposes of answering the Roman Confutation, "I invoke Augustine as if he were entirely of the same mind [*tanquam prorsus ὁμόψηφον*] because of the common opinion of him, even though he does not adequately explain the righteousness of faith."⁴ As early as the next year, Melanchthon felt free to publish this criticism in his revised Romans commentary,⁵ but if you read just the Apology, you would not know of his reservations. Fink suggests that Melanchthon, rather than being disingenuous, may not have arrived at a settled conclusion regarding Augustine quite yet and may in the meantime have been satisfied "that there [was] a deeper consistency to his line of argumentation that should be apparent to the careful reader,"⁶ even if some of the details were off.

The second critique comes from Robert C. Koons, a recent convert to Roman Catholicism from Lutheranism (the Missouri Synod), and features none of the understanding and scholarly distance shown by Fink.

> An egregious example of this cherry-picking is found in German Lutheran Reformer Philipp Melanchthon's (1497–1560) quotations from St. Augustine's *On the Spirit and the*

---

³Ibid., 231.
⁴Ibid., 232.
⁵"Augustine handled this matter inadequately (*tenuiter*). He only said that we receive the Holy Spirit by faith, and that praying in faith we obtain the help of God to fulfil the law. But it is much better to remind the reader concerning the proper role of faith, the destruction of doubt, and that for the doubting conscience, it is not possible to fulfil the law." Ibid., 234. Fink is here quoting (and translating) from Philipp Melanchthon, *Römerbriefkommentar*, in *Melanchthons Werkein Auswahl: Studienausgabe*, ed. Robert Stupperich, 7 vols. (Gütersloh, 1951-75), pp. 5, 122.
⁶Fink, "Bullshitting Augustine," 233-4.

Letter (*Apology of the Augsburg Confession,* Article IV). Melanchthon picks out a few, brief excerpts from this text, arguing that they establish that the Lutheran doctrine of justification by faith alone (apart from love) is no innovation but is wholly continuous with Augustinian theology. To read the entirety of *On the Spirit and the Letter* after reading Melanchthon is shocking: in that work, Augustine explicitly rejects the very doctrine that Melanchthon claims to find there. The gap between the plain sense of Augustine's text and Melanchthon's construction of it is so great that I found my confidence in Melanchthon's good faith as a scholar and teacher badly shaken.[7]

This is not fair to Melanchthon and is not an accurate portrayal of his use of Augustine in Article IV, as I shall show, but these are the words of one who feels misled by a mentor—and betrayed. The Apology is not just one theological treatise among many, side-by-side on the shelf with Melanchthon's 1522 Romans commentary. It has confessional status for Lutherans, who—especially at this historical remove—are exponentially more likely to have read or heard excerpts from it than from anything else Melanchthon wrote, apart from the original Augsburg Confession and his *Treatise on the Power and Primacy of the Pope*, which are also included in the *Book of Concord*. If a Lutheran assumes, because Augustine is quoted approvingly in the Apology's article on justification, that Augustine must have taught exactly the same doctrine, then certain passages in his writings could indeed be

---

[7]Robert C. Koons, *A Lutheran's Case for Roman Catholicism: Finding a Lost Path Home* (Eugene, OR: Cascade Books, 2020), 3–4.

"shocking" and might, in cases such as Koons's, contribute to a loss of faith in the Lutheran Confession.

This assumption is on robust display in a video released in March 2020 by Hans Fiene, a pastor in Koons's former denomination, on his popular YouTube channel called LutheranSatire. "The Church History Mixtape Vol. 1: Worms" recounts the story of Luther at the Diet of Worms in the form of a rap, supported by pictures and large block quotations from the Bible and historical sources. Fiene executes this unlikely combination with his characteristic wit and intelligence. At one point, Luther raps the following defense:

> It's not an innovation to say that justification
> comes from faith alone, just as Paul said in Galatians.
> Why ya fussin' and discussin' and calling this so disgusting,
> when everything was said before by Ambrose and Augustine?"[8]

The text shown on the screen at this point is the Ambrose quotation from Apology 4:103 and the Augustine quotation from Apology 4:106, which comes from the same treatise that Koons mentions, *On the Spirit and the Letter*. Here is the Augustine quotation, in full, though using a different translation than LutheranSatire does:

> The righteousness of the Law, namely, that he who has fulfilled it shall live in it, is set forth for this reason, that when

---

[8]LutheranSatire, "The Church History Mixtape, Vol. 1: Worms," March 22, 2020, video, 5:07, https://www.youtube.com/watch?v=7heceGAdsT0.

any one has recognized his infirmity he may attain and work the same and live in it, conciliating the Justifier not by his own strength nor by the letter of the Law itself (which cannot be done), but by faith. **Except in a justified man, there is no right work wherein he who does it may live**. But justification is obtained by faith . . . By the Law we fear God; by faith we hope in God. But to those fearing punishment grace is hidden; and the soul laboring, *etc.*, under this fear betakes itself by faith to God's mercy, in order that He may give what He commands . . . [9]

I have used the English translation from the *Triglotta*[10] instead of the *Reader's Edition of the Book of Concord*[11]—the translation that accompanies the rap in the video—because the *Reader's Edition* is a revision of the Dau and Bente translation from the *Triglotta* and, in this case, the revision is less accurate than the original. It replaces the bolded sentence above, "Except in a justified man, there is no right work wherein he who does it may live," with a sentence that means the opposite: "In a justified person, there is no right work by which he who does that work may live." Augustine's Latin, according to Migne's

---

[9]Phillip Melanchthon, *Apology of the Augsburg Confession* 4:106, quoting Augustine of Hippo, *On the Spirit and the Letter* 51:29. Emphasis added.

[10]*Triglot Concordia: The Symbolical Books of the Evangelical Lutheran Church*, trans. William H.T. Dau and Gerhard F. Bente (St. Louis, MO: Concordia Publishing House, 1921).

[11]*Concordia: The Lutheran Confessions, A Reader's Edition of the Book of Concord* (St. Louis, MO: Concordia Publishing House, 2005) is based on the translation by William H.T. Dau and Gerhard F. Bente and was revised, updated, and annotated by Paul T. McCain, Robert C. Baker, Gene E. Veith, and Edward A. Engelbrecht.

edition, reads "*Opus enim, quod qui fecerit vivet in eo, non fit nisi a iustificato*" ("For the work in which he who does it shall live, is not done except by one who is justified").[12] The edition quoted in the Apology has *rectum* ("right," as in the bolded sentence above) for *enim* but is otherwise identical. By replacing the good original translation with this mistranslation, the *Reader's Edition* hides a clue to Augustine's true position and encourages intelligent Lutherans, such as Hans Fiene (the LutheranSatire creator) and Robert Koons, to believe that "everything was said before by Ambrose and Augustine," so that the former makes that inaccurate claim with greater assurance and the latter is more likely to feel betrayed when he reads Augustine for himself.[13]

After the first half of this quotation from Augustine (after the ellipses), Melanchthon comments, "Here he clearly says that the

---

[12]This is the *Nicene and Post-Nicene Fathers* translation. A woodenly literal translation would be "For the work the man who shall have done which will live in it, is not done except by a justified man." This sentence does not appear in the Kolb and Wengert translation of the Apology because they used the *octavo* edition, Melanchthon's revision from later in 1531, which shortens the Augustine quotation in this passage. The sentence is fairly difficult to translate, but I cannot see by what construal the *Reader's Edition* editors could have ended up with "*in* a justified person" instead of "*except by* a justified person." The "*nisi a iustificato*" is quite clear.

[13]The *Reader's Edition* also omits the "etc." after "the soul laboring" instead of converting it into ellipses to show that Melanchthon skips a bit of the original passage here. In this case, the omitted clauses do not alter the meaning significantly, but it is still concerning to see the *Reader's Edition* concealing such markers. It smooths Augustine out, reducing the chance that he might be discovered to differ from the Apology in any way. The original sentence reads, "And the soul which labours under this fear, since it has not conquered its evil concupiscence, and from which this fear, like a harsh master, has not departed—let it flee by faith for refuge to the mercy of God, that He may give it what He commands . . . " (*Post-Nicene Fathers* translation).

Justifier is conciliated by faith, and that justification is obtained by faith." After the second half, he says, "Here he teaches that by the Law hearts are terrified, but by faith they receive consolation. He also teaches us to apprehend, by faith, mercy, before we attempt to fulfil the Law." Both summaries are accurate, but that does not mean that Augustine's understanding of justification agrees perfectly with the one Melanchthon is setting forth. He quotes these excerpts to add Patristic affirmation to the "many passages of Scripture that clearly ascribe justification to faith, and, indeed, deny it to works" (*Ap. AC* 4:107–8), as he says two sentences later. Now, Augustine did indeed "ascribe justification to faith" and did so in such a way that he could speak, as he does in the excerpt just quoted, of "one who is justified," perfect tense (*iustificato*)—not one who is *pursuing* justification with the *aid* of faith. And he did indeed "deny [justification] to works," but this was only in the sense that justification comes to the sinner "on account of no antecedent merits of his own works; . . . since it is bestowed on us, not because we have done good works, but that we may be able to do them."[14] In other words, justification is not the reward for good works, but it is the power, granted freely through faith, to *do* good works, which God might then reward. For Melanchthon and the Lutherans, on the other hand, "To attain the remission of sins is to be justified" (*Ap. AC* 4:76). For Augustine, forgiveness is a necessary part of justification, but he also includes— and gives greater emphasis to—the change in the justified that leads to righteous behavior going forward. To be justified is to be made into

---

[14]Augustine, *On the Spirit and the Letter* 16:10, in *Nicene and Post-Nicene Fathers*, vol. 5, trans. Peter Holmes and Robert E. Wallace (Peabody, MA: Hendrickson, 1994), pp. 83–114.

a doer of the law. "Justification does not subsequently accrue to them as doers of the law, but justification precedes them as doers of the law. For what else does the phrase 'being justified' signify than being made righteous . . . ?"[15]

Augustine attributes this change to the gift of the Holy Spirit, by whom "God's love has been poured into our hearts" (Rom. 5:5) so that it might "cause the soul to delight more in what He teaches it, than it delights in what opposes His instruction,"[16] and God's law might instead of "alarm[ing a man] from without . . . justify him from within." Also, we might understand "that from Him accrues to us the justification, whereby we do what He commands."[17] In the lines that Melanchthon skips in the first ellipses of Apology 4:106, Augustine calls justification a "resurrection" before the bodily resurrection, worked by the Holy Spirit, "that we may in this present world live soberly, righteously, and godly in the renewal of His grace."[18] In all three of these uses of "justify" or "justification," so strange to Protestant ears, we see that Augustine is including sanctification in his understanding of justification. The man who has believed and been baptized has been justified (perfect tense) by faith, but since justification "signifies . . . being made righteous" and this newly righteous man is still unrighteous in himself, he also *continues* to be

---

[15]Ibid., 45:26.
[16]Ibid., 51:29.
[17]Ibid., 30:17.
[18]Ibid., 51:29. "For by this faith we believe that God will raise even us from the dead—even now in the spirit, that we may in this present world live soberly, righteously, and godly in the renewal of His grace; and by and by in our flesh, which shall rise again to immortality, which indeed is the reward of the Spirit, who precedes it by a resurrection which is appropriate to Himself—that is, by justification."

justified (present tense) as long as he persists and makes progress in righteous living. Alistair McGrath concludes that there are two different kinds of "justification" in Augustine's system. "God *operates* upon man in the *act* of justification, and *cooperates* with him in the *process* of justification."[19]

The great Lutheran theologian of the next generation, Martin Chemnitz, wrote of this dual usage, "Augustine is often convinced by the testimony of Paul that the term 'to justify' is interpreted with reference to the remission of sins. But later in his life, deceived by the similarity of the words 'to sanctify' and 'to justify,' he shifted the emphasis in the direction of sanctification, having the new qualities, desires and actions of the Spirit."[20] Chemnitz then goes on to show that the Hebrew and Greek words rendered as *iustificare* and *iustificatio* in the Latin Bible have forensic meanings, referring to verdicts and declarations and not actually *transforming* unjust humans so as to make them just.[21] Alistair McGrath, writing much more recently, agrees with this analysis.

> Augustine understands the verb *iustificare* to mean "to make righteous,'" an understanding of the term which he appears to have held throughout his working life. In arriving at this understanding, he appears to have interpreted *-ficare* as the unstressed form of *facere*, by analogy with *vivificare* and

---

[19]Alistair E. McGrath, *Iustitia Dei: A History of the Christian Doctrine of Justification*, 2nd ed. (Cambridge, UK: Cambridge University Press, 1998), 28.

[20]Martin Chemnitz, *Loci Theologici* (1591), trans. J.A.O. Preus (St. Louis, MO: Concordia Publishing House, 1989), 475, col. A.

[21]Chemnitz, *Loci Theologici*, 476–477.

mortificare. [*Iustus* plus *facere* = "to make just / righteous"—E.P.] Although this is a permissible interpretation of the *Latin word*, it is unacceptable as an interpretation of the *Hebrew concept* which underlies it. The term *iustificare* is, of course, post-classical, having been introduced through the Latin translation of the bible [*sic*], and thus restricted to Christian writers of the Latin west. Augustine was thus unable to turn to classical authors in an effort to clarify its meaning, and was thus obliged to interpret the term himself.²²

So, the claim in Apology 4:76, "To attain the remission of sins is to be justified," is vindicated by the original languages. Augustine was led astray by a deficient understanding of the biblical term at the center of this doctrine, with huge ramifications for the future course of Western theology. Recovering the original forensic meaning was one of the significant contributions of the Reformation—or perhaps it would be more accurate to say, of the Renaissance, because it came from the revival of the classical humanities—and helped pave the way for the Reformation. Chemnitz writes, "In this locus [justification] the example is particularly illustrative. For when the correct terminology was lost, immediately the light of the purer teaching was also extinguished; and when in our time the correct grammatical meaning of the words in this locus was restored, the purity of the doctrine was also restored."²³ As important as this point is, however, there is much more to be said about the Augustinian doctrine of justification and the use of Augustine in the Apology of the Augsburg Confession. The

---

²²McGrath, *Iustitia Dei*, 30–31.
²³Chemnitz, *Loci Theologici*, 475, col. A.

question is nowhere near as simple as some Lutherans would like it to be on one side of the issue (We *didn't* follow Augustine. Augustine was wrong. We followed Scripture), or the other, as Robert Koons seems to think it is, with his opinion that Melanchthon is grotesquely "cherry-picking" Augustine while ignoring (or purposefully suppressing) Augustine's actual meaning in the context of his quotations.[24] The question in this essay is not how well Augustine agreed with Scripture but how well the Lutherans agreed with Augustine when they were quoting him as a supporting witness. And the answer is that they agreed with him much better than Koons thinks, though, as I have been showing, not as well as the LutheranSatire video claims.

---

[24] The Apology's other quotation from *On the Spirit and the Letter* is unambiguously on target. Because some of his opponents claimed that when St. Paul denied that we can be saved by "the works of the Law," he meant to exclude only the Jewish ceremonies, Melanchthon wrote (in Apology 4:87): "Augustine teaches correctly that Paul speaks of the entire Law, as he discusses at length in his book, *On the Spirit and Letter*, where he says finally: 'These matters, therefore having been considered and treated . . . , we infer that man is not justified by the precepts of a good life, but by faith in Jesus Christ [*nisi per fidem Iesu Christi*]' [(22:13)]." Augustine asks in his next chapter, "Is it possible to contend that it is not the law which was written on those two tables that the apostle describes as 'the letter that kills,' but the law of circumcision and the other sacred rites which are now abolished?" and concludes that it is not possible, because Paul uses one of the Ten Commandments, "You shall not covet," as his example of "the letter that kills" (Rom. 7:7,11). Note on translation: The *"nisi per fidem"* at the end of the Apology quotation would normally be rendered *"except* by faith" rather than *"but* by faith," which would seem to point to a combination of works *and* faith, but this is a quotation from Galatians 2:16 (*Vulgate*), which because of its context is translated *"but* by faith," even in the Douay-Reims Bible, the Jerusalem Bible, and the RSV Catholic Edition. Also, Augustine goes on to clarify his meaning: "in a word, not by the law of works, but by the law of faith; not by the letter, but by the spirit; not by the merits of deeds, but by free grace" (*On the Spirit and the Letter* 22:13).

The truth of the matter is that although the Lutheran doctrine of justification by faith alone—"that men cannot be justified before God by their own strength, merits, or works, but are freely justified for Christ's sake, through faith, when they believe that they are received into favor, and that their sins are forgiven for Christ's sake" (AC 4:2-3)—is much easier to prove and to keep consistent when you are using the biblical (Hebrew and Greek) definition of "justify," it is possible to articulate and defend it also using Augustine's (Latin) etymology. This is what Melanchthon does in Article 4 of the Apology—not as a subterfuge but because he is working with the same Latin terms as everyone else in the Western tradition and apparently thinks they will suffice. In Article 5, which treats the intimately related subject "Of Love and the Fulfilling of the Law," he does assert of several passages that "justify" is used forensically,[25] but he does not argue from the Greek and develop the assertion into proof for his position. He does not see the argument that impeaches Augustine's definition as a silver bullet, or even a very important arrow in his quiver.

In fact, far from faulting the Augustinian definition, Melanchthon includes the following passage, which according to

---

[25]"Here [in James 2:24] 'to be justified' does not mean that a righteous man is made from a wicked man, but to be pronounced righteous in a forensic sense, as also in the passage Rom. 2:13: 'The doers of the Law shall be justified'" (*Ap. AC* 5:131). "In this passage [Rom. 5:1], 'to justify' signifies, according to forensic usage, to acquit a guilty one and declare him righteous, but on account of the righteousness of another, namely, of Christ, which righteousness of another is communicated to us by faith" (*Ap. AC* 5:184-85).

Alistair McGrath, "has led to considerable confusion among his modern interpreters"[26]:

> Likewise, just as we ought to maintain that, apart from the Law, the promise of Christ is necessary, so also is it needful to maintain that faith justifies. **For the Law cannot be performed unless the Holy Ghost be first received.** It is, therefore, needful to maintain that the promise of Christ is necessary. But this cannot be received except by faith. Therefore, those who deny that faith justifies, teach nothing but the Law, both Christ and the Gospel being set aside. But when it is said that faith justifies, some perhaps understand it of the beginning, namely, that faith is the beginning of justification or preparation for justification, so that not faith itself is that through which we are accepted by God, but the works which follow; and they dream, accordingly, that faith is highly praised, because it is the beginning . . . We do not believe thus concerning faith, but we maintain this, that properly and truly, by faith itself, we are for Christ's sake accounted righteous, or are acceptable to God. **And because "to be justified" means that out of unjust men just men are made, or born again [*ex iniustis iustos effici seu regenerari*], it means also that they are pronounced or accounted just. For Scripture speaks in both ways.**[27]

---

[26]McGrath, *Iustitia Dei*, 212.

[27]The *octavo* edition, released in September 1531 after Melanchthon had taken suggestions from Johannes Brenz and others and made some changes to the original Apology (published in April 1531), elaborates a bit here. "The term 'to be justified' is used in two ways: to denote, being

> Accordingly we wish first to show this, that faith alone makes of an unjust, a just man, i.e., receives remission of sins. (*Ap. AC* 4:70–72)[28]

McGrath comments, "Alongside statements which explicitly define the forensic character of justification, we find statements which explicitly define justification in factitive terms."[29] As examples of the first kind of statement, he has offered two from Article 5—one of which I have already quoted in a footnote: "In this passage [Rom. 5:1], 'to justify' signifies, according to forensic usage, to acquit a guilty one and declare him righteous, but on account of the righteousness of another [*alienam iustitiam*], namely, of Christ, which righteousness of another [*aliena iustitia*] is communicated to us by faith" (*Ap. AC* 5:184–85).[30] But we don't need to go to Article 5 to find such examples. In the sentences I have not bolded, this block quotation clearly states that justification is forgiveness and that forgiveness is being "accounted righteous." Yet, along with these statements, Melanchthon offers the definition "'to be justified' means that out of unjust men just men are made, or born again" and the concession "Scripture speaks in both ways."

This stipulation that "justify" can mean two different things in Scripture makes us notice that in Article 5, when he gives examples of verses where "justify" is used forensically, Melanchthon says in each case that the usage of "here" or "in this passage." He is not ready to

---

converted or regenerated; again, being accounted righteous."
    [28]Emphasis added.
    [29]McGrath, *Iustitia Dei*, 212.
    [30]The other example McGrath has quoted comes from Apology 5:93: "for Christ's sake, we are accounted righteous before God."

claim that it is *always* so. Similarly, Augustine notes in *On the Spirit and the Letter*, the same treatise we have so far been discussing, that the word *justify* can sometimes be used forensically and that it definitely *is* used forensically in at least one passage of Scripture. When he has offered an explanation for Romans 2:13—how it is that "the doers of the law shall be justified" when, in his understanding of the word, they must *already* have been just in order to be "doers of the law"[31]—he then suggests another interpretive possibility (as he often does): "Or else the term 'They shall be justified' is used in the sense of, 'They shall be deemed, or reckoned as just,' as it is predicated of a certain man in the Gospel, 'But he, willing to justify himself,' Luke 10:29—meaning that he wished to be thought and accounted just."[32]

When we consider the way Melanchthon is clearly plugging in to Augustine's theology in this passage, without quoting him or even dropping his name (contra the allegation of "cherry-picking"), even asserting Augustine's definition as a kind of umbrella definition that *includes* the forensic use ("*Because* 'to be justified' means that out of unjust men just men are made, or born again, it means *also* that they are pronounced or accounted just"), we begin to question the justice of Robert Koons's professed disappointment with Melanchthon "as a scholar and teacher." And there is more to point out in the block quotation above. Melanchthon opens by saying that it is "needful to maintain that faith justifies," not for any of the reasons you would expect to hear first from a Lutheran—because in this way our works

---

[31] His solution has already been quoted above: "Justification does not subsequently accrue to them as doers of the law, but justification precedes them as doers of the law. For what else does the phrase 'being justified' signify than being made righteous?"

[32] Augustine, *Spirit and Letter* 45:26.

can be excluded, or because in this way we can have confidence that we are truly saved—but because "the Law cannot be performed unless the Holy Ghost be first received." This is just as Augustinian a reason as his account of "to be justified" in the same excerpt is an Augustinian definition. Nor is it only Augustinian, but it comes especially from the very treatise Koons has accused Melanchthon of misrepresenting, *On the Spirit and the Letter*:

> It is evident, then, that the oldness of the letter, in the absence of the newness of the Spirit, instead of freeing us from sin, rather makes us guilty by the knowledge of sin . . . If [the] commandment is kept from the fear of punishment and not from the love of righteousness, it is servilely kept, not freely, and therefore it is not kept at all. For no fruit is good which does not grow from the root of love. If, however, that faith be present which works by love, (Galatians 5:6) then one begins to delight in the law of God after the inward man, (Romans 7:22) and this delight is the gift of the Spirit, not of the letter . . .[33]

The same can also be said of Melanchthon's clarification that by "just men [being] *made*" out of unjust men, he means "[being] *born again*" (*regenerari*), because regeneration is the work of the Holy Spirit, in which he gives believers new life and new powers, which is why Augustine (in the same passage that Melanchthon quotes in Apology

---

[33]Ibid., 26:14.

4:106) called it "a resurrection that is proper to [the Holy Spirit]—that is... justification."³⁴

At this point, of course, Koons might ask (along with quite a few readers who are still Lutherans) how Melanchthon can honestly concede so much. How can this definition fit with justification *sola fide*? Isn't this willingness to identify justification with regeneration, this definition of justification as "making righteous" and not strictly "declaring righteous," essentially the position of "the adversaries" whom he is writing against? Can he keep his argument consistent, or is he going to have to contradict himself in the effort to hold onto Augustine even while going beyond him?

He starts to answer these questions with the final sentence of the block quotation we've been discussing. "Accordingly we wish first to show this, that faith alone makes of an unjust, a just man, *i.e.*, receives remission of sins." The "i.e." (*hoc est* in the Latin, not actually *id est*, but it means the same thing) suggests an equivalence. "Faith alone makes... a just man—that is, receives remission of sins." "To make just" means "to receive forgiveness." So is Melanchthon using factitive language (as McGrath calls it) as some kind of Trojan horse? Has all the stuffing been pulled out and replaced with forensic meaning? No. He has already said that unjust people are made just by being *regenerated*, and he is going to say it again in a few short paragraphs. "Therefore by faith alone we are justified, understanding justification as the making of a righteous man out of an unrighteous, or that he be regenerated" (*Ap. AC* 4:78). But when God grants faith to people by regenerating them,³⁵ by giving them the ability to love him

---

³⁴Ibid., 51:29.
³⁵That God is the one who gives faith to anyone who believes is an

and obey his commandments in spirit and in truth, what makes them righteous immediately is not their employment of that new ability, which has barely begun and will never be perfect. The thing that makes them righteous without qualification, truly "just men," is the remission of all their sins. This is Melanchthon's point. What he objects to is not the idea that the Holy Spirit helps believers fulfill the law, or even the idea that the gift of the Spirit is one of the things that constitutes justification, but only what he has already rejected in the long block quotation—the idea "that not faith itself is that through which we are accepted by God, but the works which follow." When we say, "faith alone," he explains a few sentences later, "It is ... *the opinion of merit* that we exclude" (*Ap. AC* 4:73).

Robert Koons includes an appendix (appendix C) in *A Lutheran's Case for Roman Catholicism* that contains eleven quotations from *On the Spirit and the Letter*, purporting to prove the following accusation from the beginning of the book: "In that work, Augustine explicitly rejects the very doctrine that Melanchthon claims to find there." Not one of the eleven proves or even supports this claim. All of them fit easily with the position that Melanchthon actually articulates in Article 4, though perhaps not with all the modern Lutheran teachers whose opinions Koons is unwittingly foisting *on* Melanchthon. What *do* contradict Article 4 are some of the short interpretations Koons interjects after each excerpt, putting in his own words what he finds telling about each one. And in almost every case

---

Augustinian commonplace, especially in his anti-Pelagian writings. It comes up at least once in *On the Spirit and the Letter*, in chapter 18:11: "By this faith of Jesus Christ—that is, the faith which Christ has given [*contulit*] to us—we believe it is from God that we now have, and shall have more and more, the ability of living righteously..."

(five out of six), the offensive element in the interjection is a claim of *merit*—either explicitly using the word (three times), claiming we can "rely on works" as long as God's grace has helped us do them (one time), or claiming that "infused grace by which the will is healed" is "*the* grace that faith procures" with no mention of forgiveness (one time).[36] In all five of these cases, the "opinion of merit" is something the Augustine quotation does not actually mention.

The closest Augustine comes in *On the Spirit and the Letter* to teaching that heaven is partially merited by "the works which follow" faith is this passage near the end of the work, where he is commenting on Psalm 103:4:

> "Who redeems your life from destruction"; this will take place at the resurrection of the dead in the last day. "Who crowns you with loving-kindness and tender mercy"; this shall be accomplished in the day of judgment; for when the righteous King shall sit upon His throne to render to every man according to his works, who shall then boast of having a pure heart? Or who shall glory of being clean from sin? It was therefore necessary to mention God's loving-kindness and tender mercy there, where one might expect debts to be demanded and deserts recompensed so strictly as to leave no room for mercy. **He crowns, therefore, with loving-kindness and tender mercy; but even so according to**

---

[36]Koons, *A Lutheran's Case*, 141–45. The three interjections that mention merit by name are the third, fourth, and sixth (pp. 142–43). The other two are the ninth and eleventh, respectively (pp. 144–45). The interjection I think contradicts Article 4 that *isn't* obviously about merit is the eighth (p. 144).

> **works.** For he shall be separated to the right hand, to whom, it is said, "I was an hungered, and you gave me meat" (Matt. 25:35). There will, however, be also judgment without mercy; but it will be for him "that has not showed mercy" (James 2:13). But "blessed are the merciful: for they shall obtain mercy" (Matt. 5:7) of God.[37]

Works are involved in the final judgment, he says, but he is not talking here simply about good works (any righteous deed done with the help of the Holy Spirit). He is talking specifically about works of mercy, which in his understanding are included in the forgiveness to which we refer when we pray, "Forgive us our trespasses, *as we forgive* those who trespass against us." So, he writes three years later (415 AD) in another work, *On Man's Perfection in Righteousness*,

> In such judgment [on the last day] all will be found righteous who with sincerity pray: "Forgive us our debts, as we forgive our debtors" (Matt. 6:12). **For it is through this forgiveness that they will be found righteous**; and[38] on this account, that [*et eo quod*] whatever sins they have here incurred, they have blotted out by their deeds of charity. Whence the Lord says: "Give alms; and, behold, all things are clean unto you" (Luke 11:41 [Vulgate]). For in the end, it shall be said to the righteous, when about to enter into the promised kingdom: "I was an hungered, and you gave me meat" (Matt. 25:35) and so forth . . . For who can justly accuse the man who wishes evil to

---

[37]Augustine, *On the Spirit and the Letter*, 59:33. Emphasis added.
[38]The *Nicene and Post-Nicene Fathers* translation omits the "and."

no one, and who faithfully does good to all he can, and never cherishes a wish to avenge himself on any man who does him wrong, **so that he can truly say, "As we forgive our debtors?"** And yet by the very fact that he truly says, "Forgive, as we also forgive," he plainly admits that he is not without sin.[39]

Now, a Lutheran would never talk this way, would never say that *we* "have blotted out" our own sins. It is confusing language, as Christ's blood is the only thing that actually blots out sin. But Augustine is not claiming that Christ procures forgiveness for certain things and then the Christian must finish the job with works of mercy. It is actually the forgiveness for which they pray that blots their sin out. But the petition for forgiveness, "Forgive us our debts, as we forgive our debtors," must be made "with sincerity"—that is, by someone who *does* forgive their debtors. This is something Jesus says in so many words in his explanation of the Parable of the Unjust Servant: "So also my heavenly Father will do to every one of you, if you do not forgive your brother from your heart" (Matt. 18:35). We read also in Martin Luther's *Large Catechism* "If, therefore, you do not forgive, then do not think that God forgives you; but if you forgive, you have this consolation and assurance, that you are forgiven in heaven, not on account of your forgiving, for God forgives freely and without condition … but in order that He may set this up for our confirmation and assurance" (*LC* 3:95, in *BC*). Augustine sees almsgiving, here and in many passages of his works, as a kind of forgiveness granted to our

---

[39]Augustine, *On Man's Perfection in Righteousness* 11:24, in *NPNF*, vol. 5, 159–176. Emphasis added.

neighbor—giving something that is not deserved as freely as *we* have received what we have not deserved. This is arguably not yet a doctrine of human merits, despite the phrasing, but rather a sign of true faith.

There is no point in hanging too much on that distinction, though, because Augustine did arrive at such a doctrine soon after, as we see in *On Grace and Free Will*, a treatise written another three years later (418 AD, six years after *On the Spirit and the Letter*). Here he does not restrict himself to works of mercy and makes much freer use of the term *merit*. He begins, however, in a place much more agreeable to Lutherans, taking Pelagius to task for teaching "that the grace of God is given according to our merits." He mentions that when Pelagius was on trial a few years previously (415 AD) in the Synod of Diospolis in Palestine, he was asked if this thesis was his, and he denied it—"but how insincerely his later books plainly show." Pelagius was dishonest on this point, Augustine alleges, because this claim was "an opinion which was so diverse from Catholic doctrine, and so hostile to the grace of Christ, that unless he had anathematized it, as laid to his charge, he himself must have been anathematized on its account."[40] This is functionally what the Pelagians claim when they argue from texts such as 1 Chronicles 28:9, "if you seek Him, He will be found of you," that human initiative precedes God's grace. "And so they labour with all their might to show that God's grace is given according to our merits,—in other words, that grace is not grace. For, as the apostle most expressly says, 'to them who receive reward

---

[40]Augustine, *On Grace and Free Will* 10:5, in *NPNF*, vol. 5, 443–465.

according to merit, the recompense is not reckoned of grace but of debt'" (Rom. 4:4).[41]

Anchored, then, by this principle that God rewards us according to his grace, and not our merits, Augustine proceeds to investigate the meaning of some passages of Scripture that might seem to favor the Pelagians. One such passage is 2 Timothy 4:6–7, in which St. Paul writes, "I have fought a good fight; I have finished my course; I have kept the faith. There is henceforth laid up for me a crown of righteousness, which the Lord, the righteous Judge, shall give me at that day." Augustine points out that before Paul could run that good race, he had first "obtained God's grace . . . without any good merits of his own, but rather with many evil merits." Once this is recognized, though, Augustine does not hesitate to treat Paul's subsequent good works as meritorious. "He enumerates these as, of course, now his good merits; so that, as after his evil merits he obtained grace, so now, after his good merits, he might receive the crown."[42] Another such passage is Matthew 16:27, which says that when Jesus returns, "Then He shall reward every man according to his works." In light of this, Augustine asks, "How can eternal life be a matter of grace, seeing that grace is not rendered to works, but is given gratuitously . . . ? How, then, is eternal life by grace when it is received from works? Does the apostle perchance *not* say that eternal life is a grace? Nay, he has so called it, with a clearness which none can possibly gainsay. It requires no acute intellect, but only an attentive hearer, to discover this."[43]

---

[41] Ibid., 11:5.
[42] Ibid., 14:6.
[43] Ibid., 19:8. "U*t non desiderent acutum intellectorem, sed attentum*

Melanchthon quotes this last sentence in Apology 4:33 as punctuation for a series of six selections of Scripture he has cited in a row to prove "that grace is not given because of our merits" (*Ap. AC* 4:29).[44] "These testimonies are so manifest that, to use the words of Augustine which he employed in this case, they do not need an acute understanding, but only an attentive hearer" (*Ap. AC* 4:33). The first two Scripture quotations in that chain of six (Gal. 5:4 and Rom. 10:3–4) appear in the context of another Augustine quotation, this time from *On Nature and Grace* (415 AD).

> For if natural capacity, by help of free will, is in itself sufficient both for discovering how one ought to live, and also for leading a holy life, "then Christ died in vain" (Gal. 2:21), and therefore also "the offense of the cross is ceased" (Gal. 5:11). Why also may I not myself exclaim?—nay, I will exclaim, and chide them with a Christian's sorrow—"Christ has become of no effect unto you, whosoever of you are justified by nature; you are fallen from grace" (Gal. 5:4); "for, being ignorant of God's righteousness, and wishing to establish your own righteousness, you have not submitted yourselves to the righteousness of God" (Rom. 10:3). For even as "Christ is the end of the law," so likewise is He the Saviour of man's corrupted nature, "for righteousness to everyone that believes" (Rom. 10:4).[45]

---

auditorem"; the *NPNF* translation renders *auditorem* here as "reader."

[44]"*Nec intellectorem acutum, sed tantummodo intentum desideret auditorem.*"

[45]Augustine, *On Nature and Grace* 47:40, in *NPNF*, vol. 5, 121–151.

Now Melanchthon is on solid ground with this longer quotation because he is quoting Augustine to support these four denials: "It is false that we merit the remission of sins by our works, . . . that men are accounted righteous before God because of the righteousness of reason, . . . that that reason, by its own strength, is able to love God above all things, and to fulfil God's Law, . . . that men do not sin who, without grace, do the commandments of God" (*Ap. AC* 4:25–28). Augustine is with him on all those points. His use of the shorter quotation ("they do not need an acute understanding . . . "), though, may be liable to the charge of "cherry-picking," against which I defended him when the subject was *On the Spirit and the Letter*.

It is true, as we have seen, that the thing Augustine said "requires no acute intellect, but only an attentive reader" was a principle that agrees entirely with Melanchthon's argument in Apology 4—St. Paul has clearly taught that eternal life is a gift of grace and, therefore, is not something that can be earned. Augustine agrees that this is quite clear. He thinks it is just as clear, however, that eternal life is awarded to good works. So, in the following chapter of *On Grace and Free Will*, he arrives at this solution for the conundrum he has posed ("How, then, is eternal life by grace, when it is received from works?"): "Even those good works of ours, which are recompensed with eternal life, belong to the grace of God, because of what is said by the Lord Jesus. 'Without me you can do nothing' (John 15:5)."[46] By this solution, Augustine preserves *sola gratia* against the Pelagians but not yet *sola fide*, which is also essential to the Lutheran

---

[46]Augustine, *On Grace and Free Will* 20:8.

doctrine of justification. It is not enough to affirm that we enter a state of righteousness by grace alone if *heaven* still cannot be earned except by *works* that we perform in the strength of that grace. If heaven must be earned by any merits other than Christ's, no matter how grace-fueled those merits are, this ends up being another way of teaching "that not faith itself is that through which we are accepted by God, but the works which follow" (*Ap. AC* 4:73).

It comes down to the question of merit. Did St. Augustine teach that Christians, once they have been justified (by which he meant forgiven and empowered by the Holy Spirit to love God and his law with a true love, productive of good works), then proceed to *merit* heaven by doing those works? We have seen him using that language already in the case of St. Paul fighting the good fight, "as after his evil merits he obtained grace, so now, after his good merits, he might receive the crown."[47] And, after he has offered the solution, "even those good works of ours, which are recompensed with eternal life, belong to the grace of God," he proceeds to illustrate it by explaining Ephesians 2:8–10, a classic *sola fide* proof text, in a way that Lutherans will find quite deficient.

> And the apostle himself, after saying, "By grace are you saved through faith; and that not of yourselves, it is the gift of God: not of works, lest any man should boast" (Eph. 2:8–9); saw, of course, the possibility that men would think from this statement that good works are not necessary to those who believe, but that faith alone suffices for them; and again, the

---

[47]Augustine, *On Grace and Free Will* 14:6.

possibility of men's boasting of their good works, as if they were of themselves capable of performing them. To meet, therefore, these opinions on both sides, he immediately added, "For we are His workmanship, created in Christ Jesus unto good works, which God has before ordained that we should walk in them" (Eph. 2:10) … **"Not of works" is spoken of the works which you suppose have their origin in yourself alone; but you have to think of works for which God has moulded (that is, has formed and created) you.** For of these he says, "We are His workmanship, created in Christ Jesus unto good works." … "Therefore, if any man be in Christ, he is a new creature: old things are passed away; behold, all things have become new. And all things are of God" (2 Cor. 5:17–18) … It follows, then, dearly beloved, beyond all doubt, that as your good life is nothing else than God's grace, so also the eternal life which is the recompense of a good life [*quae bonae vitae redditur*] is the grace of God … [48]

He does not use the word *merit* in this passage, but by explaining Paul's "not of works" the way he does, he makes the Christian's grace-filled works instrumental to receiving eternal life. And this fits with his language from an earlier passage in the same work—"The Pelagians say that the only grace which is not given according to our merits is that whereby his sins are forgiven to man, but that that which is given in the end, that is, eternal life, is rendered to our preceding merits … If, indeed, they so understand our merits as to acknowledge

---

[48] Augustine, *On Grace and Free Will* 20:8. Emphasis added.

them, too, to be the gifts of God, then their opinion would not deserve reprobation."[49]

Here, we arrive at the "bridge too far," the point that Melanchthon is aware he cannot concede to Augustine "the fancy of Augustine [*imaginatione Augustini*] concerning the fulfillment of the Law," as he says to Johannes Brenz (in the excerpt quoted from David Fink's article above), that leads to his reluctant (but thus far private) judgment that Augustine "does not adequately explain the righteousness of faith."[50] The Christians's own good works can never be an object of their confidence, no matter how correctly they learn to attribute them to the grace of God. Only the promise of God in Jesus Christ can bear that weight. "It is much better to remind the reader concerning the proper role of faith, the destruction of doubt, and that for the doubting conscience, it is not possible to fulfil the law."[51]

But Melanchthon realizing this without publishing the realization in the Apology is no reason to accuse him of being disingenuous in his quotations, as Koons does and as Fink ends up suggesting even for all his careful hedging.[52] Melanchthon knows that

---

[49] Augustine, *On Grace and Free Will* 14:6.
[50] Fink, "Bullshitting Augustine," 231–32.
[51] Quoted by Fink (p. 234) from Melanchthon's 1532 Romans commentary. See footnote 112 above.
[52] "[Melanchthon] cites Augustine 'as if he were wholly of the same mind', but never actually says so. Here we must remember that, unlike modern scholars operating under the assumptions of the historical-critical ethos, 'getting Augustine right' was never an end in itself for Melanchthon— or, one is tempted to say, for any of the combatants in the theological conflicts of the sixteenth century. The 'truth' on which Melanchthon had his sights set was the theological truth of justification by faith alone, not the historical truth of whether or not Augustine held to that view with all the precision required to meet the demands of latter-day polemics. On this question, all bets are clearly off with Melanchthon, who simply does not care in the

the great Doctor of the Church sometimes expressed himself in ways that played to his opponents' position rather than his own, but he's still convinced that the Lutheran position is much closer to Augustine's than is the position of "the adversaries." He makes it clear in Article 4 that he believes he is dealing with outright Pelagians on the opposing side, thanks to their acceptance of scholastic theories such as the doctrine that God would always send grace to aid those who "did what was in them," however little that might be (which gives the sinner the initiative in salvation) and the doctrine that, even for the unregenerate, one of those good things "in them" is the potential to love God above all things.

> Here the scholastics, having followed the philosophers, teach only a righteousness of reason, namely, civil works, and fabricate besides that without the Holy Ghost reason can love God above all things . . . In this manner they teach that men merit the remission of sins by doing what is in them, *i.e.*, if reason, grieving over sin, elicit an act of love to God, or for God's sake be active in that which is good. And because this opinion naturally flatters men, it has brought forth and multiplied in the Church many services, monastic vows, abuses of the mass; and, with this opinion the one has, in the course of time, devised this act of worship and observances, the other that. And in order that they might nourish and increase confidence in such works, they have affirmed that

---

Apology whether what he says describes the reality of Augustine's position correctly. He simply picks out snippets from Augustine's corpus to suit his purpose" (Fink, "Bullshitting Augustine," 236–37).

God necessarily gives grace to one thus working, by the necessity not of constraint but of immutability. (*Ap. AC* 4:9–11)

Their feigning a distinction between *meritum congrui* and *meritum condigni* is only an artifice in order not to appear openly to Pelagianize. For, if God necessarily gives grace for the *meritum congrui*, it is no longer *meritum congrui*, but *meritum condigni*. (*Ap. AC* 4:19)[53]

He is calling Augustine chiefly as an anti-Pelagian witness, and this role extends beyond the condemnation of such obvious neo-Pelagianisms as the ones just referenced. He also wants to clarify what Augustine *means* by "merit" and show that it is not the same thing "the adversaries" mean. For this, we need to look beyond Article 4 to Article 5, "On Love and the Fulfilling of the Law," because that is where he handles the question of what may and may not be said to "merit" and in what sense eternal life can be called a "reward."

Some talk of merit is correct, he says. "We teach that good works are meritorious, not for the remission of sins, for grace or justification (for these we obtain only by faith), but for other rewards, bodily and spiritual, in this life and after this life" (*Ap. AC* 5:73). Thus far, he agrees with Augustine, even suggesting that we may merit

---

[53]"Congruent merit" is relative human merit, attainable by good use of the free will but not so good as to obligate God to reward it. Nevertheless, since God is merciful, he always *will* reward it by granting grace to do more. "Condign merit" is actual merit because it is done not just by the human will but by the power of God's grace (concretely by the habit of love stamped in the Christian by that grace).

some rewards "after this life." But, a little while later, he clarifies that eternal life itself is not one of those rewards. "Because by our works we do not merit justification, through which we are made sons of God, and coheirs with Christ, we do not by our works merit eternal life; for faith obtains this, because faith justifies us and has a reconciled God" (*Ap. AC* 5:75). He is making a fine point, though, because the very next sentence concedes, "But eternal life is owed [*debetur*] to the justified, according to the passage Rom. 8:30: 'Whom He justified, them He also glorified'" (*Ap. AC* 5:75).[54]

How can a reward be *owed* to someone without having been *merited* by that person? Melanchthon returns to this subject later in the article, when he addresses the term *reward*. "We do not contend concerning the term reward. We dispute concerning this matter, namely, whether good works are of themselves worthy of grace and of eternal life, or whether they please only on account of faith, which apprehends Christ as Mediator." In other words, Lutherans can agree with Augustine that "eternal life . . . is the recompense of a good life," as long as it is understood that the *works themselves* do not merit such a reward but are received *as if they did* because of the doer's faith in Christ. Melanchthon explains further a few paragraphs later:

> If the adversaries will concede that we are accounted righteous by faith because of Christ, and that good works please God because of faith, we will not afterwards contend much concerning the term reward. We confess that eternal life is a reward, because it is something owed [*debita*] on account

---

[54] I have replaced the *Triglotta*'s "due" with the less ambiguous (thus more correct) "owed."

of the promise, not on account of our merits. For the justification has been promised, which we have above shown to be properly a gift of God; and to this gift has been added the promise of eternal life ... (*Ap. AC* 5:241)[55]

Eternal life is indeed *owed* to Christians, not because our works are so good as to deserve it but because God has promised to cover all the sin that makes them fall short of that and accordingly to grant us the reward of perfect righteousness—eternal life.[56]

If it seems that Melanchthon is bending over backward to justify an Augustinian manner of speaking that he might more honestly have criticized, we must remember that explaining *Augustine's* language is not his main goal here. He is explaining the language of the *Scriptures* that led Augustine to formulate his position in the first place—passages such as Matthew 16:27 (mentioned above) and Romans 2:6, both of which say that God will "render to each man according to his works." Melanchthon has no choice but to accept language that comes from the Bible itself; and once he has explained how to understand it in light of other Scriptures that teach

---

[55]The *Triglotta* has "due" instead of "owed" as a rendering of *debita*.
[56]Melanchthon also gives a second explanation for how Scripture can call eternal life a reward: "Therefore it is a sufficient reason why eternal life is called a reward, because thereby the tribulations which we suffer, and the works of love which we do, are compensated, although we have not deserved it. For there are two kinds of compensation: one, which we are obliged, the other, which we are not obliged, to render. E. g., when the emperor grants a servant a principality, he therewith compensates the servant's work; and yet the work is not worth the principality, but the servant acknowledges that he has received a gracious lien. Thus God does not owe us eternal life; still, when He grants it to believers for Christ's sake, that is a compensation for our sufferings and works" (*Ap. AC* 5:243).

justification by faith alone, he can produce an explanation that will work for Augustine's statements too, as long as he can show that Augustine meant "merit" to be understood in a similarly qualified way and not as "the adversaries" do. So he sets out to demonstrate this.

Article 5 contains four quotations from St. Augustine, and they are all chosen to make this point. The first comes after an extended discussion of the many ways that even good Christians continue to violate God's law. "Well does Augustine say: 'All the commandments of God are fulfilled when whatever is not done, is forgiven.' Therefore he requires faith even in good works, in order that we may believe that for Christ's sake we please God, and that even the works are not of themselves worthy and pleasing" (*Ap. AC* 5:51).[57] The second and third quotations punctuate a four-part argument against the doctrine of *meritum condigni*.[58] Firstly, to "imagine that good works, wrought by the aid of the habit of love, constitute a righteousness worthy by itself to please God, and worthy of eternal life," is to "have no need of Christ as Mediator" and "to transfer the glory of Christ to our works" (*Ap. AC* 5:195–96). "Secondly, the doctrine of the adversaries leaves consciences in doubt, so that they never can be pacified, because the Law always accuses us, even in good works" (*Ap. AC* 5:198). "Thirdly, how will conscience know when, by the inclination of this habit of love, a work has been done of which it may affirm that it merits grace *de condigno*?" (*Ap. AC* 5:200).[59]

---

[57] The Augustine quotation comes from *Retractationes* 19:3, vol. 1.
[58] That is, "a righteousness worthy by itself to please God, and worthy of eternal life . . ." *Ap. AC* 5:195.
[59] "Hypocrites, in their security, think simply their works are worthy, and that for this reason they are accounted righteous. On the other hand, terrified consciences doubt concerning all works, and for this reason are

> Fourthly, the entire Church confesses that eternal life is attained through mercy. For thus Augustine speaks, *On Grace and Free Will*, when, indeed, he is speaking of the works of the saints wrought after justification: "God leads us to eternal life not for our merits, but according to His mercy."[60] And *Confessions*, Book IX: "Woe to the life of man, however much it may be worthy of praise, if it be judged with mercy removed."[61] . . . But the subject is well known, and has very many and very clear testimonies in Scripture, and in the Church Fathers, who all with one mouth declare that, even though we have good works, yet in these very works we need mercy. (*Ap. AC* 5:201–3)

With the first three quotations, Melanchthon shows that Augustine qualified his talk of merit with reminders that we leave much undone—gaps that God must forgive, must fill in with his mercy, before he can judge us worthy of reward. Then the final Augustine quotation in Article 5 contrasts this qualification directly to the way merit is being interpreted by the other side.

> But here the adversaries reply that eternal life is called a reward, and that therefore it is merited *de condigno* by good works. We reply briefly and plainly: Paul (Rom. 6:23) calls

---

continually seeking other works." *Ap. AC* 5:200.

[60]Augustine, *On Grace and Free Will* 21:9. I have made a correction to the *Triglotta* translation here: "*for* our merits" (*pro meritis nostris*) rather than "*by* our merits."

[61]Augustine, *Confessions* 13:34, bk. 9.

eternal life a gift ... And Augustine says, as also do very many others who follow him: "God crowns His gifts in us."⁶² Elsewhere indeed (Luke 6:23) it is written: "Your reward is great in heaven." If these passages seem to the adversaries to conflict, they themselves may explain them. But they are not fair judges; for they omit the word "gift" ... and they select the word "reward," and most harshly interpret this not only against Scripture, but also against the usage of the language. Hence they infer that inasmuch as it is called a reward, our works, therefore, are such that they ought to be a price [*pretium*] for which eternal life is owed [*debetur*]. (*Ap. AC* 5:235–36)⁶³

Although Melanchthon has his own criticisms of Augustine's approach, wishing that he had not put so much emphasis on grace-powered works when the topic was justification and the final reward of the just, he is still making honest use of him because he is convinced that the position of "the adversaries" is a Pelagianized *corruption* of Augustine's system that has accentuated his flaws and ignored his safeguards, while the Lutheran understanding, on the other hand, is able to correct the master's weaker points by appealing to his stronger ones.

When we investigate Melanchthon's use of St. Augustine in Articles 4 and 5 of the Apology of the Augsburg Confession, we find neither a collection of cherry-picked quotations creating the illusion of Patristic support (as Koons alleges) nor a demonstration that

---

⁶²Augustine, *On Grace and Free Will* 15:6.
⁶³I have again changed the *Triglotta*'s "due" to "owed" for *debetur*.

Luther's doctrine of justification *sola fide* has all been "said before by ... Augustine" (as the LutheranSatire video claims). Instead, we find a significant volley in the battle *over* Augustine and his legacy; and whether one finds it convincing or not will depend quite a lot on whether one finds the accusations of Pelagianizing to be accurate. A Roman Catholic can call them into question, especially the claims in that last block quotation, by quoting a sentence from the Roman Confutation of the Augsburg Confession, the document to which Melanchthon was especially replying when he wrote the Apology.

Article 4 of the Confutation defines Pelagians as those "who thought that man can merit eternal life by his own powers without the grace of God" and agrees with the Lutherans that such teachers should be condemned. It then adds, contra the Lutherans, "if anyone should intend to disapprove of the merits that men acquire by the assistance of divine grace, he would agree with the Manichaeans rather than with the Catholic Church." It then quotes eight Scriptures to prove that the works of Christians *are* meritorious for salvation, "For where there are wages there is merit." Then, at the end of those Scripture citations comes the sentence I have in mind: "Nevertheless, all Catholics confess that our works of themselves have no merit, but that God's grace makes them worthy of eternal life."[64] This is an Augustinian-inspired disclaimer meant to take away the grounds for the accusation of Pelagianizing that Melanchthon goes on to make anyway. It might seem that it should cover the same ground as the quotations we have seen him marshal in Apology 5 to show how Augustine moderates his talk of merit by saying that God's forgiveness is needed for anyone to

---

[64]"Roman Confutation," *Book of Concord*. https://bookofconcord.org/roman-confutation/

be judged righteous. It's not forgiveness that the Confutation is talking about, though; it's the difference between congruent merit and condign merit. The theory is, without the extra grace that "makes them worthy of eternal life," human merit can only be congruent, i.e., approximately fitting the lines of what is required. So, God adds his grace by stamping the habit of love into the soul, and this puts the human merit over the top so that now it truly deserves to be rewarded with immortality.

We have seen Melanchthon give three arguments against this doctrine. (1) If you say that God *necessarily* adds his grace to congruent merit, then, from the human perspective, it's the same as condign merit—if you do your best, God will save you; there's just a little extra bookkeeping on his end. It ends up as "an artifice in order not to appear openly to Pelagianize" (*Ap. AC* 4:19). (2) If you think that "good works, wrought by the aid of the habit of love, constitute a righteousness worthy by itself to please God, and worthy of eternal life," then you "have no need of Christ as Mediator" (*Ap. AC* 5:195–96). Christ is given a place in your system, of course, but not *that* place. As the Apology says elsewhere, "The adversaries regard Christ as Mediator and Propitiator for this reason, namely, that He has merited the habit of love" (*Ap. AC* 4:78). You will not have active recourse to him and his cross when you need to be assured that you have peace with God, because his mediation is finished. Instead, you will be left to merit peace and salvation yourself by making proper use of the "habit of love" that he has already contributed to your effort. (3) This being the case, your conscience can never receive sure comfort. You cannot tell the difference in your own life between purely human merit (congruent) and the graced, sufficient kind (condign), so you will be left to the mercy of your personal psychology. "Hypocrites, in their security, think simply their works are worthy, and that for this reason they are accounted righteous. On the other hand, terrified consciences doubt concerning all works, and for this reason are continually seeking other works" (*Ap. AC* 5:200).

The second of these points, about having recourse to Christ's mediation and propitiation, is especially telling against any attempt to equate the Confutation's disclaimer with St. Augustine's emphasis on the need for God to forgive our sins and at the end to judge us with mercy. A constant refrain running through his anti-Pelagian works is his reference to the Fifth Petition of the Lord's Prayer. Most often, he quotes it to disprove the Pelagian claim of perfectability, because it seems obviously wrong to suggest that even the best Christian will ever arrive at the point where they no longer need to pray the Lord's Prayer, but we have seen one passage above where he applies it directly to Judgment Day. "In such judgment [on the Last Day] all will be found righteous who with sincerity pray: 'Forgive us our debts, as we forgive our debtors' (Matt. 6:12). For it is through this forgiveness that they will be found righteous."[65] The Apology's emphasis on "Christ as Mediator" is missing from this quotation (and is emphasized much less often by Augustine in general), but he says clearly that the Christians' hope before the judgment seat of God lies not in the merits that God has enabled them to accrue but in the forgiveness of their sins. Later in the same work, after touting the possibilities for growth in righteousness (in this life) so highly as to claim, "By this process, it is certainly brought about that our heart is

---

[65]Augustine, *On Man's Perfection in Righteousness* 11:24.

cleansed, and all our sin taken away," he still proceeds in the same sentence to add, "and what the righteous King, when sitting on His throne, shall find concealed in the heart and uncleansed as yet, shall be remitted by His mercy . . . If it were not so, what hope could any of us have? When, indeed, the righteous King shall sit upon His throne, who shall boast that he has a pure heart, or who shall boldly say that he is pure from sin?"[66]

Finally, we have a very Lutheran-sounding application of the Fifth Petition from *On Nature and Grace*. After saying that he would *like* to believe that sinless perfection in this life was possible for *someone*, Augustine turns to say this about everyone else: "They, however, are in a great majority, who, while not doubting that to the last day of their life it will be needful to them to resort to the prayer which they can so truthfully utter, 'Forgive us our trespasses, as we forgive those who trespass against us' (Matt. 6:12), still trust that in Christ and His promises they possess a true, certain, and unfailing hope."[67] Melanchthon is right to pit quotations such as these against the scholastic understanding of condign merit and to claim a better right to Augustine, even though the Bishop of Hippo cannot truly be considered a proponent of *sola fide* in the pure Reformation sense of the term.

The problem for the sixteenth century to untangle, in regard to Augustine's witness on the matter, was this: Augustine taught that eternal life is awarded to works done in God-given faith and love, but he also said that to the extent those works fall short, we are simply forgiven by grace. So does justification finally come by grace through

---

[66] Ibid., 15:34.
[67] Augustine, *On Nature and Grace* 70:60.

faith or by faith working through love? The Lutherans chose the first option, having experienced the results of an ecclesial and scholastic tradition that had developed the second option much further and more rigorously than Augustine ever had, in which satisfaction made by sinners themselves (down to thousands of years in Purgatory)[68] had come to replace the simple mercy of God for Christ's sake as the element in the system that made up the difference between his righteous deeds and the perfect righteousness that God actually required. All things being considered, I judge that Melanchthon was sincere when he concluded, "For we know that those things which we have said are in harmony with the prophetic and apostolic Scriptures, with the holy Fathers, Ambrose, Augustine, and very many others, and

---

[68]Augustine did begin to teach a doctrine of Purgatory in the *Enchiridion on Faith, Hope, and Love* (422), in *City of God* (427), and in some of his sermons, but it was tentative and far less developed than the late-medieval version. In 422 AD, he speculated that "some believers [may] pass through a kind of purgatorial fire, and in proportion as they have loved with more or less devotion the goods that perish, be less or more quickly delivered from it" (*Enchiridion* 69); in 427, he taught, apparently as a settled opinion, that "after the resurrection, there will be some of the dead to whom, after they have endured the pains proper to the spirits of the dead, mercy shall be accorded, and acquittal from the punishment of the eternal fire" and that the prayers of the Church would acquire the needed mercy "for those who, having been regenerated in Christ, did not spend their life so wickedly that they can be judged unworthy of such compassion, nor so well that they can be considered to have no need of it" (*City of God* 21:24). This was probably his most unfortunate contribution to Western soteriology because it opened the way to concluding that the mercy that fills in the gaps in our righteousness comes at a price of another kind. It was still a far cry, though, from the teaching that prevailed at the time of the Reformation, in which every Christian (with the rare exceptions of the saints) had to anticipate a long experience of the punishments of Purgatory before they could receive their reward. In that system, all room for pure gracious forgiveness (at least after baptism, which almost everyone had already received as an infant) had been taken up by the need for satisfaction *beyond* what Christ had made.

with the whole Church of Christ" (*Ap. AC* 5:268), and that—in the case of Augustine, at least—he was contextually justified in so saying.

"Payment for the Works of Charity": Finding Lutheran Soteriology in the Early Church

By Peter Daniel Fawcett

Since the beginning of the Reformation, the charge against Lutheran soteriology has been that it is a novelty and was unknown to the early church. While Lutheran doctrine is derived from the Scriptures and not from the fathers of the church, the church of the Augsburg Confession does treat the fathers as "witnesses, [which are to show] in what manner after the time of the apostles, and at what places, this [pure] doctrine of the prophets and apostles was preserved."[1] In his *The Lord's Supper*, Martin Chemnitz explains that he intends to build his doctrinal case

> on the basis of those Scripture passages in which it is treated and founded in its own proper setting, not through guesswork but on the basis of the clear, certain, proper, and natural meaning of those passages. Afterwards, when faith has been built in this way on this firm rock and solid foundation,

---

[1] *FC Ep.*, Rule and Norm, 2, in *Triglot Concordia = Concordia Triglotta: The Symbolical Books of the Ev. Lutheran Church, German-Latin-English* (St. Louis, MO: Concordia, 1921).

testimonies and opinions from the ancient church can usefully be added. For because we believe that the universal church, in which the Son of God works at all times, has by his Spirit raised up certain learned writers to the kingdom of heaven, who follow the natural meaning of the words, therefore by their confession, which is in agreement with the natural meaning of the divine Word, the weak may be aided and greatly strengthened.[2]

In the same way, while it is not necessary to find Lutheran soteriology in the ancient church, doing so is valuable as a rhetorical tool, and is of comfort to the believer.

The difficulty presented in attempting to find Lutheran soteriology is not one of sacramentology or eschatology; there is no shortage of early theologians who ascribe salvific power to the sacraments, nor is there a shortage of early theologians who have no place for purgatory, propose it as a personal theory but not as the belief of the church, or believe in a version of postmortem purgation that corresponds equally well to both Lutheran and Roman models.[3] The true difficulty lies in attempting to find the doctrine of justification by faith alone and in dealing with the seemingly excessive amount of confidence that is placed in good works. For example, in his

---

[2]Martin Chemnitz, *The Lord's Supper* (St. Louis, MO: Concordia, 1979), 149.
[3]Whether this is because it corresponds to both models well or poorly depends on the theologian.

treatise *Work and Almsgiving*, Cyprian speaks of almsgiving as a way of safeguarding salvation.

> The infirmity of human frailty would have no resource nor accomplish anything, unless again divine goodness came to the rescue and by pointing out the works of justice and mercy opened a way to safeguard salvation, so that by almsgiving we may wash away whatever pollutions we later contract.[4]

He then quotes Proverbs, saying that "by alms and faith sins are cleansed" (Prov. 16:6). Ambrose takes this language even further, saying

> We have more resources by which we may redeem our sins. You have money; redeem your sins. It is not that the Lord can be bought and sold. No, you yourself are venal and have sold yourself to your sins. Therefore, redeem yourself with your deeds and with your money, for sins are redeemed by almsgiving.[5]

---

[4] Cyprian, *Work and Almsgiving*, in *Saint Cyprian: Treatises*, trans. Roy J. Deferrari (Washington, DC: The Catholic University of America Press, 1958), p. 228.

[5] Martin Chemnitz, "On Almsgiving," trans. James A. Kellerman, LCMS.org (St. Louis, MO: Lutheran Church—Missouri Synod, 2005), https://files.lcms.org/wl/?id=LTlbcCfgOs97sTJqdSatUq1klDIk1QwR. This is the fourth chapter of his locus on poverty, which was part of his *Loci Theologici*. It, like all the other ethical chapters, was not included in the

According to Chemnitz, statements like these were used by his Roman opponents "who do not hesitate even today to ascribe to our alms the honor of making satisfaction for our sins and the honor of meriting eternal life."[6] However, if one examines some of the things that Chemnitz and other theologians in the Lutheran tradition said about good works themselves, one will find several ways in which they were willing to speak that may surprise modern Lutherans and could allow us to see more clearly a connection between Patristic and Reformation-era soteriology. This essay will examine the way that Lutheran theologians have described justification and good works and use this as a helpful tool for navigating certain difficult Patristic ways of speaking.

"I Have Faith, Save Me."

Before examining the difficulties, it is worth noting that it is possible to find passages that teach justification by faith alone.[7] St. Basil the Great, in his *Sermon on Humility*, writes, "Now, this is the perfect and consummate glory in God: not to exult in one's own justice, but, recognizing oneself as lacking true justice, to be justified by faith in

---

Concordia Publishing House translation. It was, however, kindly provided online by the Missouri Synod.

[6]Ibid.

[7]However, not all passages that seem to do so actually do. St. Augustine, for example, uses the word *justification* in a way that is more akin to our use of the word *sanctification*.

Christ alone."[8] Likewise, Bernard of Clairvaux, one of Luther's chief influences, writes in his sermon 22 on the Song of Songs,

> As for your justice, so great is the fragrance it diffuses that you are called not only just but even justice itself, the justice that makes men just. Your power to make men just is measured by your generosity in forgiving. Therefore the man who through sorrow for sin hungers and thirsts for justice, let him trust in the One who changes the sinner into a just man, and, judged righteous in terms of faith alone, he will have peace with God.[9]

There are even passages from fathers who would not have been known to the Lutheran reformers at the time of the Reformation. For example, in hymn 26 of *Divine Eros*, St. Symeon the New Theologian, an eastern father from the tenth century, writes,

> For even if in life I have committed every crime,
> still I admit that you are God, creator of all things.
> I worship You Son of God, the same essence of God,
> begotten from Him before all ages,
> and in the last times, from the holy virgin

---

[8] Basil, *Sermon on Humility*, in *Basil: Ascetical Works*, trans. Monica Wagner (Washington, DC: The Catholic University of America Press, 1962), p. 479.
[9] Bernard, *On the Song of Songs II*, trans. Kilian Walsh (Kalamazoo, MI: Cistercian Publications, 1983), 20.

WORKS OF CHARITY

Mary the mother of God, You were begotten like an infant,
and became human, You suffered for my sake,
and You were crucified, and, Savior, You surrendered to burial,
and rose up from the dead after the third day,
and You went up in the flesh, to the place from whence You were never separated.
so thus I believe, thus I prostrate worshipping You,
and I hope You will come again both to judge everyone
and to render to each what is due, Christ,
may my faith be reckoned before my works, my God,
and may You not look for works that fully justify me,
rather let this faith suffice for me in place of all.
this faith shall speak in defense, it will justify me,
it will render me a participant in your eternal glory.
"For one who has had faith in Me," You have said, O my Christ,
"Shall live forever and shall not see death."
and so if faith in You saves those who have despaired,
then behold, I have faith, save me, shine your divine light upon me,
and when you appear, Master, may You enlighten my
soul that is held fast in darkness and the shadow of death!"[10]

---

[10] Simeon, "Hymn 22," in *Divine Eros: Hymns of St. Symeon, the New Theologian*, trans. Daniel K. Griggs (Crestwood, NY: St. Vladimir's Seminary Press, 2010), p. 203.

Nevertheless, there are still not as many statements like these as we would like. In his *On Councils and Churches*, Luther bemoans the fact that often the fathers grasped the premise of his argument that salvation was by faith rather than works but did not explicitly state the conclusion and use the phrase *faith alone*.[11] However, as we will see, making "*sola fide*" as explicit as possible was not always Luther's priority, either.

"But This Is Slightly Too Subtle, and Is Not for Young Pupils."

Upon picking up Luther's *Small Catechism*, one might be surprised to find an absence of the phrase *faith alone*. Justification is never mentioned. If justification is the article by which the church stands or falls, how can it be absent from the one document—other than the Bible—that every Lutheran is supposed to know? Luther's answer to this question can be found in his *Large Catechism*. In the section on the First Commandment, Luther begins by explaining that the First Commandment directs us to seek all our good from God. After explaining the way that this relates to pagan idolatry and to invocation of the saints, he briefly touches upon the fact that some seek to earn God's grace by their good works, arguing that this is also sinning against the First Commandment. However, he thinks that this line of reasoning "is slightly too subtle, and is not for young pupils" (*LC* 1:23). For this reason, Luther presents *sola fide* in the *Small Catechism* not as a syllogism but as an enthymeme. It tells the reader to find forgiveness

---

[11]Martin Luther, *On Councils and Churches*, trans. C. B. Smyth (Oxford, UK: William Edward Painter, 1847), 137–150.

in baptism, absolution, and the Lord's Supper and gives no indication that forgiveness can be earned by good works. In doing so, it gives the reader everything needed to come to the conclusion that good works cannot earn salvation, without saying it outright. According to Cary, "To be justified by faith alone, in Luther's theology, is therefore to focus my attention on the word of Christ alone, and not on anything I do about it."[12] The key to forgiveness is the word of Christ. For this reason, it is possible to teach according to the doctrine of *sola fide* without explicitly mentioning it. All one has to do is to point the believer toward Christ and the sacraments, rather than to themself.

Likewise, in his book *The Cost of Discipleship*, Dietrich Bonhoeffer writes, "At the end of a life spent in the pursuit of knowledge Faust had to confess: 'I now do see that we can nothing know.' That is the answer to a sum, it is the outcome of a long experience. But as Kierkegaard observed, it is quite a different thing when a freshman comes up to the university and uses the same sentiment to justify his indolence."[13] Bonhoeffer saw *sola fide* as "the answer to the sum," not "the data for our calculations."[14] If one believes that *sola fide* must be explicitly invoked in order to teach in a way that agrees with it, then this is an impossible and dangerous idea. If, however, *sola fide* is a conclusion arising from a premise that ought

---

[12]Phillip Cary, *The Meaning of Protestant Theology* (Grand Rapids, MI: Baker Publishing Group, 2019), 155, Kindle.
[13]Dietrich Bonhoeffer, *The Cost of Discipleship* (New York, NY: Simon & Schuster, 2015), 51.
[14]Ibid, 51.

to be taught in basic catechesis—namely that forgiveness of sins is to be sought in faith through the sacramental promise—then this idea makes more sense. A Christian could live their whole life simply trusting in Christ for salvation, doing good works, and receiving the sacraments without explicitly considering the relationship between good works and salvation, just as one can believe that Christ is in the Lord's Supper without understanding the complexities of Christology. When one considers how reluctant the fathers were to delve into other religious controversies, and how unwilling they were to go beyond biblical language,[15] it should not come as a surprise that many of the fathers did not use the phrase *faith alone*.

For this reason, although certain passages that seem to directly grasp *sola fide*—sometimes even saying it directly—from Basil the Great, Bernard of Clairvaux, or Simeon the New Theologian can be comforting to the Lutheran theologian, they are not the only passages that are relevant to the search for Lutheran soteriology. Any passages that point to Christ as the Savior and to the sacraments as the way in which Christ's salvation is delivered to the believer are examples of Lutheran soteriology in the works of the fathers. However, it may still appear that there are a large number of passages that are irretrievably legalistic. While it is sometimes the case that certain passages simply cannot be salvaged, the authors of the Lutheran Confessions provide us with several methods of

---

[15]Consider, for example, the controversy over the word *homoousios*.

harmonizing certain Patristic ways of speaking with Lutheran soteriology.

"And They That Have Done Good Shall Go into Life Everlasting."
In his sermon "I Will Tear Down My Barns," Basil of Caesarea appeals to his hearers to give to the poor. Near the end of his sermon, he warns them, saying, "For you who are persuaded, the promised good things that await are evident; for you who disobey, the threatened punishments have been plainly written down."[16] This is one of many passages from the church fathers that reflect the "two-ways" style of catechesis found in the Didache, which presents the hearer with two moral paths: one that leads to life, and one to death.

> There are two ways, one of life and one of death; but a great difference between the two ways. The way of life, then, is this: First, you shall love God who made you; second, your neighbour as yourself; and all things whatsoever you would should not occur to you, do not also do to another ... And the way of death is this: First of all it is evil and full of curse: murders, adulteries, lusts, fornications, thefts, idolatries, magic arts, witchcrafts ... [17]

---

[16] Basil, "I Will Tear Down My Barns," in *On Social Justice*, trans. C. Paul. Schroeder (Crestwood, NY: St. Vladimir's Seminary Press, 2009), p. 70.
[17] Kevin Knight, ed., "The Didache," New Advent, accessed September 30, 2020, https://www.newadvent.org/fathers/0714.htm.

A Lutheran might be tempted to see a portrayal of life and death as the ends of two different ethical paths as incompatible with justification by faith alone. However, to condemn such a way of speaking would be to condemn the Scriptures. In Deuteronomy 30, Moses sets two paths before Israel, imploring Israel to choose life:

> See, I have set before you today life and good, death and evil. If you obey the commandments of the Lord your God that I command you today, by loving the Lord your God, by walking in his ways, and by keeping his commandments and his statutes and his rules, then you shall live and multiply, and the Lord your God will bless you in the land that you are entering to take possession of it. But if your heart turns away, and you will not hear, but are drawn away to worship other gods and serve them, I declare to you today, that you shall surely perish. You shall not live long in the land that you are going over the Jordan to enter and possess. I call heaven and earth to witness against you today, that I have set before you life and death, blessing and curse. Therefore choose life, that you and your offspring may live, loving the Lord your God, obeying his voice and holding fast to him, for he is your life and length of days, that you may dwell in the land that the Lord swore to your fathers, to Abraham, to Isaac, and to Jacob, to give them. (Deut. 30:15–20 ESV)

WORKS OF CHARITY

This "two-ways" doctrine can be found in the Athanasian Creed, which confesses that "they that have done good shall go into life everlasting; and they that have done evil, into everlasting fire."[18] According to the twentieth article of the Augsburg Confession, only those who are regenerate are capable of doing the truly good works God requires, "For man's powers without the Holy Ghost are full of ungodly affections, and are too weak to do works which are good in God's sight" (*AC* 20). As the Apostle Paul writes, "whatever does not proceed from faith is sin" (Rom. 14:23 ESV). On the other hand, those who are forgiven do not have their sins counted against them. For this reason, those who do good works are those who have faith, and those who do evil are those who do not. As St. Mark the Ascetic explains, "When Scripture says, 'He will reward every man according to his works' (Matt 16:27), do not imagine that works in themselves merit either hell or the kingdom. On the contrary, Christ rewards each man according to whether his works are done with faith or without faith in Himself; and He is not a dealer bound by contract, but our Creator and Redeemer."[19] One will also note that both Basil and the Didache conclude by mentioning redemption. Basil hopes that his hearers will "progress toward the good things that have been prepared for us in heaven, by the grace of the One who calls us all into His Kingdom,"[20]

---

[18] Athanasian Creed, 39.
[19] St. Mark the Ascetic, *Philokalia*.
[20] Basil, "Tear Down My Barns." One might argue that it still sounds as if Basil in his sermon is claiming that whether his hearers are saved depends on whether they give money to the poor in that particular moment. I think that he is rightly binding the consciences of his hearers in a time of

while the Didache concludes its paragraph on the way of death by saying, "Be delivered, children, from all these."[21]

"Alms Are Signs to Which God Has Added Promises."

This explanation does not solve every problem that Lutherans face. There remain the passages quoted above from Cyprian and Ambrose, which attach significant, even salvific, promises to the performance of good works. Although it would seem as if these passages cannot be salvaged, Chemnitz seems to believe something very similar, even as he rebukes Rome for using the passages incorrectly. In his *Loci Theologici*, Chemnitz lists eight spiritual promises attached to almsgiving:

> (a) God is pleased. (b) He will hear and show mercy. (c) He will redeem you from sin and free you from death. (d) You will grow in knowing God. (e) You will abound in every good work. (f) God will keep you from future sins. (g) He will give you an antidote against avarice, namely, sufficiency. (h) He will hallow your enjoyment of property.[22]

---

famine, when failure to act would mean the deaths of many in the community. Someone who failed to act in that moment would be severely damaging their soul and grieving the Holy Spirit. While they might be restored to the faith in the future, such a dire moment is not the time to soothe consciences with the possibility of future repentance.
[21] Knight, ed., "The Didache."
[22] Chemnitz, "On Almsgiving."

According to Chemnitz, the promises attached to almsgiving "were not given so that we might attach to this doctrine some ungodly notion about rewards, but so that we might arouse thoughts of mercy by considering those promises."[23] How can it be that promises of forgiveness and blessing could be attached to good works? According to the *octavo* edition of the Apology, it is because good works are, in the wider sense, sacraments: "just as Christ connects the promise of forgiveness of sins to other sacraments, so he also connects it to good works."[24]

Considering the distance between normal Lutheran theological discussion and the belief that good works can be a sacrament, it would be irresponsible to suggest the possibility of such an attachment without explaining how this could be and responding to several possible objections. I will begin by noting that the belief that

---

[23]Ibid.

[24]*Ap. AC* 4:272A. This quotation is from the *octavo* edition of the Apology of the Augsburg Confession. The *octavo* edition was the second edition of the Apology. Luther had more influence over the *octavo* edition than he did the original *quarto*. The *octavo* edition was considered the "official" version of the Latin apology until 1580. Of all the commonly used English editions of the *Book of Concord*, Kolb-Wengert is the only edition that contains the *octavo* edition. The question of whether this particular quotation ought to be considered part of the Lutheran Confessions or not is an interesting one, but it is not necessarily the most important question. I find this passage beneficial primarily as a method of integrating certain passages from the Apocrypha and certain fathers about almsgiving into a Lutheran framework. The passage can be used in this way regardless of whether it is technically part of the Lutheran Confessions or not. For more information, see Robert Kolb and Timothy J. Wengert, eds., *Book of Concord: The Confessions of the Evangelical Lutheran Church* (Minneapolis, MN: Fortress Press, 2000), 108–109.

God adds promises to good works is, in fact, in the Lutheran Confessions. Putting aside the *octavo* edition of the Apology, one will find in the more commonly used *quarto* edition that Melanchthon writes that "Alms as well as afflictions . . . are signs to which God has added promises."[25] And Melanchthon is not the only author to treat works as sacramental signs in the *Book of Concord*. In the *Large Catechism*, Luther portrays the forgiveness of our debtors in the Lord's Prayer as if it is a sacrament.

> But there is here attached a necessary, yet consolatory addition: As we forgive. He has promised that we shall be sure that everything is forgiven and pardoned, yet in the manner that we also forgive our neighbor. For just as we daily sin much against God, and yet He forgives everything through grace, so we, too, must ever forgive our neighbor who does us injury, violence, and wrong, shows malice toward us, etc. If, therefore, you do not forgive, then do not think that God forgives you; but if you forgive, you have this consolation and assurance, that you are forgiven in heaven, not on account of your forgiving, for God forgives freely and without condition, out of pure grace, because He has so promised, as the Gospel

---

[25]*Ap. AC* 8:17. Keep in mind that Melanchthon is using the Augustinian definition of *sign*, not the Reformed definition of *sign*. That is, this sign is not merely reminding the recipient of some other event, in which this event does not participate, but is in some way bringing the thing signified to the recipient.

teaches, but in order that He may set this up for our confirmation and assurance for a sign alongside of the promise which accords with this prayer, Luke 6:37: Forgive, and ye shall be forgiven. Therefore Christ also repeats it soon after the Lord's Prayer, and says, Matt. 6:14: For if ye forgive men their trespasses, your heavenly Father will also forgive you, etc.

This sign is therefore attached to this petition, that, when we pray, we remember the promise and reflect thus: Dear Father, for this reason I come and pray Thee to forgive me, not that I can make satisfaction, or can merit anything by my works, but because Thou hast promised and attached the seal thereto that I should be as sure as though I had absolution pronounced by Thyself. For as much as Baptism and the Lord's Supper, appointed as external signs, effect, so much also this sign can effect to confirm our consciences and cause them to rejoice. And it is especially given for this purpose, that we might use and practise it every hour, as a thing that we have with us at all times. (*LC*, "Fifth Petition")

Luther is here using language that is similar to the language he uses concerning absolution in the *Small Catechism*: "that we receive absolution, or forgiveness, from the confessor, as from God Himself, and in no wise doubt, but firmly believe, that our sins are thereby forgiven before God in heaven" (SC V). He presents the Lord's Prayer as a portable absolution, available to the Christian at all times.

Good works are not the same kind of sacrament as baptism or the Lord's Supper. They are also not the same kind of sacrament as absolution. They fit into Melanchthon's largest, most generous definition of a sacrament: something commanded by God to which a promise is attached. They differ from the rites normally considered to be sacraments in one crucial way: the promise is not always delivered as the action is done. In baptism, the promises attached to baptism are given at the same time as the baptism is given; but, it is not common for someone to be reading the Scriptures over you as you give alms. Rather, the promise is generally given either before or after the good work. The Christian's faith is strengthened when they remember the promise from God's word by the power of the Holy Spirit and see that it applies to them.

The most Lutheran objection to this concept would be that no one could ever know that they had done enough good works. For example, if almsgiving is a sacrament, how could one know that one has given enough? This is an objection that arises when works are seen as a method for deserving God's love, rather than as signs. Just as we do not worry about the amount of water used to baptize or bread or wine taken as Holy Communion, so we should not worry about the amount of almsgiving given. We also should not worry about someone's faith if they do not seem to be producing a sufficient amount of good works, just as someone who partakes of the Lord's Supper daily should not judge the one who partakes weekly. Just like the regular sacraments, good works do not force God to love you or to forgive your sins. It is Christ's merits that are the cause of God's favor.

In addition, because the good works in question are good works done in faith, remembering a promise of God, they cannot convert. Rather, they are a means of strengthening an already-existing faith or comforting the family of martyrs, as St. Augustine does in *The City of God*, book 8, chapter 7, comparing the promises attached to martyrdom with those attached to baptism:

> For whatever unbaptized persons die confessing Christ, this confession is of the same efficacy for the remission of sins as if they were washed in the sacred font of baptism. For He who said, "Except a man be born of water and of the Spirit, he cannot enter into the kingdom of God," made also an exception in their favor, in that other sentence where He no less absolutely said, "Whosoever shall confess me before men, him will I confess also before my Father which is in heaven;" and in another place, "Whosoever will lose his life for my sake, shall find it." And this explains the verse, "Precious in the sight of the Lord is the death of His saints." For what is more precious than a death by which a man's sins are all forgiven, and his merits increased an hundredfold?"[26]

St. Augustine here lays the forgiveness of sins and the obtaining of merits side by side. Although the modern Lutheran may be tempted

---

[26]Augustine, *St. Augustin's: City of God and the Christian Doctrine*, in Phillip Schaff, ed., *NPNF*, vol. 2, Christian Classics Ethereal Library, accessed September 30, 2020, https://ccel.org/ccel/schaff/npnf102.iv.XIII.7.html.

to see these concepts as opposites, Chemnitz does not, writing in his *Loci Theologici* that "although eternal life is a gift of God for Christ's sake, nonetheless it is at the same time a payment for the works of charity."[27] Although the law still accuses, its accusation has been washed away and it has also become for the Christian a list of works that are pleasing to God and have promises of rewards in this life and the next attached to them.

Conclusion

The works of the fathers of the early church can seem like a labyrinth at times. In part, this is a labyrinth of our own making caused by a failure to consider what the reformers said about good works. When one takes into consideration the fact that Lutherans do believe that "they that have done good shall go into life everlasting; and they that have done evil, into everlasting fire"[28] and that forgiveness and prayer can be treated in a way similar to sacraments as well as alms and other good works, it eventually becomes very difficult to find fathers who cannot be harmonized with the Lutheran Confessions, if one is willing to interpret them charitably, just as we do with pre-Nicene explanations of the Trinity. If some of their statements seem "improper, unfortunate, and ill-considered,"[29] perhaps we can learn to view some of these statements not as Nicenes viewed the Arians but

---

[27] Chemnitz, "On Almsgiving."
[28] Athanasian Creed, 39.
[29] Carl Beckwith, "Martin Chemnitz's Use of the Church Fathers in His Locus of Justification," *Concordia Theological Quarterly* 68, no. 3 (2004): pp. 271–290.

as the Nicenes viewed the pre-Nicenes, not criticizing "the lapses of those by whose labors we have been helped and whose gray hairs we ought to honor."[30]

---

[30]Ibid.

Sola Fide and the Council of Trent: Justification by Faith in the Sixteenth Century and What Can Be Learned for Today's Ecumenical Dialogues

By Laurin Fenn

Introduction

The Council of Trent convened nearly five hundred years ago to address abuses and doctrine in the Catholic Church. The Holy Roman Emperor Charles V was facing unrest in Germany because of the Lutheran Reformation and was hoping, at least initially, that the council would correct abuses and thus stem the tide of the conversion of his German subjects to Lutheran teachings. The council, however, also had to discuss important doctrines, realizing that the doctrinal issues raised by the Lutherans were important to define and that it could not only correct the doctrinal abuses.[1] Of chief importance to the Lutherans, and so to the council, was the doctrine of justification. This doctrine had never been clarified by the Catholic Church; and, even among those loyal to the pope, there was a diversity of views, some edging close to Lutheranism.[2]

---

[1] Diarmid MacColloch, *The Reformation: A History* (New York, NY: Penguin Group, 2003), 222, 227–229.

[2] Joseph Lortz observes in his book *The Reformation in Germany* that "It is not true that Luther's interpretation of the righteousness of God as the grace by which we are justified was a completely new discovery . . . All of the medieval exegetes had put forward this interpretation; and Luther must have read this the moment he began to study that passage in Romans, which so disturbed him. The trouble was that he had not really taken in what he had read." See Joseph Lortz, *The Reformation in Germany*, trans. Ronald Wells, vol. 1 (New York, NY: Darton, Longman & Todd, 1968).

COUNCIL OF TRENT

The outcome of the council determined, in some sense, the boundaries of what became the Roman Catholic view on justification, at least until Vatican II appeared to modify it. In recent times, as the Lutheran and Roman Catholic Churches have sought to find agreement on this point of division, it has become important to examine the various Catholic ideas that existed before the council that tended toward a Lutheran understanding; to ask the question of whether or not the Council of Trent actually held a contrary view to the Lutherans; and to then see, in light of Vatican II, where this now leaves Lutheran and Roman Catholic dialogue regarding justification, particularly in terms of the doctrine of *sola fide*.[3]

Sola Fide and the Catholic *Spirituali*: Contarini, Regensburg, and Pole

Prior to the Council of Trent, there were several important Catholics who desired reunion with the Lutherans and appeared sympathetic to their views. Two key players were Cardinal Contarini and Reginald Pole, both of whom were also leading members of the *Spirituali*.[4] The

---

[3] While there are other important aspects of the Council of Trent to evaluate, such as the differences of doctrine regarding concupiscence and other particularities of justification, it seems that *sola fide* is the most central doctrine and place of disagreement in the discussion of justification. (Herman Sasse, H. P. V. Renner, May 30, 1971).

[4] It may be helpful to point out that some part of Contarini's affinity for the doctrine of *sola fide* may have come from an experience he had in his twenties in which he realized that he could never do enough penance and that his "justification before God was not a matter of doing penance in a hermitage but of believing firmly in the merits of Christ's sacrifice on the cross" (Gleason, 15). The parallels with Luther's breakthrough(s) are not

Spirituali movement and everyone who was a part of it were connected in some way with Contarini or Pole. Elisabeth Gleason helpfully identifies what seems to be the center of this movement:

> Foremost was the focus on ethical and moral reform of the individual Christian who encountered God's word in the Bible, specifically the Gospels and Pauline epistles, and responded with faith and trust in the divine mercy through which man had been given the incalculable benefit of Christ's death on the cross ... [They were] certainly "dogmatically manifold," while emphasizing the practice of Christian virtues and the *imitatio Christi*.[5]

While there was diversity of dogmatic opinion, many of the *Spirituali* did hold to some idea of *sola fide* in regard to justification while at the same time believing that this did not contradict the teachings of Rome or go against the pope.[6] As alluded to in the introduction of this essay, this was not unreasonable, seeing as the doctrine of justification had not been defined by the Catholics and can be found in the works of

---

hard to tease out. Elisabeth G. Gleason, *Gasparo Contarini: Venice, Rome, and Reform* (Berkeley, CA: University of California Press, 1993), 15.
　[5]Ibid., 191–192.
　[6]Ibid., 191. In addition to Contarini and Pole, Gleason lists Sadoleto, Fregoso, Cortese, Badia, Morone, and Bembo. These figures were in Rome around 1535, when Contarini was made a cardinal, and were advocates of reform (192).

various church fathers and medieval churchmen and theologians, without even looking at the works of Luther.[7]

As a newly chosen cardinal, Contarini held a primary position in the *Spirituali* and sought reform and hoped for reunion with the Lutherans. Pope Paul III appointed him to a commission on reform, which was focused primarily on practical reforms to address abuses and was also supposed to pave the way for a general council in 1536.[8] Then, in 1541, with Charles V insistent upon a Lutheran-Catholic colloquy, Pope Paul III appointed Contarini to be the papal envoy to the Imperial Diet of Regensburg.[9] Contarini, experienced in diplomacy and wishing to make peace with the Lutherans, was quite ready to come to an agreement—especially concerning the doctrine of justification—as were the other theologians involved: Melanchthon, Bucer, and Pistorious on the Protestant side and Gropper, Pflug, and Eck on the Catholic side.[10] While Contarini was not a part of the talks,

---

[7]Lortz, *Reformation in Germany*, 207–208.

[8]Gleason, *Gasparo Contarini*, 140. This commission, focused on practical reform in the church, was in the end unsuccessful. Gleason remarks that Contarini never saw reform in Rome while he was alive and that the pope did not act on the commission's recommendations because "[the pope's] court remained entangled in nepotism and dubious political and financial deals" (175). The commission, resultantly, was "important only insofar as they survived in the thought of others who came after them" (176).

[9]Charles V was eager to have a council because he was facing multiple political pressures and wanted to reach some kind of agreement between the Catholics and Lutherans so that they could present a united front. Ibid., 189.

[10]Gleason notes that all except Eck "were men sympathetic to or even adherents of Erasmian humanism." Ibid., 225.

because he was a representative of Pope Paul III, he was consulted throughout the entirety of the colloquy.[11]

The Regensburg Formula Article 5: Double Justification

The Regensburg agreement on justification was founded on a theory put forward in the so-called Regensburg Book several months before the colloquy, during discussions between the German Catholics and German Lutherans.[12] The theory's primary author was Johann Gropper, who, according to MacCulloch, "squar[ed] the circle of the medieval theology of merit and Luther's theology of imputed merit by grace through faith."[13] The theory that he developed was called double justification and was further developed at Regensburg in Article 5 of the agreement.

The theory went like this: First, that justification comes only through Christ must be acknowledged. Then, flowing from this foundational doctrine run two different "streams," or conceptions of justice.[14] The first stream is *iustitia inhaerens*, the conception that justice is in the sinner and that the sinner begins to be justified when they cooperate with the Holy Spirit. The Holy Spirit causes the sinner to repent and believe that Christ forgives sins for all who believe in him. The role of the will here is one of assent, assent that leads to the faith that trusts in Christ's forgiveness of the sinner. It is by this faith

---

[11]Ibid., 225.
[12]MacCulloch, *The Reformation*, 229–230.
[13]Ibid., 230.
[14]*Justice, iusititia* in Latin, can also be translated to "righteousness."

that the Holy Spirit enters the sinner, remits sins, imputes Christ's justice, and gives many more benefits to the believer.[15] One may note that this *iustitia inhaerens* appears to be coming from the level of human perspective. It is also emphasized here that this justice is given by Christ and that the believer actually does not rely upon this inherent justice, but on imputed justice (*iustitia imputata*). This second aspect of double justification is that justice which is Christ's is imputed to those who have faith. This is the justice that makes a person just in the sight of God and is more important than *iustitia inhaerens*, a gift that is not a result of works. Good works, then, flow from this righteousness and are rewarded as fruits of faith.[16]

Contarini, in agreement with some conception of *sola fide*, was quite pleased with this agreed-upon theory, and saw it as a great achievement. When he saw that the agreement on justification was not gaining traction whatsoever among Catholic circles, he wrote an apologia on it in an effort to persuade the Catholics, particularly the pope, to sign on to it. He optimistically hoped it would result in a reunion between Catholics and Protestants.[17] In his apologia, he speaks of inherent justice as put forward in Article 5 as the preliminary justice "through which we begin to be just and become partakers of divine nature" and imputed justice as justice that is "given to us with Christ."[18] He then states that both of these are given

---

[15]Gleason, *Gasparo Contarini*, 227.
[16]Ibid., 228.
[17]Ibid., 229–230.
[18]Ibid., 230.

simultaneously and both are achieved through faith. He also states that what enables *iustitia inhaerens* is the Holy Spirit, who changes the will so that it turns to God in faith—which is how humans can cooperate. Gleason observes,

> He thinks that everything depends on faith, not on the construction of a logically rigorous and intellectually satisfying theory . . . Like Luther, Contarini conceives of the essence of faith as trust and hope in God's mercy. In fact, he uses the Lutheran terms *fiducia* and *assensus* in describing that faith.[19]

Contarini was far more concerned about the experience of the Christian than making a cogent theological system, in line with his *Spirituali* ideas. However, for the majority of the schooled Catholics who read this letter, a theory that was not "logically rigorous" or "intellectually satisfying" was not sufficient, and there was no burning desire for reunification driving them to accept an ambiguous theory. Regarding the latter, Contarini insightfully observed that the lines between the two camps had already been drawn and that neither side could think of or listen to the other side charitably.[20] Contarini died not long after Regensburg, having never seen come to fruition any of the reforms for which he had hoped.

---

[19]Ibid., 231.
[20]Ibid., 234.

It is clear that *iustitia inhaerens* was put forward and explained to satisfy the Catholics and that *iustitia imputata* was put forward to satisfy the Protestants. If a Catholic objected that *iustitia imputata* led to a rejection of man cooperating with divine grace or performing good works, they could be pointed to *iustitia inhaerens*, which speaks of cooperation and good works. If they objected that *iustitia inhaerens* gave too much to a person and not enough to Christ, they could be pointed to *iustitia imputata*, which states that mankind is really justified by Christ's justice, not by human effort. Perhaps the only way one can try to entangle these apparently contradictory statements is if they take the first to be purely from a human perspective; however, this still does not quite solve the problem as there is still the question of how any kind of true justice that enables cooperation with the Holy Spirit can reside in a person prior to their complete justification or how this does not amount to some effort on the person's part. Fenlon raises the question that if inherent justice does not make the person acceptable to God, why would it have any value? Contarini may have argued that it formed the basis for good works and increased grace, yet if it still did nothing to make a person acceptable before God, its value was in the very least diminished.[21] The question of whether or not faith is the only instrument that brings about justification is not clear either, though it clearly plays a significant role.

---

[21] Dermot Fenlon, *Heresy and Obedience in Tridentine Italy: Cardinal Pole and the Counter Reformation* (Cambridge, UK: Cambridge University Press, 1971), 58.

Nonetheless, this agreement did encompass the wide range of views regarding justification and satisfied both the Protestants and Catholics at Regensburg. Therefore, it can be seen as a remarkable accomplishment, particularly during a time of high political and ecclesiastical pressures. The Catholics at this time tended to be suspicious of *sola-fide* language (except for, as mentioned before, many of the *Spirituali* and perhaps a few more independently minded Catholics who mostly held their views privately). Many Protestants, conversely, were concerned that their views would not be listened to or taken seriously and were already beginning to think that reunion was impossible at this point. Yet, looking back at Regensburg and its accomplishment without knowing the outcome of Trent, one could hope that this position would be further clarified and built upon at the general council. At least it was a starting point, even if the positions were not precise and some important questions were left hanging. Such an outcome was not to be, however, for "by endeavoring to maintain the reality of inherent justice while at the same time denying it the power to render man acceptable to God, the Regensburg agreement incurred the rejection both of Luther and the papacy."[22]

Cardinal Pole and *Sola Fide*

Contarini's friend, Reginald Pole, began to take over leadership of the *Spirituali* following Contarini's death. Pole was an Englishman, practically exiled form his country due to his stance against Henry

---

[22] Ibid., 58–59.

VIII's divorce.²³ In fact, he published a book, *De Unitate*, directed to Henry VIII to dissuade him from divorcing Catherine of Aragon and calling him to repent and be saved by faith.²⁴ Interestingly enough for the discussion on *sola fide* leading up to the Council of Trent, Pole in *De Unitate* expresses his belief of justification by faith and emphasizes repentance and faith, though he does not seem to speak in terms of "faith alone."

Pole, however, did not support the compromise at Regensburg, citing in a letter to Contarini the reason that it was not sufficiently supported by Scripture. Fenlon further explains that "He found the only solution of the question in the unity of Scripture and experience . . . [The Roman *adversarias*'] refusal to examine the question in the light of Scripture and experience . . . was the root of the whole issue. If only they would realize it there would be an end to controversy."²⁵ Fenlon believed that Pole quite clearly held to the doctrine of justification by faith alone and was suspicious of the teaching that works done in a state of grace were meritorious.²⁶ Being very much an adherent of papal authority and submission to the church, even if all points of doctrine did not cohere, he did not want to come out with a position prior to the council in case it were ruled against.²⁷ It appears that Pole, a humanist churchman, believed that if

---

²³MacCulloch, *The Reformation*, 208.
²⁴Thomas F. Mayer, *Reginald Pole: Prince and Prophet* (Cambridge, UK: Cambridge University Press, 2000), 29.
²⁵Fenlon, *Heresy and Obedience*, 67.
²⁶Ibid., 97.
²⁷Ibid., 97–98. Fenlon explains, "Pole himself embodied the

Scripture were simply restated and the internal experience of the Christian in relying on Christ for salvation were accepted, then the nitty-gritty details of what happens exactly during justification would not need to be spelled out. Unfortunately for him, with the viewpoints so solidified and many Catholic churchmen and academics discounting the Lutheran view of *sola fide* (despite it also having support both in Scripture and being present in Catholic tradition), this was not a viable solution. Perhaps Regensburg Article 5 was the best that could be achieved, with its use of a combination of "Lutheran" and Catholic categories and terms; regardless, Pole could not sign on to it.[28]

---

enigmatic stance to a supreme degree—convinced of the necessity to yield to the positive essence of what Luther had to say, while being no less convinced of its compatibility with the Church which Lutherans condemned. Prudence and restraint of utterance, coupled with insistence on submission to the Church's authority, remained his guiding principles: these, and the belief that only in a General Council could reunion be effected. For a prominent churchman publicly to support the validity of Luther's fundamental tenet would at least be injudicious, in a climate of great spiritual uncertainty, to say nothing of gathering hostility . . . Paralysis of utterance now began to affect those Catholics who, in principle convinced of the possibility of reunion with the Lutherans, were nevertheless unsure how best to prepare for it outside the deliberations of a General Council" (97–98). It is here clear that Pole was in a difficult position of cognitive dissonance, to use a contemporary psychological term. He had to tread carefully to not ruffle too many anti-Lutheran feathers, disagreeing at points with both sides. What seems most convincing to him and explains some of his behavior is that, when it came down to it, accepting the authority of the church was somewhat more persuasive to him—perhaps as much for emotional and practical reasons as anything else—than a doctrinal truth he privately held.

[28]*Lutheran* is in quotations here to point out that the Lutheran position was not a novel one in the history of the church.

Pole at the Council of Trent

Pole nonetheless was quite optimistic about the impending council. He believed still that there would and could be a reunion with the Lutherans at this junction and that everywhere where Protestantism had not taken complete root would remain Catholic following the council.[29] The pope had decided to send Pole as a legate to the Council, and for a month prior to his departure for Trent, Pole composed a document outlining his hopes and goals for the council. He "declared the purpose of the council to be the clarification of dogma, the reform of Christendom, and the establishment of peace."[30] Pole thought that there could be an agreement on justification that might even be close to Luther's doctrine, writing that the doctrine of salvation by faith alone is a faith that "operates through love."[31] It seems he did not see this "working through love" as a meritorious deed but the fruit of the believer who has been justified by faith alone, though he seems to intentionally leave this controversial question open.[32] His only

---

[29] Fenlon, *Heresy and Obedience*, 102.
[30] Ibid., 103.
[31] Ibid., 109.
[32] Ibid., 112-114. It seems that refraining from specifying how faith alone and good works interact is how Pole believed the council could come to an agreement on *sola fide* while still holding strongly to the value of good works. In concluding this section on Pole's views on *sola fide*, Fenlon observes, "The particular point of departure he had chosen is, however, instructive, for it was designed to promote the doctrine of justification by faith only, while securing the value of good works. His solution had been very simply, to say: 'Faith justifies, and henceforth love directs men to good works'—a formula which left the vital question open. In particular, the crucial question whether works accomplished in the state of grace were meritorious, remained unanswered. It had not indeed been asked. It was not

objection to those Protestants preaching this doctrine was that they did so in a manner contrary to the "institutions of the Church," and he further hoped that holding the authority of the church's traditional teachings in tension with *sola fide* would actually result in a solution that would lead to peace and unity.[33]

Thus, as noted earlier, Pole saw the doctrine of faith alone to be quite important, yet the church institutions and doctrine could not be spoken against in the preaching of this doctrine. One could observe that Pole, unlike the Lutherans, did not see this doctrine as that "upon which the church stands or falls," despite his appreciation and acceptance of *sola fide*. He also did not realize the depth of disagreement with Rome that the Lutherans held because this doctrine of *sola fide* was undermined in much of the church's institutions and teachings themselves—teachings that Pole was fine with holding in tension (and contradiction) with *sola fide*.[34] Simply finding a statement that both sides could agree upon that acknowledged *sola fide* simply could not be enough at this point.

Despite Pole's optimistic hopes, the Council of Trent did not realize them in the least, and Pole's role in the discussions on

---

necessary for Pole's purpose to achieve so much; all that was needful was for the Council to assume a starting point which would unite the two conceptions: faith alone, and complete allegiance to the Church of Rome" (114).

[33] Ibid., 109.

[34] Fenlon, *Heresy and Obedience*, 123–125. Pole, for instance, believed in the doctrine of Purgatory, which the Lutherans would see as in direct conflict with *sola fide*.

justification was negligible. These optimistic hopes were quite quickly dashed as the council began discussions on original sin. The council, using scholastic distinctions and with a desire to articulate the precise dogma, was far too precise for Pole, who was far more comfortable with talk of religious experience and simple language. For Pole, a leading member of the *Spirituali*, such precision "undermine[d] the broad assumptions upon which the *Spirituali* depended in their spiritual life. Thus, as the Council's work advanced, not only did it threaten the pragmatic basis of their credo, but it gradually dispelled their dream of reunion with the Lutherans . . . "[35] Pole, along with Cardinal Girolamo Seripando, who was the leading Augustinian member of the Council, objected to the statement on original sin and concupiscence, but they were unable to make any changes to it.[36] Furthermore, it was distressing that the Protestant theologians had not even been consulted on this decree that was foundational to the discussion on justification.

In mid-July 1546, Charles V declared war on the Protestants of Germany, and at the same time, the council decided to open discussions on the doctrine of justification. This did not bode well in the least. Pole, in line with his irenic goals, made a last speech to the council, asking them to consider carefully the topic of justification and

---

[35] Ibid., 131. Fenlon later explains more about what was essential to them in the council: "the overwhelming demand for a personally assimilated faith, which would enable very Christian to experience within himself the effects of divine mercy, recalling him to a life of inner peace" (143).
[36] Ibid., 130–131. Mayer, *Reginald Pole*, 152.

to look at both sides fairly. He asked them not to dismiss an idea simply because it was called Lutheran, but to maintain an open mind to see if there might be truth in what the other side was saying.[37] A week later, Pole left Trent on leave for the purpose of restoring his health, which had been ailing, having obtained permission from the pope. Fenlon and Mayer both agree that there was likely some psychological component to Pole's request to absent himself from the council.[38] By this time, he could clearly see that the goals of the council were different from his own and that the kind of agreement he was hoping for would not come to fruition. Mayer also suggests that he left so he would not have to sign the document on justification, and his health, while being a real concern, was an easy way for him to avoid this.[39] Pole never returned to the council and was eventually relieved of his duties as legate, though he did send several letters during the fall of that year regarding justification.[40] The other *Spirituali* who were present at the council only played minor roles and did not seem to have much effect on the outcome of the council. It is unfortunate that Pole's irenic and more open-minded approach was not taken, though considering the times Pole was in, it is not at all surprising.

---

[37]Mayer, *Reginald Pole*, 152–153.
[38]Fenlon, *Heresy and Obedience*, 135. Mayer, *Reginald Pole*, 153.
[39]Ibid., 153.
[40]Hubert Jedin, *A History of the Council of Trent Vol II: The First Sessions at Trent 1545–47*, trans. Dom Ernest Graf (St. Louis, MO: B. Herder Book Company, 1957), 279. Mayer, *Reginald Pole*, 155.

Discussions at the Council: The Role of Faith

One council member who played an influential role at the Council of Trent, was a proponent of double justification, and could be seen to have some sympathies with Lutheran views was the Augustinian friar Cardinal Giralamo Seripando.[41] His approach was different from that of the *Spirituali*, who emphasized experience much more, and, unlike Pole, he was a proponent of the double justice theory. Seripando, also unlike Pole, was not part of the secular clergy and was more trained in distinctions and categories.[42] Jedin, in discussing Seripando's hopes for the council, remarked that Seripando wanted to get rid of scholastic terminology and speak in more common terms so that it could be accessible to the layperson. He wanted to emphasize experience, not the personal experience of the believer as Pole did, but rather the experiences noted in Scripture and tradition.[43] Jedin further explains Seripando's view on grace and faith:

> [F]our factors are simultaneously at work in the conversion of an adult unbeliever, (1) the grace of God freely accepted by

---

[41]One of the other members of the council, who held views probably most similar to Luther's, was Tommaso Sanfelice, but he got into a dispute with a Franciscan bishop, Zanettini, because he spoke of "slave will" and *sola fide*. Zanettini called him "either a knave or a fool" to his face. Sanfelice, temper flaring, grabbed the bishop by the beard and proceeded to shake him. Because of Sanfelice's behavior, though provoked, he had to remove himself from the council. See John W. O'Malley, *Trent: What Happened at the Council* (Cambridge, UK: Belknap Press of Harvard University Press, 2013), 109.

[42]O'Malley, *Trent*, 109.

[43]Jedin, *Council of Trent*, 188.

man without any previous preparation due to his unaided natural power; (2) repentance, in co-operation with grace; (3) God's justice; (4) the appropriation through faith of that justice ... Out of pure goodness God bestows on the sinner a grace by which he calls the offender back to himself ... The sinner is only able to respond to this call if it is accompanied by a second grace, one that heals the will and sets it free ... This grace enables him to accept the grace of the call ... God's justice intervenes, that is, God's saving will is implied in the person and in the redeeming work of Christ. Man believes and trusts in Christ and so becomes united to him and secures God's pardon of his sins ... Thus reconciled to God he receives the Holy Spirit with all his gifts, especially that of charity which enables him to fulfil the commandments . . . the remission of sin is wrought on the basis of faith and trust. Charity is God's gift to the reconciled.[44]

Seripando's view sounds Lutheran at some points, especially when he talks of the remission of sin being brought about on the basis of "faith and trust," yet he would reject that his view necessitates or implies *sola fide*. He states that forgiveness of sin and sanctification "are only logically separate, not chronologically, and as a psychological process they are simultaneous."[45] Furthermore, he would speak of

---

[44]Ibid., 188.
[45]Ibid., 188.

justification continuing in the Christian life through a struggle against concupiscence and increase in the three theological virtues. A person is only fully justified when they are reckoned so on the last day, and this justification is dependent upon God's grace and reward for good deeds done in sanctification—which is seen as a part of justification. These deeds are joined to Christ's justice because the Christian is united to Christ by faith, yet sanctification is still seen as a cooperation of a person with Christ, and a person can still be said to have merit on the last day.[46] So, while Seripando rejects *sola fide*, he does come close to it, more so than the other leading Catholics at the council.

The Thomists and the Scotists were the two other major groups aside from the Augustinians, and they had a larger showing. Fenlon points out that the Thomists were Dominicans with a theocentric theology and emphasis on logical coherency.[47] In regard to justification, they believed that faith was "an assent to revealed truth." They saw it as an "infused virtue . . . as an effect of faith,"[48] or that faith does not justify by itself but is *fides formata caritate et gratia* ("faith formed by love and grace"). To them, this meant that good works, baptism, and penance justify. Faith, therefore, clings both to the gospel and to the observation of the commandments.[49]

The final and most numerous group was the Scotists—Franciscans who wanted to emphasize the ethical and psychological

---

[46]Ibid., 188–189.
[47]Fenlon, *Heresy and Obedience*, 138.
[48]Jedin, *Council of Trent*, 177.
[49]Ibid., 177.

implications of the question of justification.[50] Their approach was to put faith in the first phase of justification, that is, the preparatory phase. With all their different starting points and views, these were the three groups that had to come to an agreement should the council reach a successful closure on justification. It should be noted that none of these groups actually held to a Lutheran view of justification, however, nor would they speak of justification in terms of *sola fide*. The categories they were working were different, and *sola fide* was far too "Lutheran" of a term for it to be accepted. It was regarded as an insult to be called Lutheran, and everyone wanted to avoid the label.

The council sought to answer six questions: (1) What is meant by justification? (2) What are its causes? (3) What is meant by being saved by faith? (4) Do works and sacraments play a role in justification, and (5) what are those roles? (6) Can the process be described?[51] On July 23, 1546, the discussion ended, and the first draft of the decree was drawn up.[52] This first draft was received with less than adequate acceptance. Cardinal Cervini, one of the three papal legates, had Seripando replace it with a second draft that the Augustinian friar mostly composed.[53]

This second draft was presented in September. In it, Seripando's most important changes regarding *sola fide* are to limit explanation on freedom of the will and to say that justification "must

---

[50]Fenlon, *Heresy and Obedience*, 138.
[51]Jedin, *Council of Trent*, 176. O'Malley, *Trent*, 108.
[52]O'Malley, *Trent*, 109.
[53]Ibid., 111.

be preceded by an active preparation, proceeding from the concurrence of grace and the human will." Like the July draft, it states that justification is not from "a declaration of man's justness, but in his being made just by faith and sacraments" and that this justifying faith is one that comes also with hope and charity. He also says that eternal life is not only a reward of merit, as the July draft says, but is also a "favour promised."[54] However, *sola fide* is condemned in one of the canons. Jedin remarks that in this draft, Seripando avoids scholastic phrasing, though he does mention twofold justice, which was important to him personally.[55]

This draft was then taken by Cervini, discussed by various theologians, and elaborated upon.[56] The alterations done to it focus on delineating the Catholic from the Protestant viewpoint. This resulted in three changes: (1) The human role in preparing for justification is seen more positively (while excluding merit prior to prevenient grace). (2) Faith—defined as trusting something to be true—is only part of the preparatory stage, rather than having a role in justification itself and being given by God to the sinner with faith and hope. (3) Justifying grace is "inherent in man."[57]

---

[54] Jedin, *Council of Trent*, 241.
[55] Ibid., 241.
[56] Ibid., 241–242.
[57] Ibid., 243. Contrast this definition of faith with Luther's: "Faith is a living, daring confidence in God's grace, so sure and certain that the believer would stake his life on it a thousand times. Martin Luther, *LW: The American Edition*, ed. E. Theodore Bachmann, vol. 35 (Minneapolis, MN: Fortress Press, 1960) 370–71.

These changes further drifted away from Protestant teaching on *sola fide*, as they place much more emphasis on a person's role in justification and adopt different definitions and categories than what the Protestants used. For instance, Luther spoke of faith as

> a divine work in us which changes us and makes us to be born anew of God, John 1[:12–13]. It kills the old Adam and makes us altogether different men, in heart and spirit and mind and powers; and it brings with it the Holy Spirit. O it is a living, busy, active, mighty thing, this faith. It is impossible for it not to be doing good works incessantly ... Faith is a living, daring confidence in God's grace, so sure and certain that the believer would stake his life on it a thousand times. This knowledge of and confidence in God's grace makes men glad and bold and happy in dealing with God and with all creatures. And this is the work which the Holy Spirit performs in faith. Because of it, without compulsion, a person is ready and glad to do good to everyone, to serve everyone, to suffer everything, out of love and praise to God who has shown him this grace.[58]

Here, it is clear that Luther does have a completely different way of talking of and conceiving of faith. He does not talk of it in terms of

---

[58]*LW*, 370–371. Luther's definition of faith is cited in *FC SD* 4:11, in *BC*.

scholastic distinctions, nor is it merely knowledge or assent, but "a living, daring confidence in God's grace."

The concessions that had been made to the Scotists and Thomists brought this draft closer to the original July draft. Also, by rejecting twofold justice, particularly the aspect of Christ's imputation of his justice to the sinner—the Lutheran part of Article 5 of the agreement at Regensburg—further distanced the council from the Lutheran position. Seripando tried to persuade the council to reconsider this objection to twofold justice, even saying that it should not be thought of as something that came from Luther, Bucer, and Calvin but as something that came from Augustine and Bernard of Clairvaux. At the same time, all the theologians present agreed that they were at the same starting point—justification took place as a "supernatural elevation, through sanctifying grace and the meritoriousness of good works performed in a state of grace."[59] This question of twofold justice was basically a question of personal piety, not essential piety.[60]

Nonetheless, the council decided to discuss it. After much discussion, it was determined that sanctifying grace is sufficient to make one's deeds meritorious before God and that inherent justice does not need any further supplement of God's grace to render those deeds meritorious. In other words, a person contributes in some way

---

[59]Jedin, *Council of Trent*, 248.
[60]Jedin notes the difference between the Catholic's position of seeing twofold justice and faith as secondary issues and Luther's position that justifying faith is the same as the faith in one's justification. Ibid., 250.

in their cooperation in sanctification to their final justification. The central idea of justification hinging on imputed justice was rejected, and along with it any hint of *sola fide*.[61] It is also here that one can see that one major difference lay in the Catholic understanding that justification includes sanctification, whereas Lutherans distinguish between the two.

Sola Fide and the Canons and Decrees of the Council of Trent

The actual canons and decrees that resulted when all was said and done did not explicitly condemn Luther, but they did condemn several of his central teachings, including *sola fide*. In chapter 5, they speak of the sinner cooperating with God's grace in conversion, which helps the sinner "convert themselves."[62] Justification is defined as both "remission of sins" and "sanctification and renewal . . . through the voluntary reception of the grace and gifts."[63] Faith must be united with hope and charity for the person to be united fully with Christ.[64] They did agree in chapter 8 that a person can be said to be justified by faith since faith is the beginning of salvation. Nothing that precedes justification merits God's grace.[65] At the same time, one must observe the commandments to be justified in the end, and this is part of

---

[61] Ibid., 250.
[62] *The Canons and Decrees of the Council of Trent* 6:5, trans. H. J. Schroeder (St. Louis, MO: B. Herder Book Company, 1941).
[63] Ibid., 6:7.
[64] Ibid., 6:7.
[65] Ibid., 6:8.

justification since sanctification is part of justification.[66] The Christian cannot rely that they are saved and, upon losing the grace of justification through sin, must go through contrition, confession, absolution, and works of satisfaction.[67] The last chapter speaks of the fruits of justification and the nature of that merit.

> For since Christ Jesus Himself, as the head into the members and the vine into the branches, continually infuses strength into the justified . . . we must believe nothing further is wanting to those justified to prevent them from being considered to have, by those very works . . . fully satisfied the divine law . . . and to have truly merited eternal life . . . Thus, neither is our own justice established as our own from ourselves, nor is the justice of God ignored or repudiated, for that justice which is called ours, because we are justified by its inherence in us, that same is [the justice] of God, because it is infused into us by God through the merit of Christ.[68]

Because this is all because of God's grace, the Christian cannot "trust or glory in himself" but must trust and glory in the Lord who gives all good things.[69] The council here speaks of infused grace and the merits of Christ and does not even mention faith at all in talking about the

---

[66] Ibid., 6:11.
[67] Ibid., 6:14.
[68] Ibid., 6:16.
[69] Ibid., 6:16.

infusion of this grace. If one compares this with the quote from Luther above, the contrast can be clearly seen, but this will be further discussed later.

> In the canons, *sola fide* is explicitly rejected:
> If anyone says that the sinner is justified by faith alone, meaning that nothing else is required to cooperate in order to obtain the grace of justification, and that it is not in any way necessary that he be prepared and disposed by the action of his own will, let him be anathema.[70]

Canon 11 also explicitly speaks against the Lutheran doctrine that is foundational to understanding *sola fide*:

> If anyone says that men are justified either by the sole imputation of the justice of Christ or by the sole remission of sins, to the exclusion of the grace and the charity which is poured forth in their hearts by the Holy Ghost, and remains in them, or also that the grace by which we are justified is only the good will of God, let him be anathema.[71]

---

[70] Ibid., 6:9.
[71] Ibid., 6:11.

Then, canon 12 rejects the doctrine that justifying faith is "confidence in divine mercy, which remits sin for Christ's sake" and that "this confidence alone" justifies sinners.[72] Canon 24 rejects the idea that works contribute anything to salvation but only are fruits of justification.[73]

The Catholic doctrine at Trent, therefore, entirely rejects what Lutherans were teaching. The Catholic doctrine starts and ends with divine grace, yet it rejects faith as the sole instrument of conveying that grace to the sinner and even speaks at length about justification without even mentioning faith. Works must be accompanied by faith since sanctification is an essential part of justification. This is so much so that a person cannot be certain of their salvation (apart from some kind of religious experience) as it depends on their inherent justice, which cannot be fully relied upon. The person does rely on God's grace for justification, yet there is no certainty attached to it. By observing God's commands, the Christian can trust that God will reward those works with eternal life.

The Lutheran Confessions and the Council of Trent

Several decades after the Council of Trent, the Lutherans wrote the following in the Formula of Concord, which shows the contrast between what was said at Trent and what became the clarified Lutheran position in contradistinction to the Roman Catholic view:

---

[72] Ibid., 6:12.
[73] Ibid., 6:24.

It is correct to say that in this life believers who have become righteous through faith in Christ have first of all the righteousness of faith that is reckoned to them and then thereafter the righteousness of new obedience or good works that are begun in them. But these two kinds of righteousness dare not be mixed with each other or simultaneously introduced into the article on justification by faith before God. For because this righteousness that is begun in us—this renewal—is imperfect and impure in this life because of our flesh, a person cannot use it in any way to stand before God's judgment throne. Instead, only the righteousness of the obedience, suffering, and death of Christ, which is reckoned to faith, can stand before God's tribunal. Even following their renewal, when they already are producing many good works and living the best kind of life, human beings please God, are acceptable to him, and receive adoption as children and heirs of eternal life only because of Christ's obedience.[74]

While it may be tempting to try to work out a way in which the Catholics and Lutherans, based on Trent and the *Book of Concord*, can agree, it seems Trent's statements and the intended meanings of those statements compared with the Formula's statement show that they could hardly be further apart on the issue of justification by faith alone. The Catholics at Trent, while rightly emphasizing grace, failed

---

[74]*FC SD* 3:32, in *BC*.

to grasp how exactly that grace was conveyed—by faith alone—as they worried about the role of works in salvation. By conflating justification and sanctification, they rejected the imputation of Christ's justice through faith as the sole basis for justification.

The Lutherans insisted upon this point while insisting upon the importance of good works as the fruits of justification. Yet these two kinds of justice (or righteousness) must be kept distinct, for the justice from Christ is the only basis upon which justification rests and the "incipient" justice, which comes from sanctification, is solely the fruit of justification and does not contribute to one's standing before God.[75] The Catholics insisted that good works played some role in the Christian's justification, so that on the last day, the Christian's works would be counted as contributing to their justification—yes, through grace—but the person's works still contributed. The Council of Trent, by determining its path at least in part by contrasting itself with the Lutherans, created an unbridgeable divide, at least for as long as the council is regarded as the final word on the subject.

Sola Fide: The Council of Trent and Ecumenical Dialogues Today

The question relevant today for Lutherans and Catholics who are trying to embark into ecumenical dialogue is how to proceed, given the Tridentine and Lutheran teachings on the doctrine of justification.

---

[75] One could compare the double justification language of the Regensburg formula on justification and see several similarities. However, here, the Lutherans make a clear distinction between justification and the justice associated with that—Christ's—and the incipient justice of sanctification being worked in us by the Holy Spirit.

With nearly five hundred years behind them, however, both Roman Catholics and Lutherans must assess the current climate.

Sasse, in a letter he wrote in 1971, mentions several of the negative changes that have occurred in the Roman Catholic Church that have obscured the doctrine of justification. As a result of Vatican II, the Catholics changed their liturgy to become more relevant; thus, they have moved further away from basing their hope on God's Word and more toward basing it on the institution of the Roman Catholic Church, which they called a "sacrament."[76] Furthermore, their doctrine of original sin has become even less scriptural when, in *Lumen Gentium*, they speak even of atheists being able to be saved through grace, thereby implicitly denying the role of faith. Sasse concludes that it seems that the Roman Catholic Church today is a different church than the church of the Council of Trent.[77] He proposes that the current church is actually describing a different doctrine of justification than the church of 500 years ago was. This difference is seen by tending toward a universalism based on the wideness of God's grace. Consequently, the church seems to reject faith in the process.[78]

Sasse hints at why Vatican II came so close to a universalism: Trent may have contained the seed of the errors that were worked out to another level at Vatican II.[79] When *sola fide* and the imputation of Christ's righteousness are rejected while *sola gratia* is adhered to, *sola*

---

[76]Sasse, 10–11.
[77]Ibid., 13.
[78]Ibid., 13–14.
[79]Ibid., 14.

gratia seems to lose its force and meaning, at least as this has been worked out alongside the forces of rationalism, liberalism, and the like. Rather than actually promoting truly good works done as a result of faith, this view does the opposite, because now one does not need to have faith in God to be saved nor to trust his grace, but can be saved regardless. One might ask, without knowing who God is or loving and trusting in him, how can one even know what "good works" are. It is ironic that the Roman Catholic theologians, so careful to preserve the importance of good works, in effect, may have unwittingly done the opposite when they formulated their decrees and canons at Trent.

Perhaps one could conclude, based on these observations, that the Roman Catholic Church has gone even further afield of the doctrine of *sola fide*, even, if possible, further than the Council of Trent. On the other hand, having gotten further away from the statements of Trent, perhaps it does provide a window of opportunity for discussing once again the subject and for seeing if the Roman Catholics may want to redefine their position.[80] Joseph Ratzinger, former Pope Benedict XVI, wrote a 2002 article titled "The Augsburg Concord on

---

[80]Lutheran World Federation and Catholic Church, *Joint Declaration on the Doctrine of Justification*, (n.p., 1999), https://www.lutheranworld.org/sites/default/files/2020/documents/original_jddj_english.pdf, 27. In the Joint Declaration, the Roman Catholic doctrine on faith in justification appears to be quite similar to that of Trent and its overall importance in the teaching of Roman Catholicism as it relates to some of the teachings that come from Vatican II is beyond the scope of this paper.

Justification: How Far Does It Take Us?" that speaks of the importance of justification and how it seems to be abandoned. He states,

> ... Christian theology is not doing its duty if it clings with ever subtler distinctions to the controversial concepts of the sixteenth century. Christian theology must remain conscious of its essential, biblical basis and of its ecclesiastical legacy, and must continue to hold fast to the redemptive potential of this legacy. It must, however, make this potential accessible to people living in the context of the modern problems of redemption [of unconcern for sin or life after death]. If we can do this, we shall soon see the quarrels of the sixteenth century need no longer be a cause of division in this matter.[81]

It seems here that Ratzinger is proposing moving beyond the language of the Council of Trent and the controversies. Following this proposal, he says he does not think it necessary to find if or where the Council of Trent can be reconciled in some way, as such a discussion becomes bogged down in detail and gets away from the simpler and clearer statements of Scripture.[82] He does agree that the doctrine of justification is important but believes it to not be as important as the overall confession of the church, which he defines as confession in the

---

[81] Joseph Ratzinger, "The Augsburg Concord on Justification: How Far Does It Take Us?," *International Journal for the Study of the Christian Church* 2, no. 1 (2008): p. 12, doi:10.1080/14742250208574000.

[82] Ibid., 13–14.

Triune God, though he does agree that justification is embedded in that confession.[83] His proposal for moving forward is that the doctrine of *Sola Scriptura* should be discussed because no communion can be achieved without determining where authority comes from.[84] He appears to be optimistic that agreement can be reached between Lutherans and Roman Catholics on the issue of justification and others.

Problems and Perspectives on the Lutheran Side

While the Roman Catholics face their own problems stemming in part from Vatican II, Sasse also talks of how the Lutherans have moved away from the centrality of the doctrine of *sola fide* by calling it a theory while forgetting it is the gospel. Sasse may have seen this in part in his day, but it seems that this has become the case even more so among so-called confessional Lutherans in North America. This can be seen in the tendency to change or abandon the liturgy, to seek

---

[83]This also comes out earlier in his article when he speaks of Luther's teaching on *sola fide* more in terms of his own subjective religious experience wrought by his search for inner peace, rather than *sola fide* actually being at the center of the gospel. By indicating that Luther's breakthrough was purely the result of a psychological (though real) need to find peace, he is able to conclude that this doctrine was fine for Luther but does not need to be accepted by all or be seen as the center of the gospel. This can be seen when he concludes his talk of Luther and *sola fide*: " . . . it remains only the experience of a particular individual and, since it is thus bound to quite distinct historical and personal circumstances, cannot simply claim to have universal reality" (Ibid., 9). On this type of argument, see C. S. Lewis, "Bulverism," in *God in the Dock* (Grand Rapids, MI: Wm. B. Eerdmans, 1979), pp. 271–277.

[84]Ratzinger, "Augsburg Concord," 20.

church growth methods, and to diminish preaching on sin and faith and the role of the sacraments.[85] Furthermore, in much of conservative Lutheranism, there seems to be a tendency toward law-gospel reductionism, where Lutherans neglect or diminish the role of works in the life of the believer. They emphasize the doctrine of *sola fide* so much that they lose track of the effects of *sola fide*—that faith produces good works. Here, they do exactly what the Roman Catholics have feared they would do. Yet, this is clearly not how Luther and our confessions speak. In speaking against the antinomians, Luther said,

> For there is no such Christ that died for sinners who do not, after the forgiveness of sins, desist from sins and lead a new life. Thus they preach Christ nicely with Nestorian and Eutychian logic that Christ is and yet is not Christ. They may be fine Easter preachers, but they are very poor Pentecost preachers, for they do not preach *de sanctificatione et vivificatione Spiritus Sancti*, "about the sanctification by the Holy Spirit," but solely about the redemption of Jesus Christ, although Christ (whom they extoll so highly, and rightly so) is Christ, that is, he has purchased redemption from sin and death so that the Holy Spirit might transform us out of the old Adam into new men—we die unto sin and live unto righteousness, beginning and growing here on earth and perfecting it beyond, as St. Paul teaches. Christ did not earn only *gratia*, "grace," for us, but also *donum*, "the gift of the

---

[85]Sasse, 11–12.

Holy Spirit," so that we might have not only forgiveness of, but also cessation of, sin. Now he who does not abstain from sin, but persists in his evil life, must have a different Christ, that of the Antinomians; the real Christ is not there, even if all the angels would cry, "*Christi, Christi*" He must be damned with this, his new Christ.[86]

If Lutherans wish to dialogue with the Roman Catholics on the topic of faith, justification, grace, and good works, going back to what Luther and the Confessions speak of regarding both justification and sanctification is of primary importance. Confessional Lutherans must be clear about the life of sanctification and how "the gift of the Holy Spirit" and faith produce good works while being clear that it is faith alone that justifies. Christ earned for us both grace (favor with God) and the gift of the Holy Spirit. This necessitates a new life in which the Christian seeks to abstain from sin, lived in faith.

While the Lutheran Church faces these problems of approaching the essence of the ecumenical dialogues with the Roman Catholics, those Lutherans who still hold to a *quia* subscription to the *Book of Concord* have not abandoned the doctrine of *sola fide*. This means that, though in certain areas some Lutherans may be distracted from justification by faith alone, their teaching on the subject has not changed and still remains the essence of the gospel—the doctrine

---

[86]Martin Luther, "On the Councils and the Church," in *LW: Church and Ministry III*, ed. Eric W. Gritsch, trans. Charles M. Jacobs, vol. 41 (Philadelphia, PA: Fortress Press, 1966), p. 115.

upon which the church stands or falls. As Sasse notes, shortly after the Vatican II Council, *sola gratia* has never been an issue with the Catholics, but the *sola fide* aspect of justification has.[87] He says that if Trent is upheld, there cannot be agreement on justification, for the doctrine of justification by faith alone is the doctrine upon which the church stands or falls because it is the gospel itself.[88] He remarks that *sola gratia* is not the sum of the gospel, but rather that it is bound together with "because of Christ through faith."[89] The justice that we receive and that justifies us is never our own, but is always Christ's, given for us through the instrument of faith that receives. It is only here that one acknowledges the depth of human depravity and the full grace of God in salvation that does not depend on human effort.[90] Sasse also observes that this topic of justification (and the closely related one of predestination) is "one of the deepest problems of mankind ... the question of the relationship between God and man."[91] It is therefore of great importance and controversy. As we have seen, this contrasts with how the Roman Catholics viewed justification as not essential—though important—in the sixteenth century, and now again with Ratzinger. It also differs with the idea seen especially since Vatican II that doctrine can develop with time, which also may be related with Ratzinger more or less admitting that we can now move

---

[87] Sasse, 8.
[88] Ibid., 8–9.
[89] Ibid., 9.
[90] Ibid., 9.
[91] Ibid., 9.

beyond Trent, as times have changed. While the Roman Catholics may have moved on from Trent, the Lutherans have not moved beyond their confessions, which clearly teach *sola fide*.

Sixteenth-Century Tie-Ins with the Ecumenical Dialogues Today

It is interesting seeing the similarities between Ratzinger today and Pole and Contarini in the sixteenth century. Pole and Contarini both desired reunion and were willing to engage with Lutherans on the subject of justification, being optimistic that such a reunion could be reached. Both held tightly to the papacy and the authority of the church. While they did hold to some doctrine of *sola fide*, they saw it more in terms of experiential Christianity and not a central doctrine that they must hold to in spite of all else. Ratzinger wishes to dialogue with the Lutherans and believes that reunification can happen. He also appears to emphasize the spiritual experience of the person, even speaking of Luther in these terms, throughout his article, speaking of what does or does not present crises to the culture today (though one would have to agree that he does so in a rather different fashion than those of the sixteenth century).

Seripando, Pole, and Contarini all wanted to use scriptural language and to avoid scholastic terminology, which is not all that different from Luther's approach.[92] Ratzinger also seems to have a similar approach in that he too wants to emphasize scriptural language and to avoid the tight distinctions as he sees them in the

---

[92]Luther and the Confessions went further by elevating Scripture over tradition.

Council of Trent (or even as a result of trying to bring the views of Trent and Lutherans together). Hermann Sasse in his letter also observes the importance of going back to Scripture when he says, "A Reformation must come out of the depth of the Word of God by which the Church lives. This applies to every Christian Church."[93] Thus, Ratzinger seems to be right when he says that, if ecumenical dialogue is to move forward, the authority in the church must be discussed once more. Does Scripture come first? Or is it on the same level as tradition and the words spoken *ex cathedra*? If the dialogue is to begin afresh from Scripture, both Lutherans and Catholics must be on the same page as to what authority Scripture holds and how the authority of tradition and the church plays into that.

While one must start off with scriptural language, as with the ecumenical creeds of Nicaea and Chalcedon, more precise language needed to be articulated in order to avoid heresy. Both the Lutherans and the Catholics of the sixteenth century did articulate clearly where they disagreed, at least in regard to *sola fide*. However, what happened at Regensburg may be instructive as well. Although Regensburg failed miserably, it did perhaps offer a starting point that may have led to something more, had it not been ignored. While it may be easy to dismiss it as being entirely too confusing or contradictory, it did show an effort to come to some kind of language that acknowledged points of agreement between them. This could have been used as the basis for further discussions, had the political climate been different.

---

[93]Ibid., 11.

COUNCIL OF TRENT

Furthermore, it also should have been clearly articulated where the points of disagreement still lie, rather than an agreement that had not quite been attained be proclaimed. It is instructive that despite an eagerness for reunion, Lutherans cannot back down on justification by faith alone—nor can victory be proclaimed apart from discussing and agreeing on the real issues that continue to divide—making proper distinctions where necessary.

Finally, if what Ratzinger proposes is what the Roman Catholic Church wants to put forward—that is, that the distinctions and controversies of Trent do not matter so much anymore, scriptural language ought to be used instead of old distinctions, and the problems of our time should be addressed—perhaps that does, in fact, lead to an opening for confessional Lutherans who must hold unswervingly to the gospel of justification by faith alone.[94] What if the Lutherans took the Roman Catholics to prior to the Council of Trent, when there was a stream of Catholic theology that acknowledged *sola fide* that stemmed from Christ and St. Paul and moved on through the early church and medieval periods? What if they did adopt the language of Scripture and the church in speaking not just about grace alone but faith alone and then went on to articulate the position as Lutherans have? What if Lutherans were able to show that the existential crisis of every individual that Ratzinger speaks of does come down to the crisis of one confronting the depth of sin before a

---

[94] The Lutheran World Federation cannot be counted as "confessional" Lutheran in the sense that these Lutherans do not hold to a *quia* subscription to the *Book of Concord*.

perfectly good God; and then that the only way for peace and consolation is through justification through faith alone because of Christ imputing his righteousness out of pure grace? In short, what if the Roman Catholics, by talking through Scripture came back to the doctrine of *sola fide* as the essence of the gospel?

This seems like it is impossible, notwithstanding Ratzinger's words of hope regarding reunion. As mentioned before, Roman Catholics continue to avoid using language of *sola fide*—even Ratzinger and the Joint Declaration still avoid using the phrase—and, especially with the current pope, a much more universalist understanding of God's grace and salvation apart from faith is promulgated. Those Lutheran-leaning theologians prior to the Council of Trent still seem to be closer to Luther in regard to *sola fide* than the Roman Catholics of our day. Historical, ecclesiastical, philosophical, and theological circumstances prevented them from having any great impact at the Council of Trent, and as a result, *sola fide* was rejected in favor of a different understanding of God's grace and faith's role in justification.

While Trent held sway, it continued to confuse justification and sanctification, and perhaps even contributed to the universalist-leaning approach found in Vatican II. On the other hand, the distancing of Roman Catholics from the Council of Trent, as Ratzinger all but acknowledges, may help to further dialogue now in a way that it could not with the unique historical and political pressures of the sixteenth century. The Lutheran Church cannot abandon its teaching on *sola fide*, but rather it can, by using Scripture and church tradition of *sola fide* prior to Trent, patiently speak with the Roman Catholic Church and seek reunion. It is only by going back to Scripture and the essence of the faith that the sin and suffering of our day can be addressed by what alone has the power to breathe life and hope: the gospel of justification by faith alone.

Defending God's Honor: The Righteousness of God in Light of Honor and Shame

By Matthew Fenn

I. Introduction

Few debates in biblical studies can touch a nerve among Lutherans like the New Perspective on Paul can. That is because the so-called New Perspective has cast itself as in direct opposition to the older "Lutheran" view. It is little wonder then that Lutherans and those of other protestant traditions have felt the need to mount a defense of the "old" perspective. However, very few have sought to enter into no-man's-land and try to find a *via media*—a Northwest Passage through the debate, which would take serious note of the New Perspective's exegetical and historical concerns yet remain faithful to the Lutheran theological tradition. Indeed, some might scoff at the attempt, likening it to mixing oil and water. Yet, that is, in part, what this essay hopes to achieve. It is indeed impossible in such a short space to seek to find rapprochement on every matter in dispute. Hence, only one particular area of dispute will be discussed, namely, St. Paul's enigmatic phrase "the righteousness of God" in the Epistle to the Romans. To accomplish this, an often-neglected area of study will be employed—what has been termed social-scientific criticism. By examining the theme of the righteousness of God in the first three chapters of Romans, especially in light of the cultural values of honor and shame, it will be demonstrated that traditional Lutheran theology and a sensitivity to the New Perspective need not be at odds.[1] To do that, a position on the occasion of the letter must be taken. Following that, it is necessary to outline the *status controversiae*.

The Occasion of Romans

There is a longstanding debate concerning the occasion surrounding the writing of the Letter to the Romans.[2] It is not the intention of this work to mount a defense of a specific position in this debate. However, when doing exegesis in Romans, a person's position on the occasion will undoubtedly affect their interpretation. Thus, for present purposes, I will briefly outline the occasion I will be assuming for my exegesis.

When Paul wrote Romans, he was en route to Jerusalem with his hard-earned collection for the poor.[3] The church in Rome was not founded by St. Paul nor by any other apostle. It appears likely that the "sojourners from Rome" in Jerusalem on Pentecost (Acts 2:10) brought their newfound Christian faith home with them and founded a Christian community in Rome.[4] Paul stated how he had longed to go to Rome so that by the preaching of the gospel among the Romans, mutual encouragement and strengthening might

---

[1] I write this paper from within and committed to the Lutheran tradition.
[2] See the positions taken in Karl P. Donfried, ed., *The Romans Debate* (Grand Rapids, MI: Baker Academic, 1991).
[3] John Ziesler, *Paul's Letter to the Romans* (London, UK: SCM Press, 1989), 10.
[4] Joseph A. Fitzmyer, *Romans: A New Translation with Introduction and Commentary*, Anchor Yale Bible, vol. 33 (New Haven, CT / London, UK: Yale University Press, 2008), 29.

occur.⁵ However, because he had been unable to do so, Paul decided to write a letter in place of a personal visit.⁶ Paul remained committed to visiting Rome but with the new purpose of using Rome as a missionary base to go on to Spain.⁷ Through personal contacts, Paul had become aware of rising tensions in the Roman church and sought to bring a solution.⁸ Thus, Paul, with his visit to Jerusalem on his mind, tailored his presentation of the gospel to fit the particular situation of the Roman church.⁹

The church in Rome was composed of Jewish Christians along with associated God-fearing Gentiles and perhaps proselytes.¹⁰ The fledgling community suffered a setback in the late AD 40s when a dispute between Jews and Jewish Christians led Claudius to expel all Jews from Rome.¹¹ Although up to this point the community had been predominately Jewish in character, the expulsion of the Jewish Christians created a situation in which this

---

⁵Neil Elliott, *The Rhetoric of Romans* (Minneapolis, MN: Augsburg Fortress Press, 2000), 85. Note that Elliott correctly sees the proclamation of the gospel serves a purpose in an established Christian community and, thus, it is not only to proselytize.

⁶Although, as I note later, it may be in preparation for a different kind of visit.

⁷Elliott, *Rhetoric*, 87. See also Elliott, *Rhetoric*, 84 n1 and Paul Barnett, *Jesus & the Rise of Early Christianity: A History of New Testament Times* (Downers Grove, IL: InterVarsity Press, 1999), 339.

⁸N.T. Wright, "The Letter to the Romans: Introduction, Commentary, and Reflections," in *The New Interpreter's Bible Commentary, Volume X: Acts to First Corinthians* (Nashville, TN: Abingdon Press, 2002), 407. See Fitzmyer, *Romans*, 79.

⁹Wright, "Letter to the Romans," 407–08. See also Elliott, *Rhetoric*, 84–86, 91–92.

¹⁰Fitzmyer, *Romans*, 29.

¹¹Ibid., 30–31. See Wright, "Letter to the Romans," 406.

was not the case upon their return after the death of Claudius.[12] Due to the increasing number of Gentile Christians in Rome, some disputes between the Jewish and Gentile Christians seem to have broken out.[13] Those quarrels seem to have revolved around questions concerning the incorporation of both Jews and Gentiles into one new community.[14] Paul had struggled with debates surrounding the relationship between Jews and Gentiles in the Christian community since his Letter to the Galatians.[15] These debates continued throughout Paul's ministry, even down to an encounter with a "Judaizing" faction in Corinth shortly before the writing of the Letter to the Romans.[16] Additionally, Paul was not certain that the Gentile money he had collected would be accepted by Jewish Christians in Jerusalem.[17] So, the major themes and contents of the Letter to the Romans were both on Paul's mind as he traveled to Jerusalem, and they were directly applicable to the Roman situation.[18]

The Righteousness from God

Perhaps it would be an overstatement to claim that a solitary friar's interpretation of a small phrase in a single verse in St. Paul's Letter

---

[12] Wright, "Letter to the Romans," 406–407.
[13] Michael P. Middendorf, *Romans 1–8*, Concordia Commentary (St. Louis, MO: Concordia Publishing House, 2013), 11–12. James D.G. Dunn, *Romans 1–8*, Word Biblical Commentary, vol. 38A (Dallas, TX: Word Books Publisher, 1988), lii–liii.
[14] Ziesler, *Paul's Letter*, 12.
[15] Ibid., 9.
[16] Barnett, *Jesus*, 339.
[17] Ziesler, *Paul's Letter*, 10.
[18] Elliott, *Rhetoric*, 91.

to the Romans could fundamentally change the church. Yet, Martin Luther's interpretation of δικαιοσύνη θεοῦ from Romans 1:17 fits that description. This breakthrough has often been recounted from Luther's own autobiographical statement in the preface to his Latin works.[19] Yet, far too often, the discussion of Luther's views is limited to the examination of the autobiographical statement, leaving some important nuances of Luther's view neglected. It is appropriate to briefly discuss Luther's understanding of δικαιοσύνη θεοῦ.

Luther was schooled in the nominalist tradition of the *via moderna*, following thinkers such as William of Ockham and Gabriel Biel.[20] While there were indeed nominalists who were Augustinian, such as Gregory of Rimini, the school of nominalists who trained Luther was not.[21] From Biel's textbook, Luther learned that the sinner was not so far gone that they could not do what lay within them and respond to God with some small moral effort.[22] These influences can be seen in the beginning of Luther's lectures on the Psalms in 1513.[23] It was during these lectures on the Psalms when Luther encountered the concept of "the righteousness of God."[24] Biel and the nominalist scholars with whom Luther was acquainted all understood *iustitia Dei* as a subjective genitive referring to God's

---

[19]Martin Luther, "Preface to the Complete Edition of Luther's Latin Writings, 1545," in *LW* 34:323–338.
[20]Gordon Rupp, *The Righteousness of God: Luther Studies* (London, UK: Hodder & Stoughton, 1953), 125. Philip S. Watson, *Let God Be God: An Interpretation of the Theology of Martin Luther* (Eugene, OR: Wipf and Stock, 1947), 21. Graham Tomlin, *Luther and His World* (Downers Grove, IL: InterVarsity Press, 2002), 31–32.
[21]Tomlin, *Luther*, 33–34.
[22]Ibid., 34.
[23]Ibid., 51–52.
[24]Watson, *Let God*, 20.

own retributive justice, whereby he punishes those who break divine law.[25]

Luther had great distress over, even hatred for, this phrase "the righteousness of God" because it seemed to him that Paul talking about the gospel revealing the righteousness of God in Romans 1:17 was a further revelation of God's retributive justice. Luther found it impossible to see how the retributive justice of God could be "good news" for sinners.[26] Sometime in the autumn of 1514, Luther found his solution.[27] He saw the righteousness of God not as a quality of God but as a gift from God. For Luther, the righteousness of God is that righteousness that God gives to us to receive passively by faith. The righteousness that God's justice demands of us is the very thing that God freely gives to us. So, Luther saw it as an objective genitive, not a subjective genitive.[28] To his delight, Luther found precedent for his interpretation in St. Augustine's anti-Pelagian work *On the Spirit and the Letter*.[29]

Far from a simplistic reading, if one looks at how Luther understood the righteousness of God in other passages in Romans,

---

[25] Tomlin, *Luther*, 57. Bernhard Lohse, *Martin Luther's Theology: Its Historical and Systematic Development*, trans. Roy A. Harrisville (Minneapolis, MN: Fortress Press, 1999), 92. Rupp, *Righteousness*, 127. If some contest this point, saying that they cannot find a nominalist who actually says this, we accept here that Luther knows what he's talking about and is not fabricating his information.

[26] Watson, *Let God*, 20. Tomlin, *Luther*, 57.

[27] Rupp, *The Righteousness of God*, 137. Lohse, *Martin Luther's Theology*, 93.

[28] Stephen J. Chester, *Reading Paul with the Reformers: Reconciling Old and New Perspectives* (Grand Rapids, MI: Wm. B. Eerdmans, 2017), 207. Tomlin, *Luther*, 57. *LW* 34:336.

[29] Lohse, *Martin Luther's Theology*, 75. *LW* 34:337.

it becomes clear that his view is a bit more nuanced.[30] In effect, Luther thought that God's gift of righteousness and his free justification of the sinner exhibits God's own righteousness.[31] God demonstrates that he is righteousness not because he punishes the wicked but because he gives righteousness to sinners as a gift.[32] Chester further notes, "The point for Luther is not to deny that the phrase 'the righteousness of God' means God's being righteous in God's self, but rather to insist that this subjective genitive sense is true *for us* only on the basis of the objective genitive sense."[33] This connection between the subjective genitive sense and the objective genitive sense for Luther is made chiefly by means of union with Christ by faith.[34] For Luther, faith in God is directly connected to God's righteousness because faith ascribes righteousness to God.[35] Additionally, faith and participation with Christ are intimately connected, as Christ "is present in the faith itself."[36] As Vainio points out, for Luther, the righteousness of God is the righteousness of Christ, and through faith we participate in Christ.[37]

What is new in Luther is not necessarily his reading of the text, but how Luther applies this text to the salvation of sinners.[38] Luther places a complete emphasis upon the saving action of God

---

[30]Chester, *Reading Paul with the Reformers*, 207–208.
[31]Ibid., 208.
[32]Ibid., 208–209.

[33] Ibid., 209.
[34]Ibid., 209.
[35]Martin Luther, "Lectures on Galatians, 1535," in *LW* 26:227.
[36]Ibid., in *LW* 26:12.
[37]Olli-Pekka Vainio, "Luther and Theosis: A Response to Critics of Finnish Luther Research," in *Pro Ecclesia* 24, no. 4 (2015): p. 63.
[38]Lohse, *Martin Luther's Theology*, 95–96.

through Christ for the sake of the sinner.[39] Many of the so-called New Perspective on Paul have taken their stand against Luther's reading of Romans, and so it is to their views that we now turn.

The Challenge of the New Perspective

In the twentieth century, there arose a challenge to the "Lutheran" reading of Romans, especially as it was espoused by scholars like Rudolf Bultmann and Ernst Käsemann.[40] It was very common to claim that the Jews sought salvation through obedience to the law and doing good works.[41] Paul in Romans was understood to oppose Jewish legalism with a message of free justification by grace alone through faith alone in Christ.[42] The work of E. P. Sanders challenges the view that Second Temple Judaism was a legalistic religion.[43] Instead, Sanders proposes the term *covenantal nomism*. This term denotes two things: first, that one was a part of God's covenant people by an act of God's grace; and second, in response to such grace, one was called upon to obey God's stipulations for remaining in the covenant people.[44] As a result of this rethinking of Second

---

[39]Watson, *Let God*, 26.

[40]David G. Horrell, *An Introduction to the Study of Paul*, 3rd ed. (London, UK: Bloomsbury, 2015), 127. While Bultmann and Käsemann were nominally Lutherans and expounded Luther's exegesis, in most other respects they represented a form of modernism quite far removed from Luther's traditional faith.

[41]Ibid., 127.

[42]Ibid., 127–128.

[43]Ibid., 128.

[44]Ibid., 130. As Horrell notes, even defenders of a Lutheran reading of Paul agree with Sanders's basic thesis. See also Horrell, *Study of Paul*, 133–136 and Stephen Westerholm, "What's Right about the New Perspective on Paul," in *Studies in the Pauline Epistles: Essays in Honor of Douglas J. Moo*, ed.

Temple Judaism, the main issue that Paul was dealing with was no longer thought to be legalism but ethnocentrism.[45] This reinterpretation of Second Temple Judaism sparked a massive reinterpretation of Paul, which was largely cast opposite to the Lutheran one. These various reinterpretations have collectively been given the nickname the "New Perspective on Paul."[46] We shall consider what the two most influential proponents of the New Perspective, James D. G. Dunn and N. T. Wright, have to say concerning δικαιοσύνη θεοῦ.

Dunn begins his discussion of δικαιοσύνη θεοῦ by noting Luther's description of his breakthrough. Despite praise for Luther's discovery of "the saving righteousness of God," Dunn claims that "Lutheran theology" is guilty of "a significant misunderstanding of Paul."[47] In opposition, Dunn proposes that the Greco-Roman idea of justice as "an ideal or absolute ethical norm" is not the background to the phrase *righteousness of God*. Instead, building upon the work of H. Cremer, the background comes from the Hebrew צדק, which denotes social relation.[48] For Dunn, God's righteousness is God's covenant faithfulness. Israel's God is righteous when he "fulfills the

---

Matthew S. Harmon and Jay E. Smith (Grand Rapids, MI: Zondervan, 2014), pp. 230–242.
    [45]Horrell, *Study of Paul*, 131.
    [46]Ibid., 132.
    [47]James D. G. Dunn, "What's Right about the Old Perspective on Paul," in *Studies in the Pauline Epistles: Essays in Honor of Douglas J. Moo*, ed. Matthew S. Harmon and Jay E. Smith (Grand Rapids, MI: Zondervan, 2014), pp. 214, 216. James D. G. Dunn, "The Justice of God: A Renewed Perspective on Justification by Faith," in *The New Perspective on Paul*, rev. ed. (Grand Rapids, MI: Wm. B. Eerdmans, 2005), p. 194.
    [48]Dunn, *Romans 1–8*, 40–41.

obligations he took upon himself to be Israel's God."⁴⁹ Specifically, God's righteousness is synonymous with his salvation. Dunn defines the righteousness of God as "God's act to restore his own and to sustain them within the covenant."⁵⁰ As such, Dunn proposes that δικαιοσύνη θεοῦ is both an objective and subjective genitive "with the emphasis on the latter."⁵¹

Wright similarly critiques Luther's view of δικαιοσύνη θεοῦ as "misleading" because "it directed attention away from the biblical notion of God's covenant faithfulness and instead placed greater emphasis upon the status of the human being."⁵² Wright notes three specific frameworks that inform our understanding of δικαιοσύνη θεοῦ. First, along with Dunn, Wright notes that covenant faithfulness and loyalty are a primary meaning.⁵³ Second, and directly connected with the idea of covenant, is the idea of the law court. This must be understood as the Jewish civil law court rather than our own criminal law court.⁵⁴ God's righteousness in this light is seen as his status as judge, specifically "to uphold the law, to punish wrongdoing, and to defend those who . . . had nobody to defend them."⁵⁵ Third, Wright notes the eschatological referent, in which God puts the whole world right.⁵⁶ Thus, because of God's

---

⁴⁹Ibid., 41.
⁵⁰Ibid., 41. Dunn, "What's Right," 216–217.
⁵¹Ibid., 41.
⁵²N.T. Wright, "Righteousness," in *New Dictionary of Theology*, ed. David F. Wright, Sinclair B. Ferguson, and J.I. Packer (Downers Grove, IL: InterVarsity Press, 1988), pp. 590–592.
⁵³Wright, "Letter to the Romans," 398.
⁵⁴Ibid., 398–399.
⁵⁵Ibid., 399.
⁵⁶Ibid., 401.

loyalty to his covenant with Israel, he acts on behalf of his oppressed people to vindicate them in their cause, and, ultimately, to restore justice to the world.[57] Thus, Wright summarizes that in light of the Jewish background, δικαιοσύνη θεοῦ "always refers to God's own righteousness, not to the status people have from God."[58]

Are these two traditions, the Lutheran and the New Perspective, diametrically opposed to one another? When determining the meaning of δικαιοσύνη θεοῦ, are we forced to make a choice of either God's covenant faithfulness or the divine gift of righteousness in Christ? It is the position of this paper that there is a way in which these two divergent perspectives can come closer together and that the cultural values of honor and shame in the Greco-Roman Mediterranean point the way forward. It is necessary, therefore, to move into a short sketch of honor and shame.

II. Honor and Shame

Introduction

Different cultures and societies value and orient themselves around different ethical currencies. While this may seem self-evident, it is not always taken into consideration when exegeting the New Testament. Because there are undeniable differences between a first-century Greco-Roman culture and a twenty-first-century post-modern culture, it behooves us to try to understand the New Testament world on its own terms. There may sometimes be bewilderment when encountering the distant culture of the New Testament world.

---

[57] Ibid., 400.
[58] Wright, "Letter to the Romans," 403.

Anthropologist Ruth Benedict is cited as noting a potential cause of such culture shock. While some societies are more focused on the individual and oriented toward justice and guilt, other societies are more focused on the group and oriented toward honor and shame. Twenty-first-century Western culture tends to the former and first-century Mediterranean culture to the latter.[59] It is important to sketch out briefly how honor and shame functioned in the ancient Mediterranean world before proceeding to read Romans in light of these cultural values.[60]

Honor

What exactly is meant by the word *honor*? In the ancient Mediterranean world, honor was a social value comprised of a person's own self-worth and their reputation in the community.[61] Hence, honor had both an individual and a corporate element. "Honor is a claim to worth along with the social acknowledgment of worth."[62] An individual could claim to have honor because they judged that they had upheld the values of the community.[63] These values might have differed from one group to another.[64] Peer pressure enforced

---

[59]Ruth Leinhard, "A 'Good Conscience': Differences between Honor and Justice Orientation," in *Missiology: An International Review* 29, no. 2 (2001): pp. 131–134.

[60]Space prohibits a complete study of honor and patronage. Additionally, it would be unnecessary, as it has been sufficiently covered by those scholars cited in the bibliography, upon which this sketch depends.

[61]Bruce J. Malina, *The New Testament World: Insights from Cultural Anthropology*, 3rd ed. (Louisville, KY: Westminster John Knox Press, 2001), 30.

[62]Ibid., 30.

[63]David A. deSilva, *Honor, Patronage, Kinship & Purity: Unlocking New Testament Culture* (Downers Grove, IL: InterVarsity Press, 2000), 25.

[64]Ibid., 25.

conformity to the community's honor code and reprimanded those who failed to conform.[65] From this, it is evident that a person's identity and self-worth were largely determined by the opinion of the community.[66]

What is more, a person's claim to honor had to have been validated and acknowledged by the community if it was not to be an empty boast.[67] The group or community before whom a person sought honor is referred to as the significant others.[68] To be honored was to be publicly acknowledged and treated with the respect one deserved by these significant others.[69] Bruce Malina likens this understanding of honor to a credit rating. "A good credit rating makes money available, allows a person to incur debt and acquire goods for immediate use, and reflects on a person's social standing in our society."[70] In a similar way, a person in the first-century Mediterranean world would have been concerned about their honor—a sort of social credit rating. A person's honor stipulated their place in society as well as essential aspects of life, such as behavior, clothing, food, and marriage.[71]

There were two kinds of honor—active and passive. Passive honor, called ascribed honor, belonged to a person without their

---

[65] Ibid., 26–27.
[66] Halvor Moxnes, "BTB Reader's Guide: Honor and Shame," in *Biblical Theological Bulletin* 23, no. 4 (1993): p. 168.
[67] Richard L. Rohrbaugh, "Honor: Core Value in the Biblical World," in *Understanding the Social World of the New Testament*, ed. Dietmar Neufeld and Richard E. DeMaris (New York, NY: Routledge, 2015), p. 146.
[68] Moxnes, "BTB Reader's Guide," 168.
[69] DeSilva, *Honor, Patronage, Kinship & Purity*, 25.
[70] Malina, *New Testament World*, 31.
[71] Rohrbaugh, "Honor," 146. Malina, *New Testament World*, 36.

having to earn it.[72] The most common form of ascribed honor was attained by virtue of birth.[73] If a person was born into an honorable or notable family, they participated in the honor that their ancestors acquired. If a person's family was unimportant or dishonorable, they participated in that disgrace.[74] This made genealogy and nationality quite important.[75] A person could also receive ascribed honor later in life by being adopted into a more honorable family.[76]

On the other hand, active honor, called acquired honor, had to be earned.[77] The most basic way one acquired or achieved honor was by being virtuous. By living up to the group's expectations and excelling above others in virtuous living, a person could make a reputation for themselves.[78] This virtue would have been practiced in public so that others in the group could see it and acknowledge it.[79]

Furthermore, acquired honor was often gained through a contest called a challenge-riposte, which was a form of "social tug-of-war" wherein a person publicly challenged the honor of an equal.[80] This could take the form of an insult, argument, or physical aggression.[81] In order to defend one's honor when challenged, one had to respond appropriately. Since this involved a public challenge, the winner of the contest was determined by the observers.[82] Therefore,

---

[72]Ibid., 32.
[73]DeSilva, *Honor, Patronage, Kinship & Purity*, 28.
[74]Rohrbaugh, "Honor," 153.
[75]Ibid., 154–155.
[76]DeSilva, *Honor, Patronage, Kinship & Purity*, 28.
[77]Malina, *New Testament World*, 33.
[78]DeSilva, *Honor, Patronage, Kinship & Purity*, 28–29.
[79]Rohrbaugh, "Honor," 155.
[80]Malina, *New Testament World*, 33.
[81]Rohrbaugh, "Honor," 149.
[82]DeSilva, *Honor, Patronage, Kinship & Purity*, 29.

a person's place on the social ladder and their privileges and responsibilities in society were gained at the expense of others. "The challenge, then, is a threat to usurp the reputation of another, to deprive another of his reputation."[83] This contest was not limited to the aggressive usurpation of an equal's honor. Every encounter outside of one's family represented a challenge to honor.[84] Good examples of a positive challenge are a gift, compliment, or invitation, as a failure to return in kind would result in dishonor.

As noted above, honor was not simply an individual concern, but it was intimately associated with the community. The community itself had corporate honor.[85] An individual's own honor was associated with the honor of their family and of their larger community.[86] A person's honor involved those who were responsible for their well-being, such as their parents, patrons, monarch, or even their god.[87] It also involved those for whom a person was responsible, such as a wife, children, or slaves.[88] This means that a challenge to one's honor was a challenge to the honor of all those associated with them. A person was not simply defending their own honor, but the honor of others as well. This also implies that dishonor and shame could also be corporate and shared by the family or community.[89]

Shame and Satisfaction

---

[83] Ibid., 35.
[84] Ibid., 36.
[85] Ibid., 42.
[86] Ibid., 42.
[87] Ibid., 42.
[88] Ibid., 42.
[89] Ibid., 42.

DEFENDING GOD'S HONOR

As tempting as it might be to equate dishonor with shame, thus making them synonymous, it is not always the case that they were equatable. Dishonor involved a lack of respect in the eyes of the community due to a real or perceived failure to live up to the community's honor code.[90] Conversely, shame was a positive quality. To have shame was to take into account one's reputation and the public perception of an intended action.[91] "It means a proper concern for one's honor and to know what can bring about its gain or loss."[92] If a person had shame, they would avoid doing things that will cause them to "lose face" in their community.[93]

Correspondingly, being "shameless" indicated a negative quality—a complete lack of concern for one's honor.[94] A shameless person did not play by the rules of the community nor think the community's standards were valid.[95] Not only was a shameless person dishonorable, but they were also treated without the normal social niceties.[96] However, being shamed was slightly different. When a person made a claim to honor and that honor was denied by the community, they were shamed.[97] This involved public humiliation and rejection. In fact, "being shamed was a social catastrophe, especially since shame for one member of a family meant shame for all."[98] In this

---

[90] DeSilva, *Honor, Patronage, Kinship & Purity*, 25.
[91] Malina, *New Testament World*, 49. This implies the necessity of a functioning conscience, which means that shame is heightened among Christians.
[92] Rohrbaugh, "Honor," 147.
[93] DeSilva, *Honor, Patronage, Kinship & Purity*, 25.
[94] Malina, *New Testament World*, 49.
[95] Ibid., 49.
[96] Ibid., 49.
[97] Ibid., 50.
[98] Rohrbaugh, "Honor," 147.

case, "being shamed" and "being dishonored" would mean the same thing. Further, it is important to realize that shame is not the same as guilt. Guilt can involve both an internal feeling of culpability for some misconduct and a status imputed by a judge. However, in first-century Mediterranean culture, the conscience was in the community, not the individual, and the result was not necessarily guilt, but public shame.[99]

If a person or group was dishonored or brought shame upon another, they were obligated to fix the situation by making restitution.[100] First, there was the need to restore honor to those who had been dishonored, and this was especially the case when social superiors, benefactors, or those in authority were the ones who were dishonored. In addition, restitution had to be made in proportion to the dishonor caused.[101] This act of restoring honor to the person from whom it was taken and making restitution is called making satisfaction.[102] The reputation of the person who had their honor

---

[99] Ibid., 148–149.
[100] Malina, *New Testament World*, 39.
[101] Malina states that the attempt to restore honor is enough, even if the actual restoration of honor is unsuccessful. Malina, *The New Testament World*, 39, 43. On the contrary, not only must the previous honor be restored, but also reparations must be made. As Anselm explains, "It is not sufficient merely to repay what has been taken away. rather, he ought to pay back more than he took, in proportion to the insult which he inflicted . . . It is not sufficient for someone who violates someone else's honour, to restore that person's honour, if he does not, in consequence of the harmful act of dishonour, give, as restitution to the person whom he has dishonoured, something pleasing to that person." Anselm of Canterbury, *Cur Deus Homo* 1:11, in *Anselm of Canterbury: The Major Works*, ed. Brian Davies and G. R. Evans (Oxford, UK: Oxford University Press, 2008), p. 283. See also Leviticus 5:14–19.
[102] Malina, *New Testament World*, 39.

impugned had to be restored to its previous sanctity.[103] If the offending person, family, or group failed to make satisfaction, then all that remained was the vengeance and punishment inflicted by the dishonored party.[104]

Patronage and Reciprocity

In the first-century Mediterranean, most of the money and land were in the possession of a small minority.[105] Most people were not as self-sufficient as many are today, nor did they have access to the modern diversity of social services.[106] Instead, people used personal connection to a patron or benefactor—a social superior who was able to provide them with what they required, often on the basis of favoritism.[107] The word *patron* derives from the word *pater*, which means "father," and from this, all patrons were considered "fathers."[108] Not just individuals but cities, and even entire provinces, received benefaction.[109] Sometimes, the desired patron was too far up the social ladder to access. In these cases, a potential client made use of a patron who had access to the higher patron, called a broker or mediator.[110]

---

[103] Ibid., 39.
[104] Ibid., 43. Anselm, *Cur Deus Homo* 1:13, 1:15, 287, 289.
[105] DeSilva, *Honor, Patronage, Kinship & Purity*, 96.
[106] Ibid., 96.
[107] Ibid., 96–97. Bruce J. Malina, "Patronage," in *A Handbook of Biblical Social Values*, ed. John J. Pilch and Bruce J. Malina, 3rd ed. (Eugene, OR: Wipf and Stock, 2016), p. 132.
[108] Malina, "Patronage," 132. *Merriam-Webster's Collegiate Dictionary*, s.v. "Patron."
[109] DeSilva, *Honor, Patronage, Kinship & Purity*, 101.
[110] Ibid., 97.

While the patron gave freely and with no thought of return, the idea of reciprocity was not thereby excluded.[111] This reciprocity however was not simply responding in kind. The patron could grant favors, such as land, material goods, political status, or military protection, and they would be reciprocated with public recognition, honor, praise, support, loyalty, or even a client's services.[112] The client would owe a debt of gratitude to the patron. It was a great dishonor not to reciprocate a patron's generosity.[113] It follows that the greater the support from the patron, the greater the debt of gratitude. The ultimate point of the favor was not to seek reciprocation but for the two parties to be united together.[114]

The Greek word χάρις, which is often translated to "grace," finds its full meaning in this context.[115] Malina notes three ways this word can be used. First, it can be used to refer to the generous and altruistic disposition of the patron or benefactor toward their client. Second, it can refer to the gift that the patron gives their client. Third, it can refer to the response of gratitude that the client returns to the patron because of being given the gift.[116] This is also the context of the Greek word πίστις, often translated to "faith." It carries the idea of trusting that the patron is rightly disposed and capable of providing

---

[111]Ibid., 106-107, 109.
[112]Malina, "Patronage," 132. DeSilva, *Honor, Patronage, Kinship & Purity*, 110.
[113]Ibid., 109-110.
[114]Ibid., 116.
[115]Ibid., 104.
[116]Ibid., 104-105.

for one's needs, along with the accompanying sense of loyalty and fidelity toward the patron.[117]

Luther and Honor and Shame

Before moving on to considering Romans, we should briefly note some striking honor-and-shame language in Luther's works. In addition to what we said concerning Luther's view of faith before, we are now in a position to see a further aspect of Luther's view of faith. Luther uses the language of honor and shame, noting that faith

> is something omnipotent, and that its power is inestimable and infinite; for it attributes glory to God, which is the highest thing that can be attributed to Him. To attribute glory to God is to believe in Him, to regard Him as truthful, wise, righteous, merciful, and almighty, in short, to acknowledge Him as the Author and Donor of every good . . . Nor does God require anything greater of man than that he attribute to Him His glory and His divinity; that is, that he regard Him, not as an idol but as God, who has regard for him, listens to him, shows mercy to him, helps him, etc.[118]

For Luther, faith attributes glory or honor to God. This means that, for Luther, faith is not only to believe in God but also to ascribe honor to him—namely, that he is faithful, trustworthy, righteous, and the

---

[117] Ibid., 115.
[118] Luther, "Lectures on Galatians, 1535," in *LW* 26:227.

supreme benefactor and giver of every good gift. Therefore, faith justifies "because it renders to God what is due Him."[119]

Additionally, with regard to the atonement, Luther accepted the view put forward by Anselm of Canterbury. This view of the atonement, advocated in Anselm's work *Cur Deus Homo* ("Why God Became Man"), sees Christ's death functioning as making satisfaction for humanity's sins that had dishonored God.[120] In his Romans lectures, Luther notes, "The death of Christ is the death of sin, and His resurrection is the life of righteousness, because through His death He has made satisfaction for sin, and through His resurrection He has brought us righteousness."[121] His Galatians lectures also follow this same language when he states, "In short, He has and bears all the sins of all men in His body—in order to make satisfaction for them with His own blood."[122] The Lutheran scholastic tradition followed Luther in the use of the Anselmic language of honor and shame in describing the atonement.[123] From this, we can see that the language of honor and shame is by no means absent from Luther's exegesis or his conception of the gospel.

A Valid Approach?

Malina, deSilva, and Rohrbaugh draw heavily from Greco-Roman sources. It can be concluded that first-century Mediterranean culture

---

[119] Ibid., 227.
[120] See Anselm, *Cur Deus Homo*, 260–356.
[121] Luther, "Lectures on Romans, 1515–1516," in *LW* 25:284.
[122] Luther, "Lectures on Galatians, 1535," in *LW* 26:277.
[123] Heinrich Schmid, *The Doctrinal Theology of the Evangelical Lutheran Church: Verified from the Original Sources*, ed. Charles A. Hay and Henry E. Jacobs (Philadelphia, PA: Lutheran Publication Society, 1889), 349–351.

was "united by a pervasive and relatively uniform value system based on complementary codes of honor and shame."[124] It can be assumed that the Gentile portion of Paul's intended audience followed standard Greco-Roman cultural mores. But what about the Jews? The ancient Near East, including the ancient Israelites, was oriented toward honor and shame.[125] The Jews, as the heirs of the Israelites, were a minority subculture and displayed the same concerns for honor as their pagan neighbors, albeit with a different code of honor.[126]

Presenting a contrary approach, Seth Schwartz argues that the Jews rejected the Roman system of patronage because benefaction was a duty of all enshrined in the Torah, and he uses the writings of Josephus, Ben Sira, and the rabbis to support this contention.[127] However, his focus on Judeans neglects diaspora Jews, who cannot be removed from the Greco-Roman culture in which they were found. The Hellenization of the diaspora Jews was thorough, as the writings of Philo and other diaspora Jews demonstrate.[128] Thus, while

---

[124] Moxnes, "BTB Reader's Guide," 168.

[125] See Saul M. Olyan, "Honor, Shame, and Covenant Relations in Ancient Israel and Its Environment," in *Journal of Biblical Literature* 115, no. 2 (1996): pp. 201–218; Matthew J. Lynch, "Neglected Physical Dimensions of 'Shame' Terminology in the Hebrew Bible," in *Biblica* 91, no. 4 (2010): pp. 499–517; David A. Glatt-Gilad, "Yahweh's Honor at Stake: A Divine Conundrum," in *Journal for the Study of the Old Testament* 98 (2002): pp. 63–74; and T.R. Hobbs, "Reflections on Honor, Shame, and Covenant Relations," in *Journal of Biblical Literature* 116, no. 3 (1997): pp. 501–503.

[126] DeSilva, *Honor, Patronage, Kinship & Purity*, 38–41.

[127] Seth Schwartz, *Were the Jews a Mediterranean Society?: Reciprocity and Solidarity in Ancient Judaism* (Princeton, NJ: Princeton University Press, 2010).

[128] Steven Weitzman, "Mediterranean Exchanges: A Response to Seth Schwartz's 'Were the Jews a Mediterranean Society?'," in *Jewish Quarterly Review* 102, no. 4 (2012): pp. 491–512. See also the data found in John M.G. Barclay, *Jews in the Mediterranean Diaspora: From Alexander to Trajan (323*

Schwartz may be correct about many Jews living in Judea, the evidence is that the diaspora Jews found in Rome would also have followed the Roman patronage system.

But is this a valid way to approach the interpretation and exegesis of St. Paul's Letter to the Romans in general? First, it is noteworthy that the language of honor and shame is more frequent and more evenly distributed in his letter than the language of righteousness and justification.[129] This emphasis reflects the values of the culture in and for which it was written. Situating the New Testament writings in the culture and society in which they were written helps to avoid the problems with a "Biblicist" perspective, which looks at the text alone, apart from the insights of history and social science. This is vital if we are to avoid anachronistically reading our own values and concerns back into first-century minds.[130] Even the historical-critical method has failed to adequately and thoroughly take social science into consideration.[131]

This criticism is equally true of the advocates of the traditional Lutheran reading of Paul and its sparring partner, the New Perspective, both of which rarely, if ever, make use of the insights of social science. In fact, Wright claims that this application of social-

---

BCE–117 CE) (Edinburgh, Scotland: T&T Clark, 1996); Tessa Rajak, "Benefactors in the Greco-Jewish Diaspora," in *The Jewish Dialogue with Greece and Rome: Studies in Cultural and Social Interaction* (Leiden, Netherlands: Brill, 2001), pp. 373–91; and David A. deSilva, "The Wisdom of Ben Sira: Honor, Shame, and the Maintenance of the Values of a Minority Culture," in *The Catholic Biblical Quarterly* 58, no. 3 (1996): pp. 433–455.

[129]Halvor Moxnes, "Honor and Righteousness in Romans," in *The Journal for the Study of the New Testament* 10, no. 32 (1988): pp. 63–64.

[130]John H. Elliott, *What Is Social-Scientific Criticism?* (Minneapolis, MN: Augsburg Fortress Press, 1993), 11.

[131]Ibid., 12.

scientific research by Malina et al. is reductionistic and guilty of a "top-down" approach filled with "large-scale generalizations."[132] Elliott notes that the problem of generalizations is a problem for almost any science, including history. Everyone works with models based on generalizations drawn from observations, and either those are made apparent from the outset or are simply unconsciously assumed.[133] So, while being aware of the limitations of this kind of study, it remains applicable and valuable nonetheless.[134] As we have now outlined honor and shame, let us move on to an examination of Romans itself.

III. Romans 1–3 in Light of Honor and Shame
Romans 1:1–7

In his typical manner, St. Paul begins the Letter to the Romans by adapting the greeting of standard Greco-Roman epistolary writing. Oddly, Paul feels the need to greatly enlarge the greeting of this letter, making it the longest greeting in the Pauline corpus.[135] Because Paul is writing to a church he did not establish nor visit himself, it has often been supposed that the length of the opening is simply the result of needing to introduce himself.[136] This view fails to account for the actual content of the opening. Instead, the extended opening serves

---

[132]N.T. Wright, *Paul and His Recent Interpreters: Some Contemporary Debates* (Minneapolis, MN: Fortress Press, 2015), 277, 280. Here Wright voices a standard objection to the use of social-science in biblical studies.
[133]Elliott, *Social-Scientific Criticism*, 41–42, 96–97.
[134]Stephen C. Barton, "Historical Criticism and Social-Scientific Perspectives in New Testament Study," in *Hearing the New Testament: Strategies for Interpretation*, ed. Joel B. Green, 2nd ed. (Grand Rapids, MI: Wm. B. Eerdmans, 2010), pp. 47–50.
[135]A.J.M. Wedderburn, *The Reasons for Romans* (London, UK: T&T Clark, 2004), 93.
[136]Ibid., 93–94.

the purpose to "create a rhetorical relationship with his readers" by means of a shared Christian identity.[137] A far more persuasive explanation is that in appealing to "matters of central Christian belief" (the central place of Jesus Christ in God's plan and the universal extent of the gospel), Paul begins to anticipate the argument of the letter.[138]

Paul introduces himself to the Romans as "a slave of Christ Jesus, a called apostle" (1:1).[139] Paul is presenting to the Roman Christians his claim to honor. Jewett notes that being a "slave of Christ" would have carried a mark of distinction and prestige to Roman ears. A "slave of Caesar" was a lucrative and prominent position in the empire. Paul is presenting himself using the honorific of a "royal official or an imperial bureaucrat."[140] Additionally, being "a called apostle" conveys the Jewish concept of the *shaliach* as a plenipotentiary representative. Paul had been invested with the full diplomatic authority of God's kingdom.[141] Paul could claim this ascribed honor because he had "been marked off"[142] from others by God himself for the purpose of proclaiming the gospel.[143] Paul's apostleship was a gift (grace) given to him in Christ, and it was also in

---

[137]Elliott, *Rhetoric*, 71, 75–76.
[138]Ibid., 71, 73–75. Ziesler, *Paul's Letter*, 55. Dunn, *Romans 1–8*, 5. Robert Jewett, *Romans: A Short Commentary* (Minneapolis, MN: Fortress Press, 2013), 9. Philip F. Esler, *Conflict and Identity in Romans: The Social Setting of Paul's Letter* (Minneapolis, MN: Augsburg Fortress Press, 2003), 135. Middendorf, *Romans 1–8*, 62–63.
[139]Unless otherwise noted, all translations of Holy Scripture belong to the author.
[140]Jewett, *Romans*, 9.
[141]Ziesler, *Paul's Letter*, 58–59.
[142]LSJ, s.v. "ἀφορίζω."
[143]Wright, "Letter to the Romans," 415.

Christ that Paul established his own identity and that also of the Romans.[144]

The "good news" for which Paul was marked off was "announced before" by God through Israel's prophetic Scriptures.[145] There, it concerned the defeat of Israel's national enemies and the return from exile.[146] In the Roman world, εὐαγγέλιον referred to the announcement of the new age of peace and salvation ushered in by the emperor's birth, accession, or victory.[147] Here is being highlighted already God's faithfulness to his promises to Israel and his own saving action in bringing it about.[148]

God's faithfulness to his promises to Israel is tied up with Jesus Christ. The life, death, and resurrection of Jesus of Nazareth constitute the gospel itself. The titles given to Jesus here are not arbitrary nor are they random details. The statement of Jesus's human parentage "of the seed of David according to the flesh" highlights that Jesus was of royal descent; additionally, by his resurrection from the dead, Jesus "was marked out as God's Son."[149] Paul is establishing Jesus's own ascribed honor, which, as we saw above, is based upon family and genealogy.[150] On the one hand, as the son of David, Jesus is deserving

---

[144]Esler, *Conflict and Identity*, 137.
[145]LSJ, s.v. "προεπαγγέλλω."
[146]Wright, "Letter to the Romans," 415–416.
[147]Moisés Silva, "εὐαγγέλιον," *NIDNTTE* 2:307.
[148]Elliott, *Rhetoric*, 74. Esler, *Conflict and Identity*, 136–137.
[149]LSJ, s.v. "ὁρίζω." Wright, "Letter to the Romans," 418. See also Romans 1:4, in John Goldingay and Tom Wright, *The Bible for Everyone* (London, UK: SPCK, 2018).
[150]I agree with Wright that, ultimately, whether Paul is quoting some known pre-Pauline creedal statement is irrelevant. If Paul is indeed quoting something, which by no means has been proven, Paul is nevertheless making

of the honor one would give to royalty. On the other hand, as the Son of God, he is deserving of the honor one would give to God. Being both the Son of God and son of David, Jesus is the ideal broker.[151] In addition to Jesus's ascribed honor, there are also hints of his acquired honor. Here, we find the seeds of the argument that culminate in 3:21–22. His "resurrection from the dead" obviously points back to the crucifixion and ultimately to his faithful obedience to death.[152] Invoking the promises from the Old Testament puts God's honor at stake. Paul is claiming already in the opening that it is the death and resurrection of Jesus through which God has kept his promises to the prophets recounted in Israel's Scriptures. Jewett notes that grace implies "unmerited access to God for those who do not deserve it, and thereby honor to those whom the world holds to be shameful." God is seen here as the great patron of Israel, and it is through his saving action in fulfillment of his promises that all Christians have his favor (grace).[153]

Romans 1:16–17

Elliott is right to see the connection between verses 1–15 (especially verses 10–12 and verse 15) and the statement of the theme in verses

---

it his own and is intending to say exactly that. Wright, "Letter to the Romans," 416–417.

[151]I am assuming that Paul wrote the Pastoral Epistles. See the arguments in Donald Guthrie, *New Testament Introduction*, 4th rev. ed. (Downers Grove, IL: InterVarsity Press, 1990), 607–649 and Luke Timothy Johnson, *The Writings of the New Testament: An Interpretation*, 3rd ed. (Minneapolis, MN: Fortress Press, 2010), 375–381. See also 1 Timothy 2:5.

[152]See also Philippians 2:6–11 and 1 Corinthians 15:1–6.

[153]Bruce J. Malina and John J. Pilch, *Social-Science Commentary on the Letters of Paul* (Minneapolis, MN: Augsburg Fortress Press, 2006), 223.

16 and 17. Paul was hindered in his desire to go to Rome and to evangelize the Romans (13), and so εὐαγγελίσασθαι in verse 15 is directly connected with τὸ εὐαγγέλιον in verse 16.[154] As his introduction states, Paul desired to proclaim the gospel in Rome but could not and as a result wrote the letter instead. Thus, Paul begins to transition into the theme of his letter, which is connected with his purpose to strengthen and encourage the Roman Christians and especially to address the rising strife between Jews and Gentiles in Rome.[155]

Paul states boldly that he is not "ashamed of the gospel" (1:16). Here, the word Paul uses is ἐπαισχύνομαι, which involves "a subjective sense of embarrassment or fear of ridicule" because of a "loss of status."[156] Hence, at the beginning of the thesis of the letter, Paul invokes the language and values associated with honor and shame. Paul did not think that the public humiliation, rejection, and ridicule that the gospel might bring would result in a loss of honor.[157] This raises the obvious question of why Paul might have been ashamed of the gospel. The simple answer implied by Paul's choice of words is that the message of the gospel might be viewed as shameful—but according to whom and for what reason?

Paul's dual audience, diaspora Jews and Greco-Roman Gentiles, would have considered the message of the gospel shameful, obscene, and unbefitting because it was intimately connected to the crucifixion of Jesus of Nazareth;[158] Paul hints at this elsewhere (1 Cor.

---

[154] Elliott, *Rhetoric*, 83–85.
[155] Wright, "Letter to the Romans," 423.
[156] Moisés Silva, "αἰσχύνη," *NIDNTTE* 1:83.
[157] Malina and Pilch, *Social-Science Commentary*, 226.
[158] Jewett, *Romans*, 18.

1:21-24). In the Roman world, crucifixion was seen as "the maximum degradation and humiliation."[159] Crucifixion said definitively and publicly that one's claim to honor was denied by Rome.[160] Adding insult to injury, the gospel message did not appeal to the honored members of Roman society but to the outcasts, fools, and barbarians (consider 1 Cor. 1:27-29).[161] In the Jewish world, the Messiah was supposed to lead a successful war for Jewish independence from Rome, not die a death cursed by the Torah (see Gal. 3:13).[162] By the inclusion of the Gentiles in the church without having to keep the Torah, the gospel seemed to imply that God had broken his promises to Israel.[163] Thus, in both the Roman and the Jewish world, God's own honor was at stake, and Paul was ready to mount a defense.

When the Christian message went out into the Roman world, what resulted was a challenge-riposte of universal magnitude. This can be seen in Paul's use of terminology. We have already noted how εὐαγγέλιον was tied up with imperial claims. Additionally, the emperor was often referred to as the savior of the world.[164] Instead of abstract dogmatic or theological concepts like gospel and salvation being used, there is a direct repurposing of terminology used in Roman propaganda.[165] Using the Romans' own language, the Christian gospel challenges the emperor's claim to honor and "turns the value system of the Roman Empire upside down."[166]

---

[159]Wright, *Jesus and the Victory of God*, 543.
[160]Ibid., 543.
[161]Jewett, *Romans*, 18.
[162]Wright, *Victory of God*, 485-486.
[163]Ziesler, *Paul's Letter*, 70. Wright, "Letter to the Romans," 426.
[164]Silva, "σῴζω," *NIDNTTE* 4:421. Jewett, *Romans*, 18-19.
[165]Ibid., 18-19.
[166]Ibid., 19. Wright, "Letter to the Romans," 404.

DEFENDING GOD'S HONOR

If the claim in both the Greco-Roman and the Jewish worlds was that the message of the gospel is shameful, then Paul's defense of the gospel had to involve proving that God has acted honorably. Furthermore, honor and righteousness are directly connected. Dunn notes, "Righteousness is not something which an individual has on his or her own, independently of anyone else, it is something which one has precisely in one's relationships as a social being. People are righteous when they meet the claims which others have on them by virtue of their relationship."[167] We can begin to see the connection between righteousness and acquired honor. After summarizing the linguistic connections between these two words, Wu notes that *righteousness* is a word that is to be associated with an honor-and-shame culture and refers to a specific aspect of honor.[168] Honor is determined by how a person acts in conformity to the group's honor code. Both honor and righteousness involve fulfilling the social and moral expectations of the group. The righteous person is honorable, and the honorable person is righteous.

This helps to solve the debate surrounding how to understand what is meant by δικαιοσύνη θεοῦ. According to the Old-Testament usage, righteousness refers to right action, not necessarily in conformity to universal ethical standards but particularly in conformity to specific covenantal obligations.[169] The meaning of righteous as being faithful to "mutual obligations or contracts" or "certain agreed upon terms" surprisingly finds evidence even in

---

[167] Dunn, *Romans 1–8*, 40–41.
[168] Jackson Wu, *Saving God's Face: A Chinese Contextualization of Salvation through Honor and Shame* (Pasadena, CA: WCIU Press, 2012), 219–221, 241.
[169] K Kertelge, "δικαιοσύνη," *EDNT* 1:326.

classical usage.¹⁷⁰ Hence, δικαιοσύνη θεοῦ refers to "Yahweh's conduct with respect to the covenant."¹⁷¹ In the Old Testament, the righteousness of Yahweh refers to a quality in God that causes him to "do the right and faithful thing by the people with whom [he] is in a committed relationship."¹⁷² This means that God is committed to and defends Israel. Further, it becomes connected with his promised salvation and deliverance of Israel from her national enemies and exile.¹⁷³ God remains faithful to his covenantal relationship despite Israel's unfaithfulness.¹⁷⁴

Additionally, the other two genitive phrases in this context, δύναμις θεοῦ and ὀργὴ θεοῦ, are both clearly subjective genitives and imply that δικαιοσύνη θεοῦ should be read likewise.¹⁷⁵ Likewise, when Paul treats the subject again in 3:4–5 and 3:25–26, it is obvious that in these passages what is being talked about is God's own righteousness.¹⁷⁶ The evidence decidedly favors reading this as a subjective genitive rather than an objective genitive or a genitive of origin.¹⁷⁷ This does not mean that there is no objective aspect to the phrase. If the phrase refers to how God acts to save his people in

---

¹⁷⁰LSJ, s.v. "δίκαιος." John Frederick, "A Critical Review of Charles Lee Irons' *The Righteousness of God*," in *Journal of Biblical and Theological Studies* 1.1 (2016): p. 53. See also Charles Lee Irons, *The Righteousness of God* (Tübingen, Germany: Mohr Siebeck, 2015), 105–106.
¹⁷¹Kertelge, "δικαιοσύνη," *EDNT* 1:327.
¹⁷²John Goldingay, *Biblical Theology: The God of Christian Scripture* (Downers Grove, IL: InterVarsity Press, 2016), 311.
¹⁷³Kertelge, "δικαιοσύνη," *EDNT* 1:328. Ziesler, *Paul's Letter*, 70–71.
¹⁷⁴Goldingay, *Biblical Theology*, 313.
¹⁷⁵Timo Laato, "'God's Righteousness' – Once Again," in *The Nordic Paul: Finnish Approaches to Pauline Theology*, ed. Lars Aejmelaeus and Antti Mustakallio (London, UK: T&T Clark, 2008), p. 49.
¹⁷⁶Laato, "Once Again," 49–50.
¹⁷⁷Kertelge, "δικαιοσύνη," *EDNT* 1:328.

faithfulness to his covenant, then the phrase moves beyond a simple quality in God and begins to extend to the grace that God has shown sinners.[178]

Romans 1:18–3:20

Romans 1:18–3:20 forms a new section in Paul's letter, which can be seen by the *inclusio* of God's righteousness being revealed in 1:17 and 3:21.[179] The rhetorical function of this section is as an *antithesis*.[180] Johnson notes that the function of the antithesis is "to demonstrate the thesis by its contrary."[181] Since the thesis is that the gospel reveals that God is honorable, remains faithful to his covenant, and has acted to save his people, the antithesis underscores this. Wu highlights that "[b]y contrasting God's faithfulness and human unfaithfulness, Paul magnifies divine honour and our shame."[182] Hence, Paul begins a lengthy section that underscores the plight of the human race in slavery to sin.[183] But, more than that, it is about "God's own problem."[184]

When people read that "the wrath of God is revealed," some conjure images of a dour and ill-tempered deity ready to eradicate

---

[178]Ibid., 1:328. Ziesler, *Paul's Letter*, 71. Schrenk, "δικαιοσύνη," *TDNTA*, 171. Dunn, *Romans 1–8*, 40–41.

[179]Esler, *Conflict and Identity*, 141.

[180]Luke Timothy Johnson, *Reading Romans: A Literary and Theological Commentary* (Macon, GA: Smyth & Helwys, 2001), 31.

[181] Ibid., 31.

[182]Jackson Wu, *Eastern Eyes: Honor and Shame in Paul's Message and Mission* (Downers Grove, IL: InterVarsity Press, 2019), 87.

[183]Ziesler, *Paul's Letter*, 73.

[184]Wright, "Letter to the Romans," 428.

those who fail to keep his arbitrary list of rules.[185] As we saw above, this is a distortion that even Luther had to overcome, but it must be kept clearly in mind that a God who is not opposed to evil is not a good God.[186] God's wrath stems from the fact that he has been personally and deliberately dishonored. So, in order to preserve his honor, God is ready to get satisfaction.[187]

God is the creator and preserver of all things by whom we were created and from whom we owe our continual existence, so it follows that we owe him "some token of appreciation."[188] God is the patron, and humanity is his client.[189] In fact, God's benefaction towards us is so great that "we all have incurred an enormous (and largely undischarged) debt."[190] When we wrong someone, we owe them some reparation.[191] This means not only that we ought to honor God as the Creator but also that when we fail to do so, we are obliged to make satisfaction on top of giving him the honor he is already due as the Creator.[192] Paul is making the point that this is exactly the position that humanity is in.

---

[185]Ibid., 431.

[186]Ibid., 431.

[187]Esler, *Conflict and Identity*, 228.

[188]Stephen Westerholm, *Understanding Paul: The Early Christian Worldview of the Letter to the Romans*, 2nd ed. (Grand Rapids, MI: Baker Academic, 2004), 67.

[189]DeSilva, *Honor, Patronage, Kinship & Purity*, 126. Wu, *Saving God's Face*, 211. Jerome H. Neyrey, "God, Benefactor and Patron: The Major Cultural Model for Interpreting the Deity in Greco-Roman Antiquity," in *Journal for the Study of the New Testament* 27.4 (2005): 471ff.

[190]Westerholm, *Understanding Paul*, 68.

[191]Goldingay, *Biblical Theology*, 327. Westerholm, *Understanding Paul*, 67.

[192]Goldingay, *Biblical Theology*, 327. Westerholm, *Understanding Paul*, 68.

Paul demonstrates that the evil with which humanity particularly provokes God to anger is idolatry.[193] By worshipping created things in the place of God, humanity had openly insulted and dishonored God.[194] They "did not honor him as God" (1:21) but instead "exchanged the glory/honor of the immortal God for images" (1:23). Instead of giving God the glory and honor that he deserves as our benefactor, humanity gave this honor to created things.[195] This is "the ultimate act of dishonor before God."[196] This is because the creation is something that humanity can manipulate to its advantage, and the implication is that God also can be manipulated by human whim.[197] Humanity had pledged its loyalty to things that are not God.[198] Further, humanity brings more dishonor upon God by not following boundaries established at creation, which regulate human sexuality.[199] "Ultimately, sin not only dishonors the Creator God, but also leaves the self mired in shame and defilement."[200] When God is not given the honor he is due, the result is that humanity itself becomes gnarled beyond recognition.[201] Thus, we begin to see that Paul in his letter is overturning standard cultural patterns of honor and shame.[202] Instead of what is honorable being determined by other

---

[193]Wright, "Letter to the Romans," 430–431.
[194]Goldingay, *Biblical Theology*, 327.
[195]Jayson Georges, "From Shame to Honor: A Theological Reading of Romans for Honor-Shame Contexts," in *Missiology: An International Review* 38.3 (2010): p. 299.
[196]Ibid., 299.
[197]Malina and Pilch, *Social-Science Commentary*, 229.
[198]Wright, "Letter to the Romans," 433.
[199]Georges, "From Shame to Honor," 299.
[200]Ibid., 300.
[201]Wright, "Letter to the Romans," 433.
[202]Jewett, *Romans*, 23, 27.

humans, Paul conceives of God as the significant other and moves honor and shame out of the murky waters of cultural relativism and into the clear water of God's objective standard.[203]

Anyone who after reading Paul's explanation of humanity's idolatry might think that it may not apply to them is addressed in the second chapter.[204] This includes the Jews who might have thought they had an advantage over the Gentiles. After all, they had the Torah, and that implies that they already had God's favor.[205] However, in 2:17–22, Paul demonstrates that the Jews had broken the Torah. As we might expect from an honor-and-shame culture, Paul focuses not on every individual but upon Israel as a whole.[206] Some Jews stole, murdered, and, it appears, even robbed pagan temples (2:22). While not every individual Jew was guilty of these specific things, some were; and, as we saw, that added to collective shame.

Then, in 2:23–24, Paul concludes that the Jews had dishonored God through their sin. The connection of sin with dishonor is important. Malina makes this important connection: "Sin is a claim to worth by standing up to God, by challenging God, by dishonoring God."[207] Sin, then, represents a challenge to God's honor by being "something that dishonors God."[208] It makes sinners the significant others in whose eyes we seek honor, instead of seeking honor from God.[209] This implies that the Jews were actually in the same boat as

---

[203]Wu, *Eastern Eyes*, 50.
[204]Wright, "Letter to the Romans," 437.
[205]Ibid., 446–447.
[206]Ibid., 447.
[207]Malina and Pilch, *Social-Science Commentary*, 241–242.
[208]Ibid. Wu, *Eastern Eyes*, 50.
[209]Malina and Pilch, *Social-Science Commentary*, 242.

those described in 1:18ff. Sin exchanges God's glory with idolatry and brings dishonor upon God. Israel's continued oppression by foreign powers demonstrates their failure to keep the Torah.[210] The Jews appealed to the Torah to show they had honor, while the Gentiles did not. Paul's basic point is that both Jews and Gentiles, in fact, lacked honor in God's eyes.[211] The Torah thus reveals the dishonor and shame of all.

For the Jews, Paul's Gospel brought God's honor into question. God made numerous promises for the blessing of Israel, such as a return from exile and a restoration of the Davidic monarchy. If God could not keep his word to Israel, how could he be trusted to keep his word to the Gentiles?[212] Paul's response was to show that it was sinful humanity that had challenged God's claim to honor. The problem, then, was how God could bless the Gentiles through Abraham if they had consistently dishonored him.[213] How could God use Israel to bring light to the Gentiles if Israel had also dishonored him?[214] If God were not opposed to evil, he would not be honorable. God's wrath and the promise that the resurrected Christ will judge the world point toward his claim to honor. If God is honorable, then he cannot allow Israel to escape the same judgment that is coming upon the Gentiles. But, if he is honorable, he also will keep his promises to the patriarchs.

---

[210] Wright, "Letter to the Romans," 447.
[211] Jewett, *Romans*, 38–39.
[212] Wu, *Eastern Eyes*, 90.
[213] Ibid., 81.
[214] Wright, "Letter to the Romans," 447.

Romans 3:21-26

In 3:21, Paul dramatically introduces a new section with νυνὶ δὲ ("but now").[215] The contents of this section begin themes that are expanded upon in the fourth and fifth chapters. Additionally, the "now" indicates that verses summarize and provide the solution for much of what Paul was arguing about the human plight in 1:18-3:20.[216] It becomes obvious that in 3:21-26 Paul restates his thesis from 1:16-17 and elaborates upon it.[217] In 1:16-17, God's righteousness is revealed in the gospel. Similarly in 3:21, "But now, the righteousness of God has been made manifest."[218] In 1:3, it is the gospel "concerning his Son," Jesus. Paul is claiming that the gospel "announces a new manifestation of God's favor."[219] Instead of wrath, the gospel proclaims that God intends to keep his promises to Israel and deal with sin.[220]

Instead of a direct reference to the gospel, we find a reference to Jesus Christ in 3:22. Here, we encounter the problem of the meaning of διὰ πίστεως Ἰησοῦ Χριστοῦ. Whose faith is it? Is it the faith(fulness) of Jesus? Or is it our faith in Jesus? Since this section is a restatement of the thesis in 1:16-17, this phrase may be read in parallel to ἐκ πίστεως εἰς πίστιν in 1:17. We find, then, that the second phrase from 3:22, εἰς πάντας τοὺς πιστεύοντας, matches up with the εἰς πίστιν of 1:17. These latter phrases refer to the human response of faith.[221] In 1:17, ἐκ πίστεως uses a preposition of source, and εἰς πίστιν uses a

---

[215] Dunn, *Romans 1-8*, 161. Johnson, *Reading Romans*, 51. Ziesler, *Paul's Letter*, 106. Wright, "Letter to the Romans," 469.
[216] Elliott, *The Rhetoric of Romans*, 147. Ziesler, *Paul's Letter*, 108.
[217] Johnson, *Reading Romans*, 51. Elliott, *Rhetoric*, 146.
[218] LSJ, s.v. "φἄνερόω."
[219] DeSilva, *Honor, Patronage, Kinship & Purity*, 126.
[220] Ibid., 126.
[221] Johnson, *Reading Romans*, 60.

spatial preposition.²²² This suggests a movement out of faith into faith.²²³

In Galatians 3:22, Paul similarly states the role of the Hebrew Scriptures in relation to sin, and he then he goes on to give the rationale "that the promise ἐκ πίστεως Ἰησοῦ Χριστοῦ might be given freely to those who believe." The similarities here to both Romans 1:17 and 3:22 are striking. For both Galatians 3:22 and Romans 3:22, if all occurrences of *faith* refer to human faith in Christ, the redundancy "through faith to all who have faith" is created.²²⁴ It is far more likely that Paul is saying that God's own righteousness has first been made manifest through the faithfulness of Jesus, even unto death (Phil. 2:8), prior to and as the basis of the act of Christian faith in him.

Johnson suggests this movement of moving out from God's own faithfulness and resulting in our response of faith reflects the dynamic of gift and reciprocity.²²⁵ Consider patron and client relationships; patrons were duty bound "to show themselves faithful or reliable such that clients could trust them."²²⁶ Clients were to express their reciprocity by means of trust and fidelity. Wu concurs that "Paul underscores the faithfulness of God our patron, while at the same time he speaks of our faith/trust as clients. Thus, we are to show faith in the faithfulness of God."²²⁷ In Galatians 3:22, Paul is saying that the validity of the promises of God is directly based upon the faithful

---

²²²Daniel B. Wallace, *Greek Grammar Beyond the Basics: An Exegetical Syntax of the New Testament* (Grand Rapids, MI: Zondervan, 1997), 368-69, 371.
²²³Johnson, *Reading Romans*, 60.
²²⁴Ibid., 60.
²²⁵Ibid., 29.
²²⁶Wu, *Eastern Eyes*, 86.
²²⁷Ibid., 86.

obedience of Jesus Christ, so that it might be given to those who have faith. Similarly, in Romans 1:17 and 3:22, we read that Christ's faithfulness is the source of and leads to human faith—that is, a trust in God.[228]

Despite the fact that God created humanity with honor, "all lack the glory of God" (3:23).[229] This is not just a reference to what was lost in creation but also to what humanity in the present fails to reach.[230] The honor and glory given to Adam and Eve have been lost.[231] "Since humanity's futile efforts have 'fallen short' of properly honoring God, they now 'lack' their own glory and are in a position of deserving shame."[232] It is all who have sinned, so this includes both the Jew and Gentile, who are on equal footing before God.[233]

Two important words that come next, ἀπολυτρώσεως and ἱλαστήριον, are the source of some scholarly debate. The first, ἀπολυτρώσεως, is often thought to refer to either redemption in the slave market or else to Israel's redemption from Egypt.[234] Likewise, ἱλαστήριον has enjoyed a heated debate, with some scholars thinking it denotes the appeasement of an angry God (propitiation), others the removal of sin (expiation), and some the place where atonement is made (the mercy seat).[235] However, the significance of how these two words and their cognates are used in the LXX—that is, how to

---

[228]Wright, "Letter to the Romans," 425. Johnson, *Reading Romans*, 29–30.
[229]LSJ, s.v. "ὑστερέω."
[230]Dunn, *Romans 1–8*, 168.
[231]Georges, "From Shame to Honor," 300.
[232]Ibid., 300.
[233]Dunn, *Romans 1–8*, 178.
[234]Ziesler, *Paul's Letter*, 111.
[235]Ibid., 112–113.

translate words derived from the Hebrew root כפר (*kpr*)—is often overlooked.²³⁶

There is a non-cultic and a cultic usage of words stemming from the כפר root. It is the very specific non-cultic usage that helps determine the exact meaning of the more-general cultic usage.²³⁷ The non-cultic usage of the כפר root "indisputably link[s] it to the notion of compensation."²³⁸ The word כפר can either be used to denote the material gift that establishes an amicable settlement between an injured party and the offending party or to describe the resulting interpersonal reconciliation.²³⁹ It involves the attempt of someone who has offended and dishonored another to avoid punishment or vengeance from the offended party by making satisfaction for their wrongdoing.²⁴⁰ The enmity that has arisen between the two parties is relaxed by an act of restitution.²⁴¹ Thus, in the LXX, λύτρωσις reflects the perspective of the offending party; by making satisfaction and offering the reparation payment, a λύτρον, the party is offering a redemption or ransom for their life.²⁴² Passages like Numbers 35:31-

---

²³⁶F. Büschel, "ἴλεως, ἰλάσκομαι, ἰλαστήριον," *TDNTA*, 362–363, 365–366. F. Büschel, "λύτρον," *TDNTA*, 543. Silva, "λυτρόω," *NIDNTTE* 3:181.

²³⁷Leon Morris, *The Apostolic Preaching of the Cross*, 3rd rev. ed. (Grand Rapids, MI: Wm. B. Eerdmans, 1965), 161–167. Silva, "ἰλάσκομαι, ἰλαστήριον," *NIDNTTE* 2:536–537. Lang, "כִּפֶּר," *TDOT* 7:296. Büschel, "ἴλεως, ἰλάσκομαι, ἰλαστήριον," *TDNTA*, 362.

²³⁸Emile Nicole, "Atonement in the Pentateuch," in *The Glory of the Atonement: Biblical, Historical & Practical Perspectives: Essays in Honor of Roger Nicole*, ed. Charles E. Hill and Frank A. James III (Downers Grove, IL: InterVarsity Press, 2004), p. 47.

²³⁹Lang, "כִּפֶּר," *TDOT* 7:292, 301, 302. Büschel, "ἴλεως, ἰλάσκομαι, ἰλαστήριον," *TDNTA*, 362.

²⁴⁰Lang, "כִּפֶּר," *TDOT* 7:295. Büschel, "ἴλεως, ἰλάσκομαι, ἰλαστήριον," *TDNTA*, 362. Büschel, "λύτρον," *TDNTA*, 543.

²⁴¹Lang, "כִּפֶּר," *TDOT* 7:295.

²⁴²Morris, *Apostolic Preaching*, 161–162, 166.

32 note that in certain cases, the only λύτρον, or כפר, that would be accepted is one's own life.²⁴³ Correspondingly, ἐξιλάσκομαι reflects the removal of the anger of the dishonored party, resulting in interpersonal reconciliation.²⁴⁴ Similarly, ἱλαστήριον can refer either to the gift or offering that makes the satisfaction possible or, more often, to the lid of the Ark of the Covenant as the place where satisfaction was made (by way of metonymy). It is likely that Paul intends both.²⁴⁵

We do well to consider the implications of the imagery of the Levitical cultus invoked by the word כפר. Although many sacrifices could be mentioned, one in particular is useful to our investigation. The אָשָׁם, 'āšām, sacrifice—best rendered as the "reparation offering"—refers to a "situation in which someone is or becomes obligated to discharge guilt by giving something."²⁴⁶ This type of sacrifice was meant "to make restitution for something that a person [had] done."²⁴⁷ The reparation offering dealt with the consequences incurred when a person impugned God's honor.²⁴⁸ In a key passage found in Isaiah 52:13–53:12, the "suffering servant" offers his life as an אָשָׁם. Goldingay notes that the focus of this passage is not that the servant is punished vicariously. Instead, both the Gentiles and

---

²⁴³Ibid., 162-163.
²⁴⁴Ibid., 158, 160.
²⁴⁵Morris, *Apostolic Preaching*, 159. Wright, "Letter to the Romans," 476.
²⁴⁶Rolf Knierim, "אָשָׁם," in *The Theological Lexicon of the Old Testament*, ed. Ernst Jenni and Claus Westermann, trans. Mark E. Biddle (Peabody, MA: Hendrickson, 1997), p. 192.
²⁴⁷Goldingay, *Biblical Theology*, 328.
²⁴⁸Ibid., 330. Lester L. Grabbe, *Leviticus* (Sheffield, UK: Sheffield Academic Press, 1997), 37.

Israelites are required to make restitution to God because of their faithlessness. However, their sin and disobedience indicate they are unable to make satisfaction to God. In addition, they fail to see their own plight and, thus, do not think they have a need to make restitution at all.[249] Isaiah's solution is then that the suffering servant can offer his own life of faithfulness as the satisfaction for their unfaithfulness.[250] The LXX uses the phrase περὶ ἁμαρτίας as a translation of אָשָׁם in Isaiah 53:10.[251] Additionally, περὶ ἁμαρτίας is used as a technical term in Leviticus.[252] In 2 Corinthians 5:21 and Romans 8:3, we find περὶ ἁμαρτίας being used to underscore the meaning of Jesus's death. It follows, then, that Paul "designated Jesus' execution as a restitution offering."[253]

It is commonly held that the offending party should take the first step toward making reconciliation. Yet, God, the offended party, "set forth" Christ as the "place and means of atonement" that enables people to enter God's favor.[254] As we have seen, our sin dishonors God and fails to give him the glory he rightly deserves. Instead of responding in wrath, God responds in grace.[255] When Jesus is presented as a reparation offering, the solution to the human plight can also be identified. As our broker and mediator, Jesus makes his

---

[249]Goldingay, *Biblical Theology*, 328.
[250]Ibid., 329.
[251]Ibid., 330.
[252]Dunn, *Romans 1–8*, 422. Wright, "Letter to the Romans," 579.
[253]Goldingay, *Biblical Theology*, 330.
[254]Wright, "Letter to the Romans," 474, 476. Moisés Silva, "προτίθημι," *NIDNTTE* 4:160. DeSilva, *Honor, Patronage, Kinship & Purity*, 129.
[255]Westerholm, *Understanding Paul*, 68.

satisfaction on our behalf for our sin.[256] "As our representative and substitute Jesus offers his perfect obedience as an offering that can compensate for our defiance and counteract its effects."[257] The faithful life and death of Jesus make it possible for humanity to make satisfaction to God for dishonoring him. "What God does in Jesus is reaffirm God's honor, by accepting the penalty for dishonoring it."[258] His satisfactory death on our behalf enables our debt to the Creator God to be paid for.[259] Because Christ remains faithful to God, even in the face of a gruesome and shameful death, he does not dishonor God.[260] Therefore, the voluntary death of Jesus upon the cross restores God's honor.[261] For Paul, Jesus's death on the cross "makes it possible for God to keep his covenant promises and so establish righteousness."[262]

Through faith, a person "attributes glory to God" and "renders to God what is due Him."[263] It is also through faith that one comes to have a share in the reconciliation that God made through the death of his Son.[264] By doing so, God revealed that he is honorable, even though he had foregone exacting satisfaction from a humanity that shamed and dishonored him.[265] It is through faith that God reckons sinners righteous. "Those reckoned righteous are worthy of divine honor."[266]

---

[256] Goldingay, *Biblical Theology*, 331.
[257] Ibid., 331.
[258] Ibid., 331.
[259] Westerholm, *Understanding Paul*, 68.
[260] Wu, *Eastern Eyes*, 90.
[261] Goldingay, *Biblical Theology*, 330.
[262] Wu, *Eastern Eyes*, 90.
[263] *AE* 26:227.
[264] Malina and Pilch, *Social-Science Commentary*, 241.
[265] Ibid., 241.
[266] Wu, *Eastern Eyes*, 61.

Hence, God ascribes honor to those who have none and bestows an honorable status on those who have not earned it.[267] "God bestows an honorable status upon humans, which would have been otherwise inaccessible due to our shameful sin. Such honor derived from adoption into a prestigious family (in this case, God's)."[268] In demonstrating that he is in fact honorable—that he has "kept faith" to Israel and the patriarchs—God also reveals that as the divine patron, his generosity to those who insulted him is unmatched.[269]

IV. Summary, Findings, and Conclusion

Paul's argument is that he is not ashamed of the gospel, because it reveals that God is honorable. God has been faithful and loyal to his covenant obligations toward the patriarchs and Israel. However, this is a faithfulness that moves him to save. Paul, then, shows by way of contrast that humanity, both Jews and Gentiles, has responded to the Creator God's benefaction by dishonoring him through its sin, chief of which is idolatry. The result is that humanity has impugned God's honor. However, instead of exacting satisfaction, God remains faithful. Jesus Christ, who is both the human heir of David and the divine Son of God, remains faithful in honoring God, even to the point of death. It is the faithful life and death of Jesus that are offered as satisfaction in compensation for the sins of the whole world. By faith, humanity comes to share in Christ and, thus, is declared to be in the right and given an honorable status. Because Christ is honorable and by faith

---

[267] Jewett, *Romans*, 66–68.
[268] Georges, "From Shame to Honor," 302.
[269] DeSilva, *Honor, Patronage, Kinship & Purity*, 127–128, 130.

Christians participate in him and are part of his royal family, his honor is their honor.

When δικαιοσύνη θεοῦ is considered in the light of honor and shame, retributive justice is not the concept being conveyed. On this point, Martin Luther was correct. Correspondingly, it should be noted that none of the advocates of the New Perspective conceive of the δικαιοσύνη θεοῦ as retributive justice either. Thus, there is widespread agreement that Gabriel Biel and the nominalist school were incorrect. It should also be observed that both sides of this discussion would agree that a simple objective or subjective conception fails to deal adequately with the range of meaning implied by the phrase. If God is the great patron who remains honorable, then it follows that he has clients to whom he is committed and to whom he gives the gift of salvation. Luther places the emphasis upon the subjective side, but he does ground this emphasis in the objective faithfulness of Christ in which the believer participates. However, Luther fails to identify the concept of God's faithfulness to his word when he reads δικαιοσύνη θεοῦ. This is unfortunate because God's faithfulness to his word is an axiom that informs much of Lutheran theology. On the other hand, the New Perspective places the emphasis on the subjective side, while noting that righteousness and salvation overlap largely. The New Perspective has not taken the time to read Luther beyond his autobiographical statement and seems to be responding to a caricature. Additionally, while it is correct to highlight that δικαιοσύνη θεοῦ refers to God's faithfulness to his covenant, this conception still is not adequate, because it is a faithfulness that motivates God to send his Son to deal with sin and save humanity. As we have seen, Paul is concerned to defend God's honor, and that largely involves God's salvation of sinners.

An honor-and-shame reading of Romans has produced a view of the atonement that is broadly consistent with that proposed by Anselm. Any attempt to charge Anselm and *Satisfactio Vicaria* with importing medieval feudalism should be dismissed as not taking account of the cultural setting of the Roman Empire. It is evident that by reading Romans in this light, while in no way limiting Paul or Holy Scripture to this language of *Satisfactio Vicaria*, this "model" of the atonement does have basis in Scripture.

From this, we see that, while Luther may have been wrong in saying that the δικαιοσύνη θεοῦ is primarily about a status we are given, the phrase does imply God's saving action toward his people in fulfillment of his word, and that does imply the bestowal of an honorable status to those who have dishonored God. It becomes clear that Luther is not always guilty of misunderstanding Paul. On the contrary, on some levels, Luther understands what Paul intends to say better than the New Perspective. This is especially the case when we realize that at times Luther uses honor-and-shame language in his exegesis of Paul, and, as we have seen, he does so throughout his career. By contrast, the advocates of the New Perspective do not have a uniform view of Pauline soteriology and tend to deemphasize soteriology in favor of focusing on the issue of Gentile inclusion into the church.[270]

Perhaps James Voelz's "levels of meaning" can help to alleviate some of the tension that has been discovered. First, there is the

---

[270]This is a topic for which reading Romans in light of honor and shame may help to point the way forward.

"sense," that is, the lexical and grammatical meaning of the words. This is what the text says. Second, there is the "significance," which asks what images or concepts are being evoked by the words, or what is going on in the "story world." Third, there is "implication," which notes that how and why an author has written something has implications to the meaning of what they wrote. Fourth, there is "application" to the present situation of the commentator or reader.[271]

When we consider what the New Perspective has discovered via Sanders concerning the nature of Second Temple Judaism and the implications that has for the occasion and argument to the Romans, we see that the New Perspective works quite a bit on the third level. However, while Luther may be wrong about Judaism, his application of Paul's soteriology to the late medieval situation and controversy is nonetheless correct. The attention to first-century Mediterranean honor-shame culture given in this paper is a response precisely to Sanders's call to be historically sensitive in our exegesis by informing our reading by attending to the historical conceptual structures within which Paul's writing makes sense. It may be possible to agree with the Sanders's specific insights into Paul and Second Temple Judaism without denying the insights of Lutheran theology. Reading Romans considering honor and shame helps keep some of that in balance.

Shockingly, even Dunn repudiates any claim that what he has been teaching contradicts basic Lutheran doctrinal formulations.[272] Instead, he claims that the insights of the New Perspective deepen our

---

[271]See James W. Voelz, "The Problem of 'Meaning' in Texts," in *Neotestamentica* 23.1 (1989): pp. 33–43.
[272]Dunn, "What's Right about the Old Perspective on Paul," 229.

understanding of Paul's teaching. While those faithful to the Lutheran tradition may not be able to accept every conclusion for which the New Perspective has advocated, this study has shown that their position does indeed shed light into the discussion on Paul's Epistle to the Romans and can help Lutherans to better articulate their faith.

Made in the USA
Columbia, SC
02 September 2021